"This outstanding book connects the reader to Judy Eekhoff's ongoing explorations of thoughtful ways to help patients who are not able to benefit from more conventional psychoanalytic treatment. Most psychoanalytic explorations depend on engaging the person in a verbal analytic process, and the patient who has no words available to reach their inner world presents a major challenge for the psychoanalytic thinker and practitioner. The challenge of understanding patients who have no language for their inner experiences calls for an expert translator, such as Judy Eekhoff. In the process of her own clinical experience, she discovers and rediscovers the language to access the deep pain of her patients.

Her work with the not known, although vividly experienced is put in a theoretical context. Ferenczi's pursuit to bridge the discontinuity between the wordless world of the very young child and the world of the adult, is brought to mind. Bion's advice on the crucial role of listening helps Dr. Eekhoff and us to appreciate the darkness of primitive states. The burden to understand falls to the analyst who intuitively creates safety and space for the potential to enter into the unspoken world of early childhood trauma, before speech, a world of undifferentiated, never formulated formless, meaningless experience.

This remarkable volume is a gift for all who are interested in finding a way to understand and work with such difficult to reach patients."

Giselle Galdi, *Editor-in-Chief*, The American Journal of Psychoanalysis

"This new book by Judy Eekhoff is a gift for anyone interested in the origins of the psyche. The book brilliantly delineates the author's understanding of the elements, processes, and media that form the foundation of mental life. It is as though the author examines mental tissue with the precision of an electron microscope, while we usually do so with an optical one. Dr. Eekhoff's capacity to express psychoanalytic experiences is extraordinary, with a passion for psychoanalysis evident throughout the book.

Psychoanalytic theories and concepts receive a sophisticated and comprehensive treatment, which the author presents in a uniquely insightful way. For example, the emotional links of love, hate, and knowledge are approached from a personal, ontological-experiential framework.

The author's appreciation and respect for the analysand's autonomy and individuality seem to serve as a guiding compass, bringing to the forefront the 'late Bion' proposal of being at one with the analysand. Dr. Eekhoff's treatment of these parameters in the book is admirable."

João Carlos Braga M.D., PhD *is a full member, training, and supervising analyst at the Brazilian Psychoanalytic Society of São Paulo and Psychoanalytic Group of Curitiba, Brazil*

"Writing is a solitary exercise from which we transform words into emotional experiences to bring warmth and passion to the author-reader encounter. In this creative dialogue, letters are precise, but silence must also speak. This book, *Bion's Emotional Links: Love, Hate and Knowledge* by Judy K. Eekhoff, beautifully promotes this intimate dialogue and takes up a wide range of concepts Eekhoff has been developing over the years; she explores the primordial affects and emotions that power intrapsychic and intersubjective relationships and expands them through her vast clinical experience. In fourteen chapters, the author achieves narrative harmony in rhythms, images, and sequences. This book constitutes an original and unique contribution to the great themes of contemporary psychoanalysis."

Jani Santamaría Linares, *Director A-Santamaría Association, A.C.; Editor of* Bion, Dreamwork and the Oneiric Dimensions of the Mind *(Routledge, forthcoming) and Co-editor of* The Bion Seminars at the A-Santamaría Association: Clinical and Theoretical Explorations *(Routledge, 2024)*

Bion's Emotional Links

In *Bion's Emotional Links*, Judy K. Eekhoff explores emotion as a bridge between unrepresented and represented states, highlighting the importance of both internal emotional and external relationships in the development of the mind.

Informed by Bion's focus on analytic technique, Eekhoff includes clinical vignettes from her own work with patients who have endured trauma. She explores somatic processes and how effective analysis can break down unhealthy defence mechanisms employed by individuals which often leads to a perpetual cycle of retraumatising the self. Eekhoff shows how, through an understanding of dreams as a representation of the inner self and hope as a means of finding and retaining one's sense of self, barriers can be broken down to free patients from a cycle of dread and dissociation. She places the individuality of the analyst at the forefront of their vital work, eschewing a dogmatic approach while carefully nurturing and respecting traditional psychoanalytic theories. Through this important work, readers will be equipped with the tools to recognize symbiotic relationships, both those in the patient's personal life and in the relationship between analyst and analysand.

Judy K. Eekhoff is an International Psychoanalytic Association-certified training and supervising psychoanalyst in Seattle, Washington, USA. She is the author of *Bion and Primitive Mental States: Trauma and the Symbiotic Link* (2021) and *Trauma and Primitive Mental States: An Object Relations Perspective* (2019).

The Routledge Wilfred R. Bion Studies Book Series

Series Editor
Howard B. Levine, MD

Editorial Advisory Board
Nicola Abel-Hirsch, Joseph Aguayo, Avner Bergstein, Lawrence J. Brown, Judy K. Eekhoff, Claudio Laks Eizerik, Robert D. Hinshelwood, Chris Mawson, James Ogilvie, Elias M. da Rocha Barros, Jani Santamaria, Rudi Vermote

---

The contributions of Wilfred Bion are among the most cited in the analytic literature. Their appeal lies not only in their content and explanatory value, but in their generative potential. Although Bion's training and many of his clinical instincts were deeply rooted in the classical tradition of Melanie Klein, his ideas have a potentially universal appeal. Rather than emphasizing a particular psychic content (e.g., Oedipal conflicts in need of resolution; splits that needed to be healed; preconceived transferences that must be allowed to form and flourish, etc.), he tried to help open and prepare the mind of the analyst (without memory, desire or theoretical preconception) for the encounter with the patient.

Bion's formulations of group mentality and the psychotic and non-psychotic portions of the mind, his theory of thinking and emphasis on facing and articulating the truth of one's existence so that one might truly learn firsthand from one's own experience, his description of psychic development (alpha function and container/contained) and his exploration of O are "non-denominational" concepts that defy relegation to a particular school or orientation of psychoanalysis. Consequently, his ideas have taken root in many places.... and those ideas continue to inform many different branches of psychoanalytic inquiry and interest.

It is with this heritage and its promise for the future developments of psychoanalysis in mind that we present *The Routledge Wilfred Bion Studies Book Series*. This series gathers together newly emerging and continually evolving contributions to psychoanalytic thinking that rest upon Bion's foundational texts and explore and extend the implications of his thought. For a full list of titles in the series, please visit the Routledge website at:

https://www.routledge.com/The-Routledge-Wilfred-Bion-Studies-Book-Series/book-series/RWBSBS

Howard B. Levine, MD
Series Editor

---

[1] Levine, H.B. and Civitarese, G. (2016). Editors' Preface, *The W.R. Bion Tradition*, Levine and Civitarese, eds., London: Karnac 2016, p. xxi.

Bion's Emotional Links

Love, Hate, and Knowledge

Judy K. Eekhoff

Routledge
Taylor & Francis Group

LONDON AND NEW YORK

Designed cover image: "On Love: My whole being is hollowed out to house you" by Hilda C. Catz.

First published 2025
by Routledge
4 Park Square, Milton Park, Abingdon, Oxon OX14 4RN

and by Routledge
605 Third Avenue, New York, NY 10158

Routledge is an imprint of the Taylor & Francis Group, an informa business

British Library Cataloguing-in-Publication Data
A catalog record for this title has been requested

ISBN: 978-1-032-89762-2 (hbk)
ISBN: 978-1-032-88770-8 (pbk)
ISBN: 978-1-003-54447-0 (ebk)

DOI: 10.4324/9781003544470

Typeset in Times New Roman
by Taylor & Francis Books

In memory of Bruce

Contents

Acknowledgements

I am grateful for the permissions to reprint the following papers in this volume with minor changes:

Routledge, Reproduced with Permission of Taylor & Francis Group

Eekhoff, J. K. (2021). Body as Dream Space. In Harrang, C., Tillotson, D., and Winters, N. (Eds.), *Body as Psychoanalytic Object: Clinical Applications from Winnicott, Bion and Beyond.* London and New York: Routledge.
Eekhoff, J. K. (2022). Psychic Equivalency as an Aspect of Symbiosis. In Levine, H. and Moguillansky, C. (Eds.), *Psychoanalysis of the Psychoanalytic Frame Revisited" A New Look at Bleger's Classical Work.* London and New York: Routledge/IPA.
Eekhoff, J. K. (2025). Perceptual Identification as analytic receptivity of unrepresented and dissociative states. In Power, D. and Power, J. (Eds.), *The Somatic-Psychic Realm (Bion).* London and New York: Routledge.

Karnac

Eekhoff, J. K. (2025). Truth and Lies: The Perversion of Truth and the Disruption of Passion. In Fortuna, T. (Ed.), *Truth and Lies in Psychoanalysis.* London: Karnac.

International Forum of Psychoanalysis

Eekhoff, J. K. (2021). Body relations and the black hole. *International Forum of Psychoanalysis*, 30(2021), 3.

American Journal of Psychoanalysis

Eekhoff, J. (2023). Between The Real And The Imaginary: Truth And Lies In The Psychoanalytic Encounter. *American Journal of Psychoanalysis*, 83, 528–546.

Eekhoff, J. (2024). Premonition: Hope and Dread in the Analytic Hour. Will be published in the 2024 December issue of the *American Journal of Psychoanalysis*, 84(4).
Eekhoff, J. (forthcoming). Catastrophe and Creativity: From Fragmentation to Emergence. Will be published in a forthcoming São Paulo Special Issue of the *American Journal of Psychoanalysis*. Koritar, Endre (Guest Ed.).

As always, I am grateful to my patients and consultees who have taught me so much of what it is to be human, of what it takes to persevere in the face of difficulties and tragedies, and to not give up hope.

I am thankful for my family who have supported me through a difficult time of mourning and demonstrated passion in the face of the turmoil of COVID, the grief of loss, and the faith in tomorrow.

So many people have aided me in my thinking and my writing. I know I cannot name all of them. I am grateful to the long-lasting Bion group facilitated by Maxine Anderson and Marianne Robinson, to the Primitive Mental States group with Dana Birksted-Breen and Susan Finkelstein, and to our "Elders Group", which includes Maxine Anderson, Elie Debbanne, and Marianne Robinson. I am also grateful for the first readers of these chapters who provided valuable feedback and stimulating questions, thus enhancing my writing.

Special thanks to Nicola Abel Hirsch, Avner Bergstein, Joao Carlos Braga, Hilda C. Catz, Giselle Galdi, Caron Harrang, Andre Koritar, Howard Levine, David Rosenfeld, and Jani Santamaria.

Special thanks to the editorial staff at Routledge, Taylor & Francis, for bringing this dream into reality. Thank you, Deepika Batra, Ayushi Awasthi, Nick Craggs and Zoe Meyer. I am immensely grateful to Patricia Teasdale for her excellent copy-editing of this manuscript.

I am especially grateful for the beautiful painting on the cover: "On Love: My whole being is hollowed out to house you" by Hilda C. Catz. *Dra Hilda Catz Ph.D Miembro titular en función Didáctica de la Asociación Psicoanalítica Argentina Directora del Departamento de Psicoanálisis y Sociedad de la Asociación Psicoanalítica Argentina Artista visual y Escritora.* It is part of a series.

Finally, I write in memory of my loved and loving late husband: Bruce K. Pollock.

Introduction

> One must bind one's own life to that of others so closely and be able to identify oneself with others so intimately that the brevity of one's own life can be overcome; and one must not fulfill the demands of one's own needs illegitimately, but must leave them unfulfilled, because only the continuance of so many unfulfilled demands can develop the power to change the order of society. But not every personal need can be postponed in this way and transferred to other people, and there is no general and final solution of the conflict.
>
> Sigmund Freud, *Jokes and Their Relation to the Unconscious*, 1905

This book explores the primordial affects and emotions that power intrapsychic and intersubjective relationships. It suggests, following Bion, that emotional relationship is essential for the birth of a mind. Psychoanalysis, which Freud in a letter to Jung (Freud, 1906) asserts is a therapy of Love, explores internal and external relationship. The exploration is an experience; it is not *about experience*. Often, patients come to us in pain about their emotional bonds with others. Especially when they have suffered early childhood trauma and abuse, they have difficulties loving and hating and knowing another human being. In reality, they have difficulty loving and hating and knowing themselves. Psychoanalysis helps them to learn about themselves via their experiences with their analyst.

This book is not meant to be a survey of the field. It originates in personal clinical experience and is informed by Bion's focus on analytic technique. It is also not meant to replace previous theories of psychoanalysis. The theories we use are intimately connected with our analytic identities and these chapters do not offer new theories. I am not even sure these chapters offer new models, although there may be implications in my focus on very primitive processes underlying pathologies. Rather, I am presenting what Levine (2019, in Eekhoff, 2019) names "a metapsychology of process". These processes are also extremely personal and unique between each analyst and analysand. Each of us can only be ourselves. We become the kind of analyst we are based on who we are.

My focus is also on the analyst's gaining access to the outer regions of inner space. Under normal circumstances, these regions are inaccessible, clouded by dissociative and splitting processes. However, helping patients who have more access than they can bear requires analysts to also know these places. These outer reaches are available to those who have suffered trauma in early childhood because their ordinary defenses failed to protect them from their unformed and unorganized nature. The ongoing access to these outer regions of inner space continues their trauma, overwhelming them again and again. In the place of the usual defenses, extreme protections of somatic defenses are evoked, enabling psychic survival. Psychic survival by means of somatic defenses comes at huge cost: relationships are superficial. Behavior and even emotions are mimicked, originating from the outside instead of the inside of a person. Even words are *words about words* instead of words that express emotional truth.

Analysts working with these very primal manifestations often attest that their traumatized patients are difficult to reach and hard to find. Faith and security in the human need for contact and the analytic process that reveals it provides a psychological holding for those of us engaged in this very difficult work. The freedom of mind and constancy of spirit required is humbling. The breadth and depth of emotional experience discovered in each and every analytic relationship is profound. The discipline required to remain curious in the face of violent primal affects and emotions is daunting. At the same time, the satisfaction derived from the privilege of our intimate work is immeasurable.

In **Chapter 1, "The Essence of Being"**, I emphasize my beliefs in the importance of an ontological focus of analytic attention. This is not in place of our more traditional epistemological emphasis. Essential to the uniqueness of every individual is 'some-thing' that cannot be categorized or even accurately named. This 'some-thing' enables us to engage meaningfully with ourselves and our intimate others. Its expression takes many forms, but the 'some-thing' itself does not change. No relationship will alter it, no tragedy will destroy it. At the end of a successful analysis, it will be there, perhaps more visible for others to experience. I wonder whether one's unconscious is expressed by one's essence of being. Perhaps the unconscious contains aspects that are changeable and can become known and others that are the background essence of the Self. Bion (1970) says that at the end of a successful analysis, the essence of the person remains. Freud said the same.

The chapter also speaks of Being and its relation to symbiosis with others. Healthy symbiosis includes a relationship between two bodies, two somas, two beings, two psyches.

Chapter 2, "Love, Hate, and Curiosity", includes my differentiation of affect, emotion, and feeling. The chapter provides context for the way in which the ontological emphasis on being interacts with the epistemological search for meaning via the emotions engendered by the internal and external experiences of reality. Processes of representation and symbolization become the means for both deepening relationships to self and others and increasing satisfaction with life via an ability to tolerate frustration. Clinical examples are given.

Chapter 3, "Body as Dream Space". This chapter discusses the role of the body in health and the way in which healthy somatic processes can be conscripted by the mind and used defensively. It explores how psychoanalysis is increasingly examining the role soma plays in representation and symbolization. Just how that 'mysterious leap' occurs is unknown. However, the chapter asserts that the body is a background object that provides a psychic space for dreaming. As such, the body is a space where thoughts can be found. A clinical example is presented.

Chapter 4, "In Defense of Hope" explores what I believe to be a neglected element of psychoanalysis. Hope is the living edge of growth and creativity. At the same time, it can be a defense against despair, which is hope's conscious manifestation. Further, I am linking hope to a truth principle (Grotstein, 2004), that includes an instinctive drive to find personal truth. The drive for personal truth is also a drive to procreate, to be creative and alive. Perhaps we analysts do not write about hope more frequently because we recognize it as a conscious defense against uncertainty and entropy. Perhaps this is so because hope can be a defense, an omnipotent bulwark against reality, rather than (as I also think of it) a primary affect, experienced in the body and a precursive aspect of representation and symbol formation, a precursor to desire and renewed life, which begin in the body. Hope is an element of the use of the senses via dreaming processes to create and recreate the mind (Monteiro, 2023). Hope is the two psyches (Bollas, 1987) behind every analytic intervention. The chapter includes a clinical example.

Chapter 5, "Premonition: Hope and Dread in the Analytic Hour". Analytic awareness of the process of meaning-making involves tracking premonitions and intuitions to their sources. As precursors of symbolic processing, premonitions are essential elements in any relationship, including the analytic relationship. They provide unconscious communication that informs and amplifies internal and external body and object relations. These relations facilitate depth and dimensionality between and within persons. They also enable the representational processes to establish psychic structure. When traumatized, a person can lose faith in these processes and defend against relationship. Exploring precursors of the emotional experiences of hope and dread enables the analytic dyad to re-vitalize lost potentials and the representation of experience. A clinical example is given to demonstrate the application of these ideas.

Chapter 6, "Psychic Equivalency as an Aspect of Symbiosis". This chapter explores the healthy functioning of symbiotic relationship. It recognizes undifferentiation as a state of mind that is accessed all of our lives and is not pathological evidence of dissociation. Undifferentiation is not only a beginning stage of development. Symbiotic relationship and psychic equivalency provide structure and comfort in phantasy as long as these states of mind remain fluid. Symbiosis is an aspect of the frame and the setting of analysis.

Chapter 7, "The Primordial Symphony of Life: Truth and the Body", continues my examination of the interaction between mind and body in the search for truth. It focuses on the emotions of love, hate and knowledge as they inform and elaborate a sense of self that originates in a somatopsychic dialectic. The movement of emotion begins as an integration of soma and psychic and becomes a symphony by the harmony and disharmony the instincts bring to affective and emotional experience. The background sound and sensation of life are the precursors to the image making and figurability within the symbolization process.

Chapter 8, "Perceptual Identification as Analytic Receptivity of Dissociative States". In this chapter, I describe in detail a highly dissociated patient to illustrate my belief that early, continuous traumatization leads to the patient's overreliance on the defensive use of primary dissociation. Primary dissociation differs from other, better known defensive processes such as splitting, projective identification, or repression. Primary dissociation forecloses somatopsychic cohesion and integration, involves precocious mental development, and disrupts normal processes of projection and introjection. This latter disruption destroys the usual means of unconscious to unconscious emotional communication crucial to the analytic process and necessitates the analyst's sensitive use of perceptual identification, a term Freud (1900) introduced in *Interpretation of Dreams*, which I use to describe these processes. The case report illustrates these challenges, my efforts to overcome them by employing perceptual identification, and the importance of understanding very early mind-body dissociation and the limits it places on more traditional analytic technique.

Chapter 9, "Between the Real and the Imaginary". When reality is too much to bear, bodymind unity can fracture, creating self-deceptions, distortions, and disguises of emotional experience that amount to unconscious lies. Without clarity regarding what is real and what is imaginary, emotional truth is difficult to discern. Lies disrupt the development of a subjective sense of self, making it difficult to trust sensations, emotions, or thoughts. In the absence of this trust, a patient may form a delusion that they do not exist. Working psychoanalytically with patients traumatized in infancy and early childhood requires the analyst to experience a somatic link between herself and the patient, thereby enabling a process that was inhibited and, in some cases nearly aborted, to resume functioning. Clinical material is presented illustrating a negative hallucination of 'not existing' following an emotional experience that could not be borne as well as bodymind dissociation that separated the patient's psychic pain from her childhood narrative. I conclude that these methods of coping with trauma prevent the grieving necessary for truth to become bearable and the mind to grow.

Chapter 10, "The Perversion of Truth and the Disruption of Passion", explores the relationship between truth and lies. Lies are the bodyguard of truth, protecting us from the absolute truth we cannot bear. In addition, the chapter describes the means by which our body relations and our object relations aid us in developing an apparatus for thinking. It emphasizes object relationships as mediators of affect and emotion. The emotions of love, hate, and curiosity, as components of passion, are bridges between the mind and the body as well as between self and other. When one or both members of a couple are insufficiently differentiated, a fusion occurs that perverts relationship. Mimicry takes the place of authentic relationship. The person becomes a lie that and healthy symbiosis is compromised. Unfortunately, when lies are the bodyguards of truth, distortions and delusions also interfere with relationships that promote meaning-making and growth. When each member of a dyad is individuated, their emotional relationship is passionate. A clinical example is given.

Chapter 11, "Body Relations and The Black Hole". This chapter uses a clinical example to demonstrate primal body relations used as defenses against psychic death. The psychic Black Hole is a primitive psychosomatic representation of undifferentiation and loss of the vanished mother of infancy. It is evoked during a psychic collapse, originated when awareness of the reality of separation from the mother comes in too soon. Its repetition creates an implosion into the self instead of an explosion into the receiving other. The catastrophe that it marks is an overwhelming affective storm which has resulted from a loss of the containing (m)other and a subsequent annihilation of the self. As a sign or a signal used for self-regulation, the Black Hole marks a deficit in the ability to symbolize that evokes states of meaninglessness, nothingness, and hopelessness.

Chapter 12, "Missing Emotional Links". Analysts working with borderline or psychotic patients frequently describe being unable to think in the session. This occurs especially when the patient has a delusion of not existing. Such delusions often originate in infancy when the infant's emotional development and acquisition of healthy defenses is thwarted by trauma. Early infantile trauma, occurring before speech, remains as implicit memory in the body and in unconscious phantasy. It is often accompanied by experiences of undifferentiation, formlessness, and meaninglessness. Defenses themselves remain primitive and do not evolve to meet increasingly more and more complex problems of living. This means that the veil between primal states of mind and ordinary everyday adult states of mind is inadequate. A clinical example of working with these unrepresented or poorly represented states of negative hallucination is given.

Chapter 13, "Time, Space and Dimensionality as Somatic Representations". This chapter explores the undifferentiated and symbiotic (Bleger, 1967, the undifferentiated and archaic (Loewald, 1979) analytic relationship and its therapeutic function in the ongoing development of the mind. It traces some of these ideas to the work of Hans Loewald. Loewald's prescience in drawing our attention to somatic underpinnings in language and to archaic levels of the mind always found in relationship foreshadowed current developments in analytic thinking around object relationships. Object relationships profoundly impact the development of the mind via represented and unrepresented states.

It expands on Loewald's "archaic level" of the analytic relationship, focusing on what has frequently been termed 'the psychotic core' (Eigen, 2004) of the dyad. I concur with Loewald that these levels manifest as normal aspects of relationship throughout all of our lives. These deeply unconscious links influence the therapeutic action at a nonverbal level. The communication of the primal link is unconscious to unconscious and outside of language. The derivatives, I believe, are in the soma. When outside of language, words are used as words for their sensual qualities and their associative link to the lost mother of infancy. They are not primarily used for their symbolic meaning. Words are also used as links to primordial unity and the *somatic surround*. The paper explores the defenses of stopping time and space as a means of dedifferentiating. Further the chapter links the undifferentiated aspect of relationship to post-Bionian field theory. A clinical example is given.

Chapter 14, "Catastrophe and Creativity: from Fragmentation to Emergence". This chapter uses Ferenczi's search for truth and the courage he exhibited in seeking it with his patients and his colleagues to explore catastrophe and creativity. Further, I am following Ferenczi's lead into the primordial, exploring a search for truth, that if it is successful will result in both a catastrophic loss and creative gain. In entering the primordial, Ferenczi takes us into experiences of undifferentiation that bring us to the very origins of a self. It is an ontological journey outside of time and space. I also explore fragmentation and how coming apart can lead to finding a means through the chaos to emerge into one's potential.

Conclusion

In reviewing these chapters as I have just done, I am aware of how having an emotional life of loving and hating and knowing others creates turmoil and catastrophe that leads to truth and beauty. I am in awe of what it is to be human.

Familiarity with the primordial never leaves us, but rests silently in our bodies, as background to the truth. We access it in moments of beauty discovered in art, poetry, music, or sexuality. Truth and beauty go together and cannot be separated. Unfortunately, they can be attacked, and with disastrous consequences as we know from the years when Ferenczi's ideas were banned from psychoanalytic discussion. Attacks on truth are as catastrophic as is truth itself. Each of us knows this from our personal experiences with each other as well as of our observations of the political and environmental catastrophes around us.

References

Bion, W. R. (1970). *Attention and Interpretation*. London: Tavistock. [Reprinted London: Karnac, 1984.]

Bleger, J. (1967). *Symbiosis and Ambiguity: A psychoanalytic study*. Churcher, J. and Bleger, L. (Eds.); Rogers, S., Bleger, L., and Churcher, J. (Trans.). London and New York: Routledge, 2013.

Bollas, C. (1978). The Aesthetic Moment and the Search for Transformation. *Annual of Psychoanalysis*, 6: 385–394.

Bollas, C. (1987). *The Shadow of the Object: Psychoanalysis of the Unthought Known*. New York: Columbia University Press.

Eigen, M. (2004). *The Psychotic Core*. London: Karnac.

Freud, S. (1900). The Interpretation of Dreams. *S. E. Volume 4*: ix–625. London: Hogarth. [Trans.: Crick, J. Oxford, UK: Oxford University Press, 1999.]

Freud, S. (1906). The Freud Jung letters (Dec 6, 1906, pp. 12–13).

Grotstein, J. S. (2004). The seventh servant: The implications of a truth drive in Bion's theory of 'O'. *International Journal of Psychoanalysis*, 85: 1081–1101.

Levine, H. (2019). Forward. In Eekhoff, J. K., *Trauma and Primitive Mental States, An Object Relations Perspective*. London and New York: Routledge.

Loewald, H. W. (1979). Reflections on the psychoanalytic process and its therapeutic potential. *Psychoanalytic Study of the Child*, 34(55): 155–167.

Monteiro, J. S. (2023). *Bion's Theory of Dreams: A Visionary Model of the Mind*. London and New York: Routledge.

Chapter 1

Essence of Being

There is *'some-thing'* in us or that <u>is</u> us. What exactly this 'some-thing' is, we do not know and cannot name. The 'some-thing' is ineffable. There is an essence, a soul, a spirit, a 'some-thing' that makes each of us uniquely ourselves. There are no satisfactory words for this 'some-thing', because it is outside of the symbolic order. However, this some-thing is essential for the experience of having a subjective sense of Self. This 'some-thing' is infinite in its manifestations and its potentials. Because this essence is outside the symbolic order, and nameless, psychoanalysts have mostly not considered the *Essence of Being* relevant to psychoanalysis. Yet, I believe it is at the core of what all analysts do, whatever theory grounds their work.

Essence of Being

Exploration into the Essence of Being occurs in every analytic session wordlessly. Discovering wordless places within ourselves and responding to them contributes to our ongoing development. These discoveries occur in an instant and are fleeting. Being present to the 'some-thing', to the essence, has increasingly become explored by contemporary analysts. They use words such as *'being with'* (Reis, 2021), *'presencing'* (Eshel, 2013), and *aesthetics of being* (Bollas, 1978). The *aesthetics of being* is an aspect of the *aesthetic frame* (Bollas, 1978; 1987).

Aesthetics of Being is *Moment*, outside of cognition, outside of symbolization. Moment is when two essences meet in deep rapport (Bollas, 1978). Moment also occurs during contact of self with self. Aesthetics of Being <u>is</u> existence. Being is not about survival, but *Presence*. Essence is present from the instant of sentience and an aspect of the primal position. Moments of Being (Bollas, 1978) are moments "when time becomes a space for the subject". These may also include *authentic pleasure* (Rezze and Braga, 2019). These moments do not accumulate without relationship. They are intricately interwoven in body relations with an actual live other. The Essence of Being meets the essence of another, in what Meltzer (1983) calls *aesthetic reciprocity*, which he identifies as occurring in the first gaze between infant and mother. Bion (1952) postulates that "a physical and mental activity is undifferentiated" (p. 236).

DOI: 10.4324/9781003544470-1

He (1965) says, "The thing in itself is not mediated by the senses which means that it is the unknown... the *essence* [italics mine] is not known because all of our perceptions come into it" (p. 4). When all of our perceptions come into the Essence of Being, a transformation occurs that may bring us closer to or further away from our essential selves. This is a Transformation in O. Analytic process enables a search for the truth of our Being. Such a search occurs in the mystery of a here-and-now relationship that goes beyond appearances and is outside of language. The mystery is found in our *at-one-ment* (Bion, 1970) with ourselves and our subsequent ability to be *at-one-with* another object or to be at-one-with Nature.

Freud knew about this some-thing I call Essence. In fact, his first choice of a word for the ego was the German word for soul. His inner circle dissuaded him from writing about it. Ferenczi too knew about it and ventured to also muse about this 'some-thing'. His analysand, Elizabeth Severn, called it *Orpha* and in doing so was associating essence with a positive life force – a mothering aspect of every human being that made psychically surviving difficult things possible. Perhaps Ferenczi (1932) was closer to essence when he wrote about *Astra*, although his original intent in the choice of that word was to describe a defensive experience of being lost in space. He was writing about becoming further away from Self. I think of Astra as becoming undifferentiated, and not in a pathological sense, but in a Bionian return to the earliest proto-mental experience. Jung too knew 'some-thing' existed inside every human being that was bigger than words could say. He spent his life writing about *Spirit* and found it an essential element in being human. This 'some-thing', whatever we name it, is internal to us human beings. Our soul or spirit or essence is the innermost permanent core of who we are. It is our fundamental nature, our Being. This vital Essence of Being-ness is infinite and beyond description.

Essence of Being is mysterious. It cannot be altered or changed via analysis, but it can evolve or be uncovered, discovered, and experienced as truth about one's self. Each person's Essence is unique to them. Essence cannot be mimicked or counterfeited. It is neither conscious nor unconscious. It just is. It is truth about Self. It exists in what Bion (1977, Vol 10, p. 197) calls an *inaccessible* part of mind, but becomes manifest in its derivatives. It is found in undifferentiated moments of symbiosis. Symbiosis (Bleger, 1967) involves a bodily relationship of essences, or should I say *being-nesses*? Essence of Being is also found in the body and the somatopsychic expressions of embodiment. It is not symbolic.

An analytic process comes from true relationship between both members of the dyad. Transference is only an aspect of this relational process. Any true relationship is intuitive, with responses coming automatically, uncensored and unclaimed. It includes physical and emotional proximity, a body relationship as well as an object relationship. *Intuitive psychoanalysis* is at once ordinary as well as mysterious. Intuitive analysis involves relationship of psyche and soma and of mind and body of each member of the dyad as it is occurring in the present here-and-now rapport. It is emotional, intellectual, and physical. It cannot be otherwise, whether or not it is acknowledged. Surrounding the physical, emotional, and cognitive processes is the atmosphere of the Essence of Being. The Essence of Being is primal and primary. Existence is. Meaning is derived from the simultaneity of symbiosis of two subjects (Botella and Botella, 2005, p. 179). Symbiosis, as Bleger (1967) maintains, is an aspect of all of our relationships all of our lives.

Becoming

Essence of Being emanates becoming. Perhaps Freud (1900) was signaling such a place when he described the navel of the dream as being inaccessible. It might have frightened him since we know he struggled with the idea of *oceanic feeling* (Ackerman, 2017). An oceanic feeling is one of being united with infinity, with the universe. Imaginably this is what Winnicott (1956; 1960) was attempting to understand when he wrote about *True Self*. Bion (1965) writes of the unknown essence. Essence of Being is inaccessible in its totality; however, our Essence, Spirit, Soul of Being is background for everything we do and feel. Essence of Being is foundational to all that we are and all that we present in every intimate moment. Our *unknowable essence* is transformed by our perceptions and by our discovery of a *transformational object* (Bollas, 1987). Bollas (1978; 1987) believes that character is a derivative of *aesthetic moment*. This is a very different idea than character arising as defense against overwhelming forces of nature and nurture. Essence is Being is what makes analysis with difficult-to-reach patients possible.

Soul murder or death of Essence is not possible in my way of thinking. For this reason, I believe psychoanalysis is able to help everyone somewhat – not every analyst can help every analysand, however if Essence cannot die, but exists beneath the layers of trauma, then analysand and analyst can find each other. Granted, the detritus of defense and deficit will build resistances in both people. The task will not be easy. However, this faith in *relationship of essences* gives me patience as well as hope and security in the analytic process and the dyadic relationship.

Aesthetic Reciprocity

Aesthetic reciprocity is found to a greater or lesser degree in every intimate relation when two essences meet. When I say this, I am expanding on Meltzer (1983), who refers to the reciprocity of immediate connection and love-at-first sight of mother and baby. I believe aesthetic reciprocity is an instantaneous rapport: a relationship of essences resulting in an immediate emotional link. Love-at-first-sight occurs between lovers. Hate-at-first-sight occurs between enemies. Curiosity-at-first-sight occurs when attention is riveting and captured by the object. Aesthetic reciprocity as expression of the proto-mental affects of love, hate, and knowledge unconsciously occurs in our consulting rooms with every patient. It is Moment. It is oneness and undifferentiation. It is fleeting oceanic sensation. It is fusion and merger, as I differentiate them (Eekhoff, 2019).

Essence of Being is most perceivable in reciprocity with one other actual human individual. Our senses and sensibilities transform our essence into responses to our experiences. Our very presence unconsciously transmits our Essence. These transformations of essence include our perceptions of the world and our expression of ourselves and the world in music, art, and poetry. Life is inspiring. It then takes imagination and awareness to make use of this inspiration.

Aesthesia is awareness – a mental responsiveness to our emotional responses to life, that includes our insight and intuition informed by our affects and emotions. As such, Essence of Being is revealed by our emotional awareness as expressed in love, hate, and knowledge. These emotional links bring us closest to our true selves, to our essences. These emotions link us to being and becoming embodied. They are relational both inside and outside of our selves. In analysis, emotions and their expressions drive the analytic process. They also drive our epistemophilic instincts and the process of representation and symbolization (Levine, 2012; Levine and Powers, 2017). But first is Being, then becoming. This is ontological and not symbolic.

Analytic Passion

Analytic passion arises when two people meet intimately. Analytic passion requires two people in contact (Bion, 1962b). Honest contact is not always pretty, nor is it neat and organized. It is a messy somatopsychic expression of the Essences of Being of two people who unconsciously meet in symbiotic union. Observing the manifest union (Loewald, 1980; Civitarese, 2023) is an aspect of analytic encounters. Both members of the dyad do this, but typically it is the analyst's responsibility to speak of it. The analysand may or may not do so, depending upon their inclination in the moment or their capacity to find language. Ferenczi (1932) wrote at length about the enormous responsibility this fact places upon the analyst. Honest contact inevitably produces change (Ferenczi, 1909). Growth inevitably includes pain and, as Bion (1965) has said, true contact is catastrophic. True contact upends previous organizational structures and unconscious beliefs. Being in relationship requires faith in a process of becoming more than what we were – of the continual and inevitable nature of *Being in Transition* (Bergstein, 2020). Everything is changing in every moment. Since everything is changing, faith is required to tolerate not knowing what is happening next.

Faith is also a requirement for honesty in relationship. Even our patients who proclaim they have no faith in us or the analytic process contradict this proclamation by coming faithfully and paying us for our work with them. They recognize, even when they do not know it, that our analytic relationship is not about the mechanics of problem solving or communication about a difficulty. It is about intimate contact and discovery of what is happening between and within two people. Analysis is having faith and love and hope in the waiting for thought to arise.

The Interpretation of Facts

Faith is not about why or how or what. Attention to the why, the how and even the what of relationship is an intellectual approach to the mechanics of relationship. The why we are the way we are is related to our Essence of Being, and therefore is unknowable. Sometimes, we are drawn to exploring the 'why' as a means of understanding the context and the culture out of which a person emerges. There may be value in that. The danger is that when we attempt to know why we are the way we are, we reduce reality to a cause-and-effect experience. In doing so, we unconsciously support our omnipotent beliefs of being able to control our relationships and our development.

Bion (1977) says, "...psychoanalysis needs to be carefully done, because the situation is so precarious and because it is so difficult to find the minimum conditions for achieving wisdom either in oneself or in one's collaborator – namely the patient" (pp. 180–181). As analysts, we are reminded by him to be cautious and careful. We are <u>being</u> in relationship with the patient. Being is not about behavior. Being is not symbolic interpretation of facts.

We are also not particularly interested in the 'how' of our analytic relationships. The 'how' is related to the behavior that is presented and although analyzable, behavior is not a matter of Faith. Behavior is perhaps more related to our ability or lack of it to contain our emotions and think about them. Bion (1958; 1992) says this is directly related to our ability to tolerate frustration. Being able to wait is possible only if we can tolerate frustration. Frustration of not knowing, of not being in control, of being strangers to our Selves and having big emotions for seemingly no reason, is inevitable.

Perhaps we analysts are somewhat more interested in the 'what' of the immediate analytic experience in that it can place us within the immediate *somatic surround* of the emotional experience instead of outside of it as an observer. 'Some-thing' is happening here and the moment we observe it, it is already past and some-thing new is occurring. Observation is a key element of curiosity and a necessary component of self-reflection as long as we as analysts are *participating observers*. We are simultaneously *observing partici-pants*. Only later, after the session, might we be able to think about our experience and derive meaning from it. In the here-and-now of the session, we are in the relationship and in the experience.

A mechanical approach to analysis, without a faith-based belief in its efficacy, leaves out the personal and focuses on what is known or knowable rather than on what is unknown and mysterious. It focuses on the intentional instead of the unpredictable. Faith in the process of relating contains a belief in the inevitability of change if two people truly meet. Faith enhances our curiosity and creativity, enabling us to pay attention to the mystery and the essence of being-and-becoming who we are.

Faith and Trust

Faith enables us to be open, loving, kind, and compassionate. It also puts us in touch with our darker sides – our hatred and our aversion. This inevitably evokes terror and dread in both members of the analytic dyad. Making contact with some-thing, with Essence, with Being, even fleetingly is being in touch with the infinite, *being the infinite*. Contact with being the infinite is awesome, inspiring, and terrifying. Faith in the Essence of Being is a state of Being not primarily a state of mind. It is momentary undifferentiation and waiting. It is not fragmentation or disintegration or even primary narcissism. Bion (1970) would call faith in the Essence of Being 'O'.

Faith and trust are the stuff of dreams and dreaming, of fantasy and phantasy, of truth and imagination. They are also the background essential for inspiration and creativity. The Essence of Being lies at the center of every intimate relationship and inevitable change. Change embodies our hope of a future. Faimberg (2013a; 2013b) calls this "As yet". Loewald (1980) also looks to the future as a means of being in the present. The present and future are the poetry and the perfume of the Essence of Being. Dreams, while both awake and asleep, are the processes of representation where Essence of Being is revealed. In *Dream Life*, Meltzer (1983) says, "But it is the poetry of the dream that catches and gives formal representation to the passions which *are* the meaning of our experience so that they may be operated upon by reason" (p. 47). Faith in Moment emerges as trust in the future.

Clinical Examples: Dennis, Brian, and Ada

Finding clinical examples of Essence of Being is not easy. The people who have shared these intimate moments with me sometimes are barely able to articulate their experiences. I too am attempting to describe ineffable experiences that are mysterious, indescribable, and life-changing. They occur between two people while simultaneously creating catastrophic internal change in structure and the vertices through which we experience ourselves and others.

Dennis

I have written about Dennis in Chapter 11, "Between the Real and the Imaginary". Several times he has reported leaving our sessions and dancing to the music of Elvis Presley. Sometimes he moves through his house saying, "I'm alive. I'm alive!" I believe that the sessions I am speaking of demonstrate access to his Essence of Being which enables his aliveness.

In the first session of the week, Dennis told me our work last week had really shaken him. Over the weekend, he had awakened with many dreams which he could not now recall. He did remember being deeply sad and teary about his life. The morning of our session, he awoke feeling alive. He said he had a fleeting experience of himself in the future – with potential. It was a feeling he had never had before. He looked forward to our session so he could tell me and did not feel the dread that has become customary in the few minutes before.

The next day, he told me how important it was that he could tell me about his experience of having potential, given that he was 81 years old. He felt he could be himself in the future. He wondered if this fleeting feeling of future potential was something new or something he had lost and regained. Momentarily he felt he was, fleetingly, in touch with a part of himself that existed as a young child but that he'd never known due to all the abuse and neglect in his family. He said, "This is the me I might have been, and I am in awe to find myself now with potential again. It must have always been here". Instead of 'it' always being there, I might have said his Essence of Being was always with him.

Brian

Brian, a scientist, came to see me because his wife told him it was analysis or divorce. He had sympathy for her, telling me that he thought he was pretty stiff and unfeeling. He had a difficult medical history from birth onward and thought he had 'shut down' when in the incubator. He just didn't feel much, neither good or bad things.

Brian told me he knew he existed because of his daughter. One of the few times in his life when he did feel something about himself was when his daughter was born. Moments after her birth, he looked into his daughter's eyes and saw a person there. He was terrified. He realized that he had never known himself as the person his infant daughter already was. The terror was also that in that moment of eye contact, he could also feel himself – a self he had never known. She seemed to recognize his Self in him, and that recognition and mysterious miracle brought him in touch with his own essence of Being. Meltzer (1983), and I agree with him, would call this aesthetic reciprocity.

Ada

I have written about Ada (see Chapter 3). Until now, I have not wondered about her experience of coming into her body as being an example of a fleeting awareness of her Essence. I have described it as an experience of existing, but now I wonder. Ada sensed a presence that terrified her and only later did she realize it was her. She frequently told me there was nothing inside of her because she was a sieve and what went in went out just as fast. There was a nothingness inside. As her analysis progressed, she began able to notice her Self. At first this was quite disturbing. She went from a feeling of emptiness to a feeling of fullness. Having some-thing inside of her was terrible and terrifying. She became claustrophobic in relation to her own sense of some-one inside of her. This was not a welcome change. She responded to her own aliveness with aversion, oscillating between experiences of being full and empty, empty and full. She had never before experienced the Essence of herself, her Presence. When she discovered this was she herself, she cried as she had never cried before.

Discussion

I have come to believe that Essence of Being is an essential ineffable element of presence. Presence is an integrated embodied somatopsychic existence in the world, that includes the alive mysterious, *inaccessible self.* To be present is to be fully in the moment with soma, psyche, and essence. I say Essence because as I have indicated, I do not like to use the words spirit or soul due to their being saturated with religious implication. Perhaps this caution is unnecessary. I may in fact be talking about something that religions have always known. Contemporary theologians describe the "God-in-us". The Bible says, "The body is the temple of the Holy Spirit" (First Corinthians 6:19–20). Perhaps the Holy Spirit referred to in the Bible is an attempt to name the Essence of Being that is expressed when we are present to ourselves and others.

Essence is not a concrete inanimate object. Essence is not discoverable with our senses. Rather Essence is alive, pulsating, constantly transforming 'something' that is uniquely personal. Essence of Being is profoundly mysterious and awesome in its force and constancy. Essence manifests in someone's ability to be present to life. Essence in relationship creates emotional experience, depth, and intimacy.

Essence can be hidden. *Denial of Essence* and focus on the concrete aspects of living interferes with presence. Denial impedes growth and development when it does not use concreteness as a means to verify reality and enable a representational process to evolve. Bion (1962b, pp. 50–51) says, "The concretization, by contrast, can be seen as a form of publication which facilitates correlation by common sense; that is, by stating something so that it is recognized as an object of one sense that can yet be tested as an object of another sense. The criterion for the statement must be its value in facilitating testing by more than one sense or by the senses of more than one person". The testing of reality via relationship becomes a means of testing for truth. Further, Bion (1965) adds, "the qualities of any object are a function of its relationships" (p. 44).

Meaning is derived from relationships, both internal and external. Concrete descriptive language enables determining both the context and the specific relationship of the experience. The idea that any word has only one meaning and is always used in the same manner by all who use it denies the alive, constantly changing experience of *Essence-in-Transition*. Concrete language is designed to describe the material and the finite on the way to a description of the immaterial and the infinite. Of course, the process can also move in the opposite direction from deductive to inductive and inductive to deductive. Psychoanalysis in its awareness of constantly changing reality is concerned with the unknown and the infinite. I concur with Bion (1977) when he says, "Psycho-analysts must become accustomed to open-ended theory, to infinite, not finite space" (p. 22).

Conclusion

This introductory chapter has laid the foundation for the rest of this book. I am focusing on an ontological exploration of what it is to be human. In exploring Essence of Being, I have asserted that it cannot be destroyed and so is always present no matter how inaccessible. My belief in Essence of Being gives me faith in the life-altering Presence found in all relationships. I believe this makes psychoanalysis possible with patients who are hard to reach and hard to find.

References

Ackerman, S. (2017). Exploring Freud's Resistance to the Oceanic Feeling. *Journal of the American Psychoanalytic Association*, 65: 9–31.

Bergstein, A. (2020). Violent Emotions and the violence of life. *The International Journal of Psychoanalysis*,100(5): 863–868.

Bion, W. R. (1952). Group dynamics: a review. *International Journal of Psycho-Analysis*, 33, [Reprinted in Klein, M., Heimann, P., and Money-Kyrle, R. (Eds.). *New Directions in Psychoanalysis* (pp. 440–477). London: Tavistock Publications, 1955. Reprinted in *Experiences in Groups* (1961).]

Bion, W. R. (1958). On Arrogance. *International Journal of Psycho-Analysis*, 39: 144–146.

Bion, W. R. (1962a). A psycho-analytic theory of thinking. *International Journal of Psycho-Analysis*, 43: 306–310. [Reprinted as "A theory of thinking", in Bion, W. R., *Second Thoughts* (pp. 110–119). London: Karnac, 1984.]

Bion, W. R. (1962b). *Learning from Experience*. London: Heinemann. [Reprinted London: Karnac, 1984.]

Bion, W. R. (1965). *Transformations*. London: Heinemann. [Reprinted London: Karnac, 1984.]

Bion, W. R. (1970). *Attention and Interpretation*. London: Tavistock. [Reprinted London: Karnac, 1984.]

Bion, W. R. (1977, Vol 10, p. 197). Levine, H. B., Reed, G. S., and Scarfone, D. (Eds.). (2013). *Unrepresented States and the Construction of Meaning: Clinical and Theoretical Contributions*. London: Karnac.

Bleger, J. (1967). *Symbiosis and Ambiguity: A Psychoanalytic Study.* Churcher, J. and Bleger, L. (Eds.); Rogers, S., Bleger, L., and Churcher, J. (Trans.). London and New York: Routledge, 2013.

Bollas, C. (1978). The Aesthetic Moment and the Search for Transformation. *Annual of Psychoanalysis*, 6: 385–394.

Bollas, C. (1987). *The Shadow of the Object: Psychoanalysis of the Unthought Known.* New York: Columbia University Press.

Botella, C. and Botella, S. (2005). *The Work of Psychic Figurability: Mental States without Representation.* Weller, A. with Zerbib, M. (Trans.). Hove, East Sussex, UK: Brunner–Routledge.

Civitarese, G. (2023). *Psychoanalytic Field Theory: A Contemporary Introduction.* London and New York: Routledge.

Eshel, O. (2013). Patient-Analyst "Withness", On Analytic "Presencing," Passion and Compassion in States of Breakdown, Despair, and Deadness. *Psychoanalytic Quarterly*, 82: 925–963.

Eekhoff, J. K. (2019). *Trauma and Primitive Mental States: An Object Relations Perspective.* London and New York: Routledge.

Faimberg, H. (2013a). The as Yet Situation in Winnicott's Fragment of an Analysis (1955): 'You Father Did Not Make You the Honor of … Yet'. *The Psychoanalytic Quarterly*, 82(4): 849–875.

Faimberg, H. (2013b). 'Well, You Better ask Them': The Countertransference Position at the Crossroad. In Oelsner, R. (Ed.), *Transference and Countertransference Today.* London and New York: Routledge.

Ferenczi, S. (1909). Introjection and transference. In *First Contributions to Psychoanalysis* (pp. 35–93). New York: Brunner/Mazel, 1980.

Ferenczi, S. (1932). *The Clinical Diary of Sándor Ferenczi.* In Dupont, J. (Ed.); Balint, M. and Jackson, N. Z. (Trans.). Cambridge, MA: Harvard University Press, 1988.

Levine, H. B. (2012). The colourless canvas: Representation, therapeutic action and the creation of mind. *International Journal of Psycho-Analysis*, 93: 607–629.

Levine, H. B. and Powers, D. G. (Eds.). (2017). *Engaging Primitive Anxieties of the Emerging Self: The Legacy of Francis Tustin.* London: Karnac.

Loewald, H. (1980). *Papers on Psychoanalysis.* New Haven, CT: Yale University Press.

Meltzer, D. (1983). *Dream-Life: A Re-examination of the Psycho-analytical Theory and Technique.* Strathclyde, Perthshire, UK: Clunie Press.

Reis, B. (2021). The analyst's listening for, to, with. *International Journal of Psychoanalysis*, 102: 219–2356.

Rezze, Cecil José and Braga, João Carlos (2019). Authentic Pleasure. In Alisobhani, Afsaneh and Corstorphine, Glenda (Eds.), *Explorations in Bion's 'O': Everything We Know Nothing About.* The Routledge Wilfred R. Bion Studies Book Series. 1st Edition, Kindle Edition. London and New York: Routledge.

Winnicott, D. W. (1956). On Transference. *International Journal of Psychoanalysis*, 37: 386–388.

Winnicott, D. W. (1960). The Theory of the Parent-Infant Relationship. *International Journal of Psychoanalysis*, 41: 585–595.

Chapter 2

Love, Hate, and Curiosity

Bion's Model of the Development of the Mind

We are all different. In spite of these differences – of race, age, gender, class, character, culture, history, etc. – we have one thing in common. We all need human connection. Granted, we are also unique in the ways in which we personally respond to that need for connection with others. Some of us are gregarious and out-going. Others are introverted and solitary. Some prefer group interactions. Others prefer one-on-one. Some are satisfied with proximity; others long for and seek emotional intimacy with physical and sexual closeness. Still others live as if they need no one. Whatever the behavioral expression around this physical and emotional need for others, the instinctive need is a given. The need for others remains whether or not it is denied, split-off, or dissociated. Human beings are social mammals who need each other. This interdependency keeps humans physically vital, emotionally thriving, and intellectually active.

The reality of profound dependence that continues throughout life (Winnicott, 1963; Bleger, 1967/2013) led Klein (1946; 1952; 1975) to focus on relationship as well as intrapsychic instincts. She learned this from her clinical experience with small children. She paid attention to their bodies and the concreteness of psychic reality as it was manifested in the children's unconscious phantasies about their mother's body as well as their own. She found evidence of these phantasies in their play and in the transference. Klein used their play much as she used the free associations of her adult patients. Her ability to observe signs of deeply unconscious processes and respond emotionally to these resonated with her little patients. Some of this she also learned from her experience with her analyst Ferenczi, who might be credited with the discovery of Object Relations. Klein and Fairbairn continued Ferenczi's clinical research into the importance of the external world in the creation of the internal one.

Bion (1958b; 1962a; 1962b; 1963; 1970) elaborated the processes present in the birth of mind. Learning from experience, according to Bion (1962b), occurs via emotional relationship. He linked the birth of the mind to emotions, using love (L), hate (H), and knowledge (K) to represent them. His intuitive grasp of the process foreshadowed neuroscientists' research into the

DOI: 10.4324/9781003544470-2

necessity of emotions for learning (Damasio, 1999) Bion, like Freud and Klein, was able to perceive and emotionally respond to deeply unconscious processes, tracing their origins to fetal states of body and mind. He placed emotions at the center of the communicating and thinking processes.

Further, he believed that the mother's ability to receive and interpret the infant's emotional communications is internalized by infants, which helps them to develop a sense of existing. He maintains that it is not just the information that is learned, but that the process itself is internalized. The internalization of the process of meaning-making from sensory and emotional experience creates what he calls an "apparatus for thinking" (Bion, 1962a; 1963; 1965). The apparatus for thinking originates in the body's experience of trying to order and understand infinite sensory experiences (Eekhoff, 2022). The bridge between sensory experience and making use of those concrete facts is mysterious. However, I believe an important component of that mysterious bridge is emotion. Reverie and meaning-making of a baby's somatic emotional experience is the essence of a mother's love. We might add that reverie and meaning-making of an analysand's somatic emotional experience is the essence of an analyst's love.

The ability to think, as I understand Bion (1962a; 1962b), then comes from love as expressed by reverie. The presence or existence of both mother and infant and the actual physical relationship between them is essential. The experienced emotional relationships between the mother's breast and the infant's mouth, the mother's skin and the infant's skin, the mother's mind and the infant's mind, are primal. These primal experiences build ego strength. Reverie, in Bion's usage, is always a function of love because it requires both radical openness and trust. The mother's trust is in both the infant and herself. Her faith is in the processes evolving between them. The mother's presence and use of reverie enables the infant to build a tolerance for emotions, not just a tolerance for frustration. Then, with tolerance of both emotion and frustration, in the physical absence of the mother's reverie and love, a thought can be formed. Thoughts require a thinker to enable the accumulation of emotional experience. The thinker develops a tolerance for not knowing.

When tolerance for emotion is inadequate, due to a *catastrophic miss* for whatever reason between infant and mother, extraordinary protections (Mitrani, 2001) are required. Extra ordinary protections enable the child to cope with devastating, overpowering sensations and emotions. The catastrophic miss between the two may include physical and emotional traumas that interrupt the development of ordinary protections. An aspect of what may then become 'missing' when extra-ordinary protections are used is the affective seeking of contact with another. Instead, relationships are met with indifference.

Indifference is not found in the unconscious, nor is it possible without mentalization that erases affect and emotion. Indifference is a defence against traumatic experience that includes a loss of self or other. It signals the presence of a catastrophe. Indifference is not a deficit, but the defense results in deficits. Patients who cannot tolerate frustration often behave indifferently, which impedes the development of a thinker to think the thought. Indifference also marks a lack of tolerance for emotions of love, hate, and knowledge.

The Emotional Link

Bion (1977) tells analysts to pay attention to the link. To do so requires paying attention to love, hate, and curiosity. I associate awareness of existence to love and life; fear of annihilation to hate and death; and curiosity to the capacity for concern. All are present, even when one or the other foregrounds. Love, hate, and curiosity present differently depending upon the vertices from which they are perceived: they are perceived and expressed differently in the primal position than in the paranoid-schizoid position or the depressive position. However, all three are present in all positions. Love, hate, and curiosity put us in touch with primal states of body and mind.

In this chapter, I am focusing on the vertices of the paranoid-schizoid position or the depressive position described by Klein, as well as the vertex of the primal position elaborated by Ogden, Bleger, and myself. Grotstein (2007) claims that Bion's 'O', which occurs both before and after these positions, is a transcendent position. I will leave that discussion for another time. Noticing the vertices from which my patient and I experience each other enables me to ascertain the nature of the emotional link between us. The positions are vertices through which experience is organized.

In the primal position, the emotional link is more somatopsychic. Existence itself – being and becoming – is the focus of attention. In the paranoid schizoid position, where anxiety is high, the emotional link is more reactive, making thinking, feeling, and doing equivalent. The survival of the self is primary. The emotional link in the depressive position includes more space for emotion and for thinking. Thinking, feeling, and doing are more often differentiated from each other. The other is of primary concern. All positions are always present in the psyche and foreground and background depending upon the circumstances.

I also hope to demonstrate that these three emotional processes chosen by Bion as representative of all emotional life intersect and interact to create a passionate engagement with others and with the world. Emotions are fluid, constantly shifting and changing with intimacy and connection. They also are intense and anything but predictable. They evolve from the innate mammilian affects researched and named by Panksepp (1998) as seeking, rage, fear, panic, lust, play, and care. Affects are not unique nor are they personal. We share them with all mammals and, of course, all humans.

Emotions which are transformations of affects are uniquely personal. Although they are both conscious and unconscious, I believe emotions are primarily unconscious. They effect unconscious phantasy. Emotions are in constant flux. They are the links in every relationship. Feelings which are the personal ideas and beliefs derived from both affects and emotions are less fluid, more likely to be shared by groups, and often seemingly difficult to alter. They include a large cognitive component as well as their emotional origins and are primarily conscious. Some patients are able to have feelings while seemingly not experiencing emotions. Patients will say, "It's just how I feel", implying that their feelings are absolute truth and unchangeable.

As elements of relatedness necessary for intellectual development, affects and emotions fuel the mysterious link between soma and psyche (Eekhoff, 2019). These mysteries perpetuate being and becoming as well as maintain going-on-being (Winnicott, 1960). Emotion moves the mind to make abstractions from concrete facts. Without emotions as internal links, facts do not come together nor do they accumulate significantly. Without emotional responses to the sensory realities of experience, facts are not usable for problem-solving or for thinking. Emotions can be abstracted and put into words. These words are *about* an emotional experience. They are not *the* experience. These can even be words about other words about emotions. Without emotions as links, two people can have a transactional relationship that lacks passion. Emotions are foundational elements of passion, imagination, and dream thought.

The Need to Communicate

Human beings need to communicate. They need to communicate with both themselves and with others. Communication involves many nonverbal aspects of relationship as well as verbal. The somatic expressions of affects and emotions are present long before language. They are found in images and dreams. They are somatically in the breath and in the body. The way a body moves, gestures, or engages reveals the underlying emotional state. The eyes and the face also reveal our deepest affects and emotions. They express interest or curiosity, openness to intimacy, or closedness to emotional contact. The eyes express presence as is found in emotional interaction or absence as is found in indifference or dissociation. The eyes recognize others as human, or not. Emotions drive unconscious communicative projections, introjections, and identifications, thereby also driving the representation and symbolization processes. Under normal circumstances, ordinary defenses enable emotional communication.

Love (L), Hate (H), and Knowledge (K) express innate human needs for connection and communication (Bergstein,2020). They tie the instinctive need for and expectation of intimacy with a sense of existing, fostering subjective experience. Love, hate, and knowledge interact with the vertices through which we subjectively relate to the world. They put experience into perspective. Together they enhance communal meaning-making. Just how these links occur is mysterious. As puzzling is the mysterious leap between body and mind, also accomplished via these emotional forces (Monteiro, 2023).

Somehow in humans, the instincts and the mind are internally joined via unconscious emotional responses, creating a multi-dimensional soma-topsychic structure. In this chapter, I have chosen to focus on 'curiosity' (Fisher, 2011) as an essential element of knowledge. In doing so, I hope to highlight the processes of getting to know and getting to be known by another person and by one's self; however, getting-to-know without love or hate is insufficient for being and becoming.

Love, hate, and curiosity promote emotional and intellectual development by ensuring internal cohesion and external intimate relationships. They arise from the depths of our existential presence and, in unison, help create internal structures out of which we experience the world. They are responsible for the vertices we use to order, classify, and subordinate information. Emotional responses determine the dimensionality of internal space. Affects and the emotions of love, hate, and curiosity paradoxically put us in the intensity of the moment. When functioning together in harmony to connect with an alive other person, these emotions create passion. Passion always involves relationship with another person (Bion, 1963).

Passion

Passion, as Bion and I are using it, can be an aspect of sexuality, but the two are very different. Passion and sexuality are not the same. Passion is a soma-topsychic state that is never violent. Passion is an expression of love, hate and curiosity entwined. Passion, according to Bion (1963), is always about at least two people. He says,

> Awareness of passion is not dependent on sense. For senses to be active only one mind is necessary: passion is evidence that two minds are linked and that there cannot possibly be fewer than two minds if passion is present.
>
> (p. 13)

The intensity of passion cannot be held alone. Passion seeks expression and involves communication with both self and other. Passion includes sign, signal, and symbol. In that way, passion is an emotional and mental process of integration and meaning-making. It is related to emotional truth and, hence, is central to creativity. Passion is the ontological expression of being and becoming. Passion is linked to *aesthetics of being* (Bollas, 1978, 1987).

As truth is often psychically disorganizing, passion is painful, revealing truth that one becomes newly attuned to inside and outside oneself. Therefore, passion upsets the established psychic order. No wonder Bion also says that when any two people meet, it is catastrophic. In spite of the pain derived from the loss of a previous psychic organization, Bion (1963) says that by passion he means, "the component derived from L, H, and K. I mean the term to represent an emotion experienced with intensity and warmth though without any suggestion of violence" (pp. 12–13). It is not therefore the violence of emotions (Bergstein, 2020) that passion represents that causes pain. Rather passion carries truth. The personal truth that we are forever in transition is terrifying. The truth that life is transitory is incomprehensible.

Passion is vitalizing because it puts us in touch with our primal selves, with affective states that we normally may be only vaguely aware of. Being in touch with the primal, our mammilian humanity, is humbling even as it is energizing. This is the enlivening emotional world of reverie, imagination, and intuition. Psychoanalytic reverie is very different from artistic reverie in that it is not only private and personal, but evoked in a shared space with another.

Psychoanalytic reverie is unconscious communication peeking through and creating turbulence and transformation in both participants. It resembles a state of primary maternal preoccupation, although is not the same, in that one's attention, openness, and receptivity to the personal and shared experience is then material for understanding by both participants. Passion is the mysterious communicative link we so desperately long for from ourselves and to ourselves as well as from others and to them.

Love, as an element of passion, is a link that includes hate and curiosity. Without those, love becomes a means of losing the self in the other. I say 'in' because Bion's observations of container and contained also relate to passion. A wide-open psychic container has no boundaries. It is infinite. Perhaps those who are falling in love describe being ripped open or torn apart or terrified by their vulnerability because they have lost their usual psychic skin. Sometimes, they also feel as if their two bodies are one. In becoming one with their lover, they have opened to infinity. The lover seems essential for being in the world. At another level, the lover is essential for survival. For this reason, often initially, love involves a symbiotic attachment that includes withdrawing from the rest of the world. The same is true when a couple has a pregnancy and then a baby. Opening to the baby often includes shutting out the world for a time.

However we define it, love involves radically opening to another person. It is an emotion half conscious and half unconscious. Love occurs against the will. Falling in love with a baby is instantaneous. Lovers are not chosen but found. Consumed and taken over by love, the loved one, whether family or friend, becomes more important than anyone else. For a brief timeless moment, the other and the union is all there is. In the isolation, there is peace and safety. There is no need for vigilance or for differentiation. The concomitant loss of self and the grief over that loss are momentarily delayed by the symbiotic pleasure of being in the other and feeling the other in the self. This is first love. Of course, I am naming only one aspect of love, an aspect many never consciously experience. For many, love is softer, quieter, and less disturbing.

Love without the mediation of hate and curiosity interferes with differentiation and results in a destructive fusion with other that denies the reality of separateness. Oceanic bliss can involve a loss of going-on being. Symbiosis, a natural and healthy aspect of relationship from birth to death (Bleger, 1967/ 2013), becomes extreme and foregrounds. The irony is that oneness as is found in all symbiotic love can be a death of the self if hate and curiosity are lacking. For change to happen, the symbiotic structure must be disrupted. Such disruption, brought on by true emotional contact, is catastrophic since it troubles the internal *organization of experience*. Psychic equivalency (Eekhoff, 2022) is an attempt to keep everything the same.

Hate, as an element of passion, enforces limits and boundaries and moves individuals out of the protective bubble of love. Envy of the loved one and the very traits that stimulated the attraction, threatens the union. Terror of being subsumed by the other and lost forever inside of them arises as psychic and physical boundaries are radically opened. Terror and hatred as its expression maintains psychic boundaries, asserts individuality, and fosters differentiation. An oscillation between open and closed psychic borders regulates the intensity of the passion. Hatred ensures this movement so the *oceanic bliss* of oneness in love is challenged. Psychic shifting of perspectives and constant fluidity between emotional forces promotes change and development. Hatred in families drives healthy competitive dynamics and contributes to sibling rivalry, oedipal conflict, and the ability to emancipate.

Hate without the intersession of love and curiosity is destructive. Hate without mediation aggressively resists change and promotes envy. The comfort of psychic patterns such as are found in container and contained relationships may become hidden and/or distorted when attacks of hate predominate. The capacity for concern does not evolve, resulting in attacks on relational links. Acknowledgment and realization of otherness is avoided. These attacks are on one's own mind and the mind's ability to use somatic experience to grow and develop (Bion, 1959; 1963).

Hate might take the form of an aversion of the very existence of the other. It might be self-envy where the self is annihilated and the person is controlled by an unconscious phantasy of not existing. Psychic attacks of hatred are found in the avoidance of actual personal relationship with both self and other. As an expression of hate, these attacks seek to eliminate difference and to promote a psychic phantasy of oneness. The difference in hate's phantasy of oneness and love's phantasy of oneness is the aggression by which it is maintained.

Curiosity enables self-regulation. As the third element of passion, it provides emotional distance from both love and hate. The curious benign witness is separate from love and hate, which when observed can be understood. Distance enables perspective and hence also encourages a fluid interaction that mediates and moderates love and hate. Curiosity as a drive to know and be known enables a tolerance of excessive, potentially overwhelming, emotion. It also acknowledges not knowing and implies a tolerance for uncertainty fueled by faith in oneself and the other. Curiosity fuels an attraction that includes desire and interest. It focuses attention and drives communication. The wish to know and be known mediates fear and the approach avoidance dance of intimacy. Curiosity creates a witness, thereby adding perspective, providing space for reflection and realization.

Curiosity without love and hate is obstructive, turning the other into a possession to be used and abused for personal gain. It becomes perverse, manipulative, and arrogantly judgmental. Voyeurism follows. Bion (1958a) describes how analysis itself can become highjacked by a perverse curiosity and an arrogance about knowing. Obsessive processing, in reality describing, of the self becomes an autistic defense against the link.

Curiosity conjoined with love and hate becomes a source of continual renewal. The effortless intermixing of the three expands possibilities for the recognition of new and creative experience. Curiosity provides a focus and aids the differentiation process. It fosters attraction for others and paying attention to them. Curiosity, as well as love and hate, is directed not only at the other person, but also towards the self. Self-love and self-hate are moderated by self-curiosity. Together, they enable mourning.

Passion, the union of love, hate, and curiosity, enables persons to learn more about themselves as they are getting to know the other. Getting to know speaks to the movement and the fluidity of emotions. Getting to know also contributes to the accumulation of attachment, dimensionality, and depth. Passion as a product of love, hate, and curiosity is both creative and destructive. Old ways are uncovered and altered. New ways are bearable because of the pleasures of passion. Passion keeps the 'apparatus for thinking' flexible and in use. Passion includes an oscillating container and contained relationship between two people. Body relations and object relations heal unintegrated unrepresented sources of pain and fuel the symbolic and creative processes.

Trauma as Disrupter of Passion

Trauma, which I define as an internal and external event that is too much for the mind to bear, disrupts emotional links and hence communication. The intense emotions unleashed by a failure of the defensive barriers to protect the psyche from overwhelm, further traumatize the person. Ordinary defenses fail. Traumatic experience is traumatic because it attacks the container and contained relationship between self and other. Trauma destroys the internal and external links. When under extreme duress and without the aid of a mediating other, such as occurs with early childhood trauma, the intensity of love, hate, or curiosity overwhelms body and mind unity. Emotional shutdown results. Mental processing ceases. The triad of emotions are split off from each other and often from consciousness altogether.

An emotional shut-down can take many forms. The emotions can be defensively separated, split-off from each other and projected uncontained out into the universe, causing a depletion. Ferenczi (1932) named this process *astra*. Without a receiving other as container, emotions may be split off and projected into the body, causing many somatic symptoms. In extreme cases, the senses themselves are separated from each other, dismantled and perceived singularly (Meltzer, 1975a; 1975b) in order to manage the emotional intensity. The chaos of sensory experience and the infinite number of perceptions associated with them become split- off from emotions. There are splits of splits of splits. Ferenczi (1933) describes this as atomization. The shutdown in response to chaos also separates the linking function of emotions from the mind. It interferes with both projection (Ferenczi, 1909; Bion, 1957; 1958a; 1959) and introjection (Ferenczi, 1909).

When even fragmentation and splitting fail, dissociation of mind and body arises as an extraordinary means of protection. Dissociation between body and mind brings relief, but unfortunately it also brings indifference. Dissociation occurs before the mind has symbolized the experience, making mourning the trauma unfeasible. Indifference does not require mourning as a means of processing the losses from the trauma.

While this dissociation of sensations and emotions succeeds in protecting the person from traumatic overwhelming experiences, simultaneously, the mind becomes inoperable and relationship with others is lost. The intensity is compounded by the chaos of unordered somatic experience. When the overwhelming intensity is not too great, and is mediated by a loved other, the power is transformed into a representational process (Brown, 2019). The need to get rid of intensity which cannot be borne drives the psyche to symbolize. Representation and symbolization enhance creativity.

If the intensity is insufficiently mediated by internal or external containment, as can happen with acute or chronic trauma, the body and mind float apart. Psychic existence cannot be perceived. Subjectivity is lost. Ontological anxiety, anxiety about existence itself, creates nameless dread and meaninglessness and nothingness without words. Deficits develop, as do primal pathological defensive structures. Representation and symbolization are constricted. These primal defenses, which are primarily somatic in manifestation, and the resultant deficits of development arise from unmediated access to *ontological anxieties* (Molinari, 2024). Emotional intensity, whether derived from love, hate, or curiosity, is then experienced as pain that cannot be borne. Being and becoming is thwarted.

Clinical Example: Edith

Edith came to see me after having a falling out with her previous analyst, whom she said was homophobic. She wasn't sure about seeing a woman, telling me women were too emotional. She hoped I was not the touchy feely type, but I had come highly recommended by a former psychology professor. She confessed she 'stalked' me online, had driven past my office to time the distance from her house, and called me several times. She hung up before leaving a message. She didn't like my voice, and so chose someone else to see.

Then she was unhappy with the male therapist she chose. Eventually she decided to call again. Later, I learned this break-up with her former male analyst had occurred more than five years previously. Clearly, Edith's reason for seeking treatment was unknown.

She informed me in the first session that she would not use the couch. She'd done that before and wasn't sure it helped. She would come twice a week, but not more. All this was reported matter-of-factly, without any emotion or even modulation in her voice. I too responded matter-of-factly, neither silently interpreting this as paranoia or as taking charge. I didn't know. There seemed no malice nor emotion in these pronouncements. They were just facts. And so, I waited and listened. After three years, she agreed to come four times a week. After seven years, she began to use the couch.

Edith was a tall, handsome woman, dressed impeccably. I was struck by her beauty. At 36, she appeared to be in her mid-20s. Her face was open and unlined. Her smooth face, in spite of seeming flat, was strikingly beautiful. She had dark black hair, flawless pale skin, dark and searching eyes. Her physical beauty without emotion was an enigma. Her unreachable soul, the essence of her, called to me like a Michelangelo. A statue is not alive, but still, the spirit is in the stone.

Her eye contact was steady, neither too much nor too little. She looked at me, stone-faced. I might have been a speck on the wall. I did not feel seen as a person. Nor was I chilled by her gaze. Mostly, I felt perplexed. She, like my patient Dennis (Chapters 4 and 9), did seem to blink excessively, like a newborn unaccustomed to the light. I could not find meaning in her blinking. Her voice was pleasant. She had a large vocabulary, although at times she mispronounced words, seemingly transposing syllables. Again, I did not name this.

Although I felt mildly curious about her, I felt little else. I felt more curiosity about my own minimal responses to her. She did not seem to split and project, at least not that I could feel. Edith reported. I did not know why she came. She said little of her history. Her description of her life was vague. She did tell me she had recently graduated from college with a major in psychology. The professor who gave her my name was someone she valued highly and who also told her what to read.

Completing requirements for graduation had taken her more than six years because "My memory is not so good. Maybe I have a learning disability". Since she had to put herself through school, she also had worked full-time, so studying was difficult. She was a head waiter at an up-scale waterfront seafood restaurant. She liked her job as it paid well and "gives me a built-in friend network". In her spare time, she collected psychology books and biographies of psychoanalysts, which she read repeatedly. She read nothing else – neither fiction nor nonfiction. She did not read a newspaper. Once she said, "I should have become a psychologist". When I wondered if she wanted to be like me, she changed the subject as if I had not spoken.

Slowly over time, Edith told me stories of poverty and abuse in her childhood. I felt she did this because she thought patients were supposed to speak of childhood when with an analyst. She grew up in the Midwest in a fundamentalist Christian family, the middle of nine children. She said her parents did not live their faith in that, in spite of her mother teaching Sunday school and her father serving as elder in the church, they behaved quite unchristian at home. The only book in her home was a Bible which was read daily at the dinner table after the meal. Slowly over months and years, the details of the physical, emotional, and sexual abuse she suffered were revealed.

She wondered if both her parents were mentally ill. When they weren't physically fighting with each other, they were yelling at the kids and beating them. Often, the children went hungry to bed, while the parents ate dinner. The children fought with each other and early on Edith purportedly became the target of the others. Her sisters dressed her in their clothes, then told her how ugly she was. Her brothers pushed her around. Once, her older brother knocked her to the ground, got on top of her and wouldn't let her up, insisting that she liked it. Once he broke her arm. Her mother blamed Edith, telling her she got what she deserved. Initially, she was not taken to the doctor for her injury. Only when a teacher noticed her bruised and twisted arm and called her parents did her mother reluctantly bring her to a doctor. Her parents were angry about the attention she got and the cost of the appointment. Another time, her sister also appeared with bruises, but she didn't know how she got them. Their parents said she was clumsy.

She lost her virginity to a popular girl in college. They dated for a while and then drifted apart. Other girls asked her out. So did boys. She always said yes and sometimes 'made-out' with them. Her mother told her she better not get pregnant. She felt there was no chance of that and yet her passivity meant that having unprotected sex did happen. During this time, she knew she preferred girls, but felt afraid of sinning. She was ashamed of what she called her lust. She dated men who asked her out. When they broke up with her, she was not bothered, even when she liked them. Once she even went with a boyfriend to look at rings.

All these stories were told without emotion and without many details. Edith seemed indifferent to her own experiences. The details were filled in slowly. In fact, as the stories were elaborated, I increasingly began to have emotions. I was no longer so blank. I believe these emotions were mine, not countertransference or the reception of projective identifications. I began to be more curious about Edith and looked forward to our sessions.

In spite of this, I still felt that when she looked at me, she did not see me as a person. Later, I wondered if my mild curiosity was stimulated by my looking at her blank, flawless face. She seemed almost a mannequin, if not a stone statue. Over time, I slowly began to think of her as unborn or newly born. Her beauty, her vagueness, and her innocence were those of a newborn. In spite of not feeling seen, I often felt I was the only person in the room. Yet slowly, as happens when getting to know a baby, I was beginning to imagine the person in her. I do not think she would have recognized the Edith I envisioned.

She told me her previous analyst had told her that she was a very odd person, who seemed naive and immature. Edith didn't know why the doctor had said this, or even if this were true. My experience was that she lived in a kind of contented bubble, being neither upset nor pleased. She looked innocent, untouched by life. She liked routine and felt uncomfortable if anything disrupted the schedule. I might have named her discomfort about a broken schedule anxiety. She would not have called it that. More likely she would have said she didn't like change. It was just a fact.

After several years, she remarked off-handedly that something was missing in her, but that was not why she came to see me. She came to therapy because she liked to think of herself as someone who came to therapy. I said she came instead of going to church. She agreed. She liked psychology. Reading about psychology was as much a part of her regular schedule as was coming to see me. Soon after this statement that something was missing in her, she began to come four times a week.

Any attempts on my part to interpret the transference were ignored. She would blink rapidly and continue talking where she left off. It was as if I had not spoken. Eventually I came to feel as if I weren't there. This was in sharp contrast to my earlier feeling of being the only one present. When I suggested that she barely noticed me, her reply was that I did not bother her. Weekends did not bother her either. Previously announced holiday breaks also were unremarkable. Unexpected breaks caused either by her or by me were an imposition because her routine was broken. That imposition had nothing to do with me. She told me she sometimes wondered if I were as good as she was told, because I talked more than her previous analyst had, but "whatever". She didn't mind my talking as she liked the sound of my voice. She did wonder if what we were doing was psychoanalysis. Again, this was stated without emotion. There was no recrimination in her wondering.

I was impressed by what, at first, I thought was self-reflection. She could describe her moods and states of mind. She seemed a good observer of details about herself. I attributed this to her previous six-year analysis. Yet, these observations didn't go anywhere. Self-reflection did not produce insight. I came to believe that what I mistook as self-reflection was a self-observation *without* reflection. It was merely description. Although she sometimes used psychological language, she didn't seem to really know how it applied to her. It was up to me to reflect upon her recognitions. When I did, she seemed largely to ignore me or even not hear me.

While writing about Edith, I suddenly had the insight that she was truly alone inside his own psychic world. Other people did not exist. Her interest in psychology was an interest in herself. This seems obvious in retrospect. But I think I could barely imagine such a barren psychic existence. Perhaps I was also narcissistically wounded by her failure to recognize me as a person.

In spite of feeling as if I did not exist for her, it took me a long while to recognize that she simply didn't notice anyone else or have any interest in them. Again, perhaps my own sense of my own existence interfered. I was horrified by her isolation. She was not. She had no idea that she impacted me or anyone. She lived as if she were the only person in the world or perhaps more accurately, she was everyone and everyone was her. This undifferentiated state contributed to her moment-to-moment concrete life. She had whole areas of unrepresented states and operated by borrowing symbols, not making them. To relate to another was something she had not yet learned. I wondered if she had in fact had an analysis, since I learned she'd never gone more than twice a week. I felt empathy for her former analyst, obviously in identification with how difficult this was for me.

She also brought me dreams, but had no associations to them. They were stripped of any emotion. She would tell me a dream and move on, as if describing having gone to the grocery store. A dream, like any action she would report, was a concrete event. When I attempted to explore these dreams, she'd gently change the subject, sometimes saying, "That is all". I felt she knew analysts wanted dreams, so she brought me dreams. I wondered about these stories she told. Were they dreams? Memories? Hallucinations? As a side note, I want to emphasize that knowing analysts wanted dreams had nothing to do with her awareness of me as a person or as an object. It was just what was done.

After perhaps another year, she told me she had never loved and wondered if this was related to what was missing in her. Again, this was said without feeling. She had no curiosity about this fact nor seem to be bothered by this reality. It was just true. I thought she could not love if she didn't recognize others as existing, but I said nothing. I silently noted that she had described a cause and effect when she linked not loving with having something missing in her. This was unusual in that previously her concrete reporting was of unchanging reality. What happened just was. Facts were not related to each other.

Again, many months later, she began to wonder who she was or *if* she was. This wondering seemed to include a hint of an emotion and was accompanied by a dream of being at work and not being listened to, "as if I were invisible". Using my own frequent feelings of not existing for her, which I had previously interpreted with seemingly no impact, I ventured an interpretation about her behavior with me and with others as evoking feelings in us of our not being important to her. This time, she stopped talking, blinked a lot, and replied, "Probably true, no offense".

I think in focusing on others, instead of herself, I missed an opportunity to describe what seemed to be her own lack of existence, but perhaps she felt my unspoken response to her because she proceeded to talk about being invisible. She linked it to her dream. I wondered if this were a transference response or direct feedback about my having missed her.

She went on to talk about feeling invisible with her new boyfriend. They had interesting dates to the theatre or the museum. They both loved fine food and went to special restaurants, but had not made love. When she wanted to, her boyfriend did not. When her boyfriend wanted to, she did not. They kissed upon meeting and leaving, nothing more. Sometimes they slept together. I said it was as if there were only one of them present at a time. She replied, without feeling, "You say the oddest things". I smiled, feeling that I had just been acknowledged. She cocked her head like a little girl and looked at me.

It is difficult to convey the concrete nature of our relationship. COVID changed our routines which she did not like. When it necessitated our shifting first to phone and then to Zoom, she was again indifferent to the change, except as it affected her schedule. She found Zoom convenient. She missed working out three or four hours a day at her club, and of course could not go to work, but she was fine. Again, she appeared indifferent although the pandemic elicited fear of dying in her. I believe this was an affective response, not an emotional one. COVID made her frightened of getting sick and dying. When her boyfriend abruptly left town, Edith didn't seem to mind.

Apparently, Edith had saved money, because not once did she discuss her financial reality. She continued to pay me my fee without comment. I shifted us to Zoom, because I felt that phone sessions where she could only hear my voice were not enough for her. She was compliant, again it seemed all the same to her. Whereas I struggled with our lack of sensate contact: no three-dimensional sight of her, no smell of her, no peripheral sounds of her breathing or moving since Zoom cancelled those out, she apparently did not struggle. She carried on as if nothing were different.

If there was anything different, it was her routine. She missed her routine, not the people she no longer saw. She substituted running for going to the gym. She began biking hours a day. Our online visits substituted for coming in person, but remained at the same times. She said she missed the drive to me because she thought about the session then. Without the drive, she felt unprepared. I was in the same place, even though she was not. Unlike other patients who attempted to have sessions in their cars, while walking outdoors, or from random places in their homes, she always contacted me from her home office. I believe that the physical distance between us actually made her feel safer. When I attempted to speak to that, she replied that she didn't feel unsafe with me. I wondered if she ever felt unsafe with anyone and she replied, "Not anymore". I recognized that comment as a statement about her childhood. As usual, she did not elaborate, while I tucked this information away.

Discussion of Edith's dynamics

Over the years, I tried to understand my responses to Edith. Being psychically with her early on required me to become as psychically dead and emotionally indifferent as she was. This was horrible for me. I could not tolerate such an existential absence of my 'self' for long. After such moments, I felt drained and despairing. It seemed we were two subject-less entities. Sometimes, I wanted to interpret at a higher level, accuse her of doing this to me. I wanted to interpret her aggression or envy or hatred. Had I done that, I believe it would have re-traumatized her, even if she did not show it. I would have been naming my own emotional response to being non-existent to her. I intuited that emotional responses in relation to me just weren't to be found in her – at least not then. Love, hate, and curiosity were missing. There was no passion between us. There was mind-numbing indifference.

In spite of her indifference, and in spite of feeling I did not exist for her, I came to care about her. I was curious and eventually could have moments of reverie when with her, where I felt an 'at-one-ment'. This is analytic love, arising out of symbiotic non-symbolized psychic proximity and attunement. Reverie requires nothing less. My love seemed to arise out of a deep appreciation for her innocence, helplessness, and seemingly lost potential. Her beauty continued to move me, but I am not sure it was related to my love for her. It seemed an innocent beauty of being untouched by the world, perhaps of unrealized potential. Perhaps it reminded me of newborns. My love did not seem to arise from the reception of her projective identifications, which were few. I wonder whether my reverie was possible because Edith's generalized indifference did not feel dangerous to me.

At other times, I was aware of feeling intense frustration and a wish to tell her what to do. I think that was analytic hate. I hated her otherness and had difficulty accepting her extreme passivity and indifference to life. I hated that I became passive and indifferent in order to be with her. These responses did not feel like counter-transference responses, although I had those too. Bion (1963) says, "Passion must be clearly distinguished from counter-transference, the latter being evidence of repression". Then he tells us that passion is "one of the dimensions of a psycho-analytic object and therefore of a psycho-analytic element" (p. 13). Passion, whether present or absent, assures that the experience is not in the intellectual realm of words. Passion is in the body and the mind. It is intensely relational and intensely personal. My love and my hatred were links to Edith, enabling me to find her.

From our first meeting, I experienced analytic curiosity. I genuinely wanted to know her. At times, unmediated by love or hate, my curiosity arose as an obstruction between us, embodying a kind of arrogance that I could reach her. Only when I submitted to the truth of the reality that I had no control over my understanding or knowledge about Edith, nor over her openness or even awareness of me as a separate person, did my curiosity also become a genuine link between us. Initially, my curiosity made of me an *obstructive object* (Bion, 1958a).

I believe that over time, Edith and I engaged in a passionate relationship. We became linked by love, hate, and curiosity. Our connection changed both of us. Initially, this was not true. The first analytic emotions arising in me were me in *union* with her, resonating at a deep primal level. I experienced rage, terror, panic, and seeking after her. These intense affects were not my counter-transference, which arises from my symbolic inner world of objects. Initially, these affects were nowhere to be found in her. They were in me as a separate human being, not as a container of her projections. Her deadness was deeply disturbing. I had only my analytic intuition and my commitment to the psycho-analytic process to hold me through the agony of her coming alive.

Later the analytic psychotherapy became a more classic analysis, but, in the beginning, my contact with Edith was primarily a sensory contact. Proximity was primary. The setting and the frame (Bleger, 1967; Eekhoff, 2022b; Moguil-lansky and Levine, 2022), my office and my person as an object in it, were more important than our relationship. These were a constant until COVID.

At different moments, our sensory contact reflected the primal position, the paranoid-schizoid position and the depression position. Our sensory contact provided a floor for experience (Ogden, 1991; Eaton, 2005) and a center of gravity (Eekhoff, 2019) for Edith. My initial responses to her were primitive and bodily. They were sensual and sensate. I had in-the-moment-responses to her that were minimally intellectual. Being present with her required both my physical and emotional self. It was not from a symbolic order. It was an experience of proximity and presence. It was two Beings, together.

This is difficult to describe. I am clumsy here in my attempts. I recognize that nothing is pure; however, I want to pay attention to the body and the affective responses I had. I say affective and not emotional, because these were quite different from my emotional responses which came from my own responses arising from repression and my own splitting and projective and introjective responses. My animal instincts of seeking, rage, fear, panic, lust, play, and care (Panksepp, 1998) were terrifying to me. Being with Edith somehow mysteriously gave me access to these primitive affects that I had long ago repressed or split off from my awareness. As Tustin (1986) says, working with these patients forces us to go places we never should go, to learn things about ourselves we never want to know.

I was not only a witness to her absence, but also, I was present to her beauty and her innocence. Her wide-open blankness was something I experienced as lost potential. Perhaps seeing her blankness as potential might have been defensive on my part, perhaps not. I recognized it as dissociation. I felt it was a potential, nonetheless. The enormous power unleashed in me was more than my omnipo-tent defenses against the reality of her trauma and its effect on her. It was the barely mediated awareness of my own animal nature. The other link was not one I could hold, but I became aware of Edith's states of undifferentiation.

Indifference

Edith was a patient who was very difficult for me to reach. Edith's indiffer-ence to whatever happened to or around her was profound. I was stunned by it. Since I did not believe indifference existed in the unconscious nor in the body, I could only think of it as a massive defense. When I stopped trying to help her, accepted her as she was, I was able to just be with her. Then I felt her lack of sophistication as arising not as a cultural or class expression, but as a newborn's lack of knowledge of the world. It seemed to me that her innocence and lack of emotional development arose from massive dissociation. Her dissociation protected her from painful realities she could not bear. Her dissociation also occasionally put her into states of seeming undifferentiation. These states contributed to my feeling that she was innocent and not dangerous.

This feeling of mine was very different than I might have found if she were massively splitting and projecting into the universe rather than into me. Her dissociation showed in her apparent lack of aging, something she was very proud to display. Her face and her body were not touched by the pain of living. She was 'forever young'. I came to believe that her history included far more trauma than I could begin to imagine. If she were to access it, she would begin to age. I feared she would also rage and in fact, much later, she did.

The dissociation and resultant indifference also seemed to have created developmental deficits that made learning difficult for her. She was extremely concrete. She could learn in a rote manner, which helped her. I was amazed that she had graduated from college and been able to learn enough to pass her courses. She told me she took word-for-word notes and memorized them for exams. She also seemed able to take on responsibilities at work and do well, perhaps somewhat related to her obsessive need for order. Her genuine interest in herself and her obsessive reading of psychology books seemed to be an identification with her psychology professor who was kind to her. She appeared to have some self-curiosity which may have brought her to analysis; however, I may be misinterpreting her identification with and mimicry of her psychology professor as self-curiosity. Eventually, it seemed she also had an identification with me.

Somatopsychic dissociation interferes with the capacity to transform physical experiences of the body into emotional experiences that become the foundation of all learning. I believe that Edith's extreme defensive structures created and used to protect herself from affective and emotional pain arose out of somatopsychic dissociation. She exercised hours a day, even when she could no longer go to the gym. The exercise seemed to be a means of deadening her senses. She was not in touch with her body. She reportedly did not feel hunger, in spite of working around food. She did not use drugs or alcohol. The idea of being sexual was more important than being sexual. Although she occasionally had one-night stands, she mostly masturbated and did not enjoy pornography. She told me her mind was without fantasies during masturbation, focusing only on sensation. Perhaps coincidentally, but more likely not, many years into her analysis, she said she'd also heard my name from one of her 'hook-ups'. This woman was a psychiatric resident in supervision with me.

For Edith, it was not only that experience could not be borne, it was that in the somatopsychic dissociation, the capacity to process experience was not adequately developed. Learning from experience (Bion, 1962b) was impeded. Facts could be noted, but not used by her. What she called her learning disability was dissociation and indifference. Without an ability to classify and subordinate her experience, she had an inability to remember it. Without an ability to remember, accumulation of experience was difficult, if not impossible. Mimicry substituted for introjection. I would add that Edith's concreteness meant she did not have images or imagination.

I have found this also with other patients with a history of childhood trauma. Instead of being informed by reality, the perception of reality is distorted. Trauma in the form of intense affects and emotions causes a catastrophic implosion or explosion of the mind. The secondary destruction stops the transformative processes by destroying the mind's ability to remember and accumulate knowledge. Emotion is necessary for learning. Remembering and accumulating knowledge are essential for being able to think. Without access to emotion, the movement from sensation to image to imaginative conjecture is lost. Without sufficient transformative means, catastrophe destroys creativity. Identification with others is limited but helpful, in that mimicry is a first step towards recall. Reverie, imagination, and symbolization suffer when dissociation destroys emotional links.

The emotional reality of pain and pleasure requires transformation of experience in order to be communicated. The innate need to communicate drives humans via projective and introjective identifications to relate intimately with other persons. Finding language to express unnamed states of body and mind to self and to other is containing. When relationships, both internal and external, are disrupted, as must have happened between Edith and her parents, the experience of existence – of being and becoming – is also disrupted.

I cannot imagine that Edith ever saw herself in her parents' eyes. And so, the processes of dreaming, alpha functioning, and meaning-making were automatically disrupted. The dreams that Edith faithfully brought me were almost all about work and seemed to be memories of actual events rather than emotional responses to them. I came to wonder whether these were dreams at all. With few emotional links, her vitality failed and her ability to envision did not evolve.

Instead of emotional aliveness, psychic deadness presented itself as indifference and profound resignation. Yet, something must have been alive in her. She came faithfully and paid immediately. I wanted to be with her and listen to her stories. Gradually over time, her stories became more detailed. My interest and seeming lack of a need for her to be different ignited something like *putting the pieces of herself together*. Edith began to suspect something was missing in her. She loved movies and reported that she noticed she did not love nor hate as the characters on screen did. She had a mild curiosity about that and perhaps my curiosity about her was in resonance with hers.

I could say much more about Edith, she did eventually fall in love and marry. She suffered greatly on her way to loving, as did I. Curiosity came first, then hate, something not easy for either of us. I took solace from Bion's (1962b) reminder that hate only comes after love. There were many evidences of her growing love for me. She would have the slightest smile on her face as we both appeared on screen. She would tilt her head, much as a small child does, when listening to me. Overtime, she came to miss me between sessions. Soon, she was pressuring me to resume in-person sessions and eventually she used the couch. With her emerging emotions, came more and more realizations of just how bad her childhood had been and just how much she had missed. Grieving what was and what was not in her childhood took courage. Mourning enabled her to resume living. Living, which entailed loving, hating, and being curious was not an easy thing for her, but one she rejoiced in.

Discussion

Extraordinary protections such as indifference and somatopsychic dissociation are often somatic or autistic defenses. Another defense may be a delusion of not existing, of dying before being born. Psychic existence is required for a sense of being and going-on-being, and therefore necessary for the growth of emotional capacities to love, to hate, and to be curious. An emotional life is necessary if one is to remember, to know, to dream, and to think. Further, if we extend Bion's model of container and contained from the mother and infant dyad to the analyst and analysand dyad, we realize that Bion (1962b) made a shift from Freud's one-person psychology and Klein's one-and-a-half-person psychology to a two-person psychology. Bion wrote about reverie – analytic love, hate, and curiosity.

Unconsciously identifying those around us who are able to tolerate the intensity of our evolving existence is crucial for psychic survival. Those persons become the object of our love, hate, and curiosity. They help us moderate passionate affective and emotional experiences. Ideally these are intimate family members, who welcome physical and emotional proximity, receive positive and negative projective identifications, and are able to return them to us in manageable form. Lovers are always the object of our love, hate, and curiosity, so too are family and friends. The objects of our emotions are also our analysts and analysands.

Sometimes the objects of identifications are strangers from another race or culture who are used as the objects of negative projective and introjective identifications. When that is so, containment is more difficult. The play of emotions is interrupted and hate is unmediated by love and curiosity. Without enough containment, primal affects replace representational emotions. Violence becomes the means of reducing the internal overwhelming unconscious affects to bearable proportions. Unfortunately, violence breeds violence. There are gang wars, drive-by shootings, indiscriminate viciousness, and senseless war. The COVID-19 pandemic and the chaos that ensued unleashed unmediated affects. Our collective terror of and awareness of mortality unleashed a Pandemic of Violence.

Bion's focus on emotional links requires two people passionately engaged with one another. Love, hate, and curiosity entwinned are the elements of passion. In speaking of reverie as evidence of love, Bion is describing love between an analyst and patient. Both the analyst and the analysand love. It follows that both also experience hate and curiosity. Getting to know each other intimately, and then being able to communicate it, is the heart of psychoanalytic practice. Bion (1962b; 1963) also tells us that when two people meet, there is an emotional turbulence that results from the continuing evolution that inevitably follows.

The passion generated by loving, hating, and being curious about our patients requires a great deal from us. It is the source of the pain and suffering we feel when working with our agonized patients. It requires us to be disciplined, well trained, and well analyzed. Hopefully, it keeps us humble and in touch with a psychoanalytic method that holds and contains us.

Passionate Emotion as Clinical Realizations

This common need to be passionately in relationship with others enables us as analysts to work deeply with very withdrawn or undrawn (Alvarez, 2006; 2010; 2012) individuals who bring us a variety of dilemmas in their treatment. Often these individuals are trauma survivors who appear indifferent and unengaged with relationships. Sometimes, in spite of their analysands faithfully coming, being committed to the routine of their appointments, and compliant in their relationships, analysts wonder why they come.

Perhaps, this is why when we clinicians meet patients who display little or no emotion, we are concerned. For us, it is even worse when our patients evoke little or no emotion in us. As difficult as it is, we would prefer big emotions to none. Hatred of emotions (Bion, 1959, p. 311) contributes to an inability to split and project. Without this ability, love, hate, and curiosity are left without psychic objects. Without objects, there can be only a minimum subjective experience of Self. Instead, there is mimicry and isolation. The patient experiences the analyst as non-existent. I believe this is a post-traumatic response. From the patient's perspective, two subject-less bodies are in a room.

Trauma stimulates resignation that there is no receiving other. Trauma fosters a despair that there is no container that can hold the emotional intensity without breaking. Both hate and love contaminate the container, making recognizing or knowing the truth difficult. With such contamination, the container does not provide a crucible for thinking. Love and hate are compromised. Curiosity is dulled. The container cannot hold.

When two persons cannot alternate becoming the contained and the container, the introjection that nourishes the mind is restricted. An absence of curiosity leads to a loss of the search for truth about the world, but more specifically about the other person or about the Self. Since according to Bion, knowledge and curiosity are conjoining emotions, psychic development is curtailed when curiosity is lost or contaminated by love or hate. Being contaminated by an emotion is different than being mediated by one. In contamination, differences are blurred and individuation lost. The container itself cannot hold or receive. The contained cannot be mediated by its time spent within a container.

As analysts, our own, taken-for-granted but perhaps unacknowledged, need for relationship aids us in our observations, our sensitivities, and our responsiveness to our patients. Our benevolent curiosity enhances our faith and hope in the relational processes hidden in analysis with hard-to-reach patients (Joseph, 1975; DeMasi, 2015). The union of love, hate, and curiosity opens us to contain and be contained in ways we could never imagine, resulting in a passionate engagement with our patients in the here and now of the session. Always, passion results in surprise. It also results in turmoil which produces change. This change is also in the containing functions of our minds. Our analytic containers are forever strengthened and changed as is our receptivity. Receptivity effects what we are able to allow to enter our psychic containers. Passion makes the *psychic-container-of-the-self* become deeper, stronger, and more flexible. It enables us to tolerate frustration and the violent intensity of emotional connection. All of history both of the self and of the universe is in this connecting aesthetic moment.

Conclusion

This chapter has examined the role of emotion in the development of the mind. It has explored the role of passion, which unites love, hate, and curiosity in a two-person experience of body and mind, of soma and psyche. Passion is an essential element of psychoanalysis. Emotion, not affect and not feeling, is the mysterious link between the body and the mind. Emotion is also the link intra-psychically and inter-subjectively between internal objects and external objects (persons).

The chapter also describes emotion as a link to the primal, enabling analysts to understand and treat early defenses and deficits. The combined emotions of love, hate, and curiosity are links to the mammilian affects of seeking, rage, fear, panic, lust, play, and care (Panksepp, 1988). As a very active link, emotion drives learning (Bion, 1965; Damasio, 1999). Emotion is central for the development of the mind, linking two or more people, places, or things together and fueling the symbolization process. The relating emotions of love, hate, and curiosity enable us to approach our own uniquely personal truth.

Trauma interferes with the emotional links. The chapter provides a clinical example of a patient who purportedly suffered extreme physical, sexual, and emotional abuse in childhood. She appeared indifferent to relationships. Her trauma left her highly dissociated and difficult to reach. In spite of an ability to describe herself, she could not reflect on her experiences. The clinical example focuses on the analytic relationship that initially did not seem to exist because of a delusion that neither the analyst nor the patient existed.

In addition, the paper asserts that faith and security in the human innate need for contact as found in our mammilian affects enables us to work deeply with any patient. Faith and trust in the analytic process that reveals our human need for connection and communication provides a psychological holding for those of us engaged in this very difficult work. The freedom of mind and constancy of spirit required is humbling.

I have discussed how within each analytic relationship, analysts are called upon to face their own worst fears and frailties. The breadth and depth of emotional experience discovered in each and every analytic relationship is profound. The discipline required to remain curious in the face of violent primal affects and emotions is daunting. These affects bring us back to our bodies and can flood our minds. Frequently, we must observe ourselves unable to think and caught in the turmoil of intense affective storms. Still, the satisfaction derived from the privilege of our intimate work is immeasurable. Love, hate, and curiosity enrich us, making us better containers for ourselves and others.

References

Alvarez, A. (2006). Some questions concerning states of fragmentation: unintegration, under–integration, disintegration, and the nature of early integrations. *Journal of Child Psychotherapy*, 32(2): 158–180.

Alvarez, A. (2010). Levels of analytic work and levels of pathology: The work of calibration. *International Journal of Psycho-Analysis*, 91: 859–878.

Alvarez, A. (2012). *The Thinking Heart*. London: Routledge.

Bergstein, A. (2020). Violent Emotions and the violence of life. *The International Journal of Psychoanalysis*, 100(5): 863–868.

Bion, W. R. (1957). The differentiation of the psychotic from the non-psychotic personalities. *International Journal of Psycho-Analysis*, 38: 266–275. [Reprinted London: Heinemann, 1967; London: Karnac, 1984, pp. 43–64.]

Bion, W. R. (1958a). On Arrogance. *International Journal of Psycho-Analysis*, 39: 144–146.

Bion, W. R. (1958b). On hallucination. *International Journal of Psycho-Analysis*, 39: 341–349.

Bion, W. R. (1959). Attacks on linking. *International Journal of Psycho-Analysis*, 40: 308–315.

Bion, W. R. (1962a). A psycho-analytic theory of thinking. *International Journal of Psycho-Analysis*, 43: 306–310. [Reprinted as "A theory of thinking", in Bion, W. R., *Second Thoughts* (pp. 110–119). London: Karnac, 1984.]

Bion, W. R. (1962b). *Learning from Experience*. London: Heinemann. [Reprinted London: Karnac, 1984.]

Bion, W. R. (1963). *Elements of Psycho-Analysis.* London: Heinemann. [Reprinted London: Karnac, 1984.]

Bion, W. R. (1965). *Transformations.* London: Heinemann. [Reprinted London: Karnac, 1984.]

Bion, W. R. (1970). *Attention and Interpretation.* London: Tavistock. [Reprinted London: Karnac, 1984.]

Bion, W. R. (1977 [1989]). *Two Papers: The Grid and Caesura.* London: Karnac.

Bleger, J. (1967). *Symbiosis and Ambiguity: A psychoanalytic study.* Churcher, J. and Bleger, L. (Eds.); Rogers, S., Bleger, L., and Churcher, J. (Trans.). London and New York, Routledge, 2013.

Bollas, C. (1978). The Aesthetic Moment and the Search for Transformation. *Annual of Psychoanalysis,* 6: 385–394.

Bollas, C. (1987). *The Shadow of the Object: Psychoanalysis of the Unthought Known.* New York: Columbia University Press.

Brown, L. J. (2019). Trauma and representation. *International Journal of Psycho-analysis,* 100: 1154–1170.

DeMasi, F. (2015). *Working with Difficult Patients: From Neurosis to Psychosis.* London: Karnac.

Damasio, A. R. (1999). *The Feeling of What Happens: Body and Emotion in the Making of Consciousness.* New York: Harcourt Brace.

Eaton, J. L. (2005). The obstructive object. *Psychoanalytic Review,* 92(3): 355–372.

Eekhoff, J. K. (2019). Affective bridges between body and mind. In *Trauma and Primitive Mental States, An Object Relations Perspective.* London and New York. Routledge.

Eekhoff, J. K. (2022). Psychic Equivalency as an Aspect of Symbiosis. In Moguillansky, C. and Levine, H. (Eds.), *"Psychoanalysis of the Psychoanalytic Frame Revisited" A New Look at Bleger's Classical Work.* London and New York: Routledge/IPA.

Ferenczi, S. (1909). Introjection and transference. In *First Contributions to Psychoanalysis* (pp. 35–93). New York: Brunner/Mazel, 1980.

Ferenczi, S. (1932). *The Clinical Diary of Sándor Ferenczi.* J. Dupont (Ed.); Balint, M. and Jackson, N. Z. (Trans.). Cambridge, MA: Harvard University Press, 1988.

Ferenczi, S. (1933). Confusion of the tongues between the adults and the child—(The language of tenderness and of passion). In *Final Contributions to the Problems and Methods of Psycho-Analysis* (pp. 156–167). London: Karnac, 1994.

Fisher, J. (2011). The Emotional Experience of K. In Mawson, C. (Ed.), *Bion Today* (pp. 43–63). London: Routledge.

Grotstein, J. S. (2007). The Concept of the 'Transcendent Position'. In *A Beam of Intense Darkness* (pp. 122–134). London: Karnac.

Joseph, B. (1975). The patient who is difficult to reach. In Feldman, M. and Spillius, E. B. (Eds.). *Psychic Equilibrium and Psychic Change: Selected Papers of Betty Joseph* (pp. 75–87). London: Tavistock/Routledge, 1989.

Klein, M. (1946). Notes on some schizoid mechanisms. *International Journal of Psycho-Analysis,* 27: 99–100.

Klein, M. (1952). The origins of transference. *International Journal of Psycho-Analysis,* 33: 433–438.

Klein, M. (1975). Envy and Gratitude and Other Works 1946–1963. Masud, M. and Khan, R. (Eds.). *The International Psycho-Analytical Library*, 104: 1–346. London: The Hogarth Press and the Institute of Psycho-Analysis.

Meltzer, D. (1975a). Dimensionality as a parameter in mental functioning: Its relation to narcissistic functioning. In Meltzer, D., with Bremner, J., Hoxter, S., Weddell, D., and Wittenberg, L. *Explorations in Autism*. Strath Tay, Perthshire, UK: Clunie Press (pp. 6–29). [Reprinted for the Harris Meltzer Trust, London: Karnac, 2008.]

Meltzer, D., with Bremner, J., Hoxter, S., Weddell, D., and Wittenberg, I. (1975b). *Explorations in Autism: A Psychoanalytic Study*. Strath Tay, Perthshire: Clunie Press. [Reprinted for the Harris Meltzer Trust, London: Karnac, 2008.]

Mitrani, J. L. (2001). *Ordinary People and Extra-ordinary Protections*. Philadelphia: Brunner-Routledge. New Library of Psychoanalysis.

Molinari, E. (2024). *Binocular Vision: An Inquiry into Psychoanalytic Techniques and Field Theory* (pp. 1–184). London and New York. Routledge.

Moguillansky, C. and Levine, H. (Eds.) (2022). *"Psychoanalysis of the Psychoanalytic Frame Revisited" A New Look at Bleger's Classical Work*. London and New York: Routledge/IPA.

Monteiro, J. S. (2023). *Bion's Theory of Dreams: A Visionary Model of the Mind. 1–225*. London and New York: Routledge.

Ogden, T. H. (1991). Some theoretical comments on personal isolation. *Psychoanalytic Dialogues*, 1(3): 377–390.

Panksepp, J. (1998). *Affective Neuroscience: The Foundations of Human and Animal Emotions*. New York: Oxford University Press.

Tustin, F. (1986). *Autistic Barriers in Neurotic Patients*. New Haven, CT: Yale University Press, 1987.

Winnicott, D. W. (1960). The theory of the parent-infant relationship. *International Journal of Psychoanalysis*, 41: 585–595.

Winnicott, D. W. (1963). From Dependence towards Independence in the Development of the Individual. In *The Maturational Processes and the Facilitating Environment: Studies in the theory of Emotional Development* (pp. 83–90). London: Hogarth Press.

Chapter 3

Body as Dream Space

In his paper "A Theory of Thinking", Bion (1962a, p. 306) states "...thinking has to be called into existence to cope with thoughts". He goes on to admit that this is not the typical way to conceptualize the process of thinking and highlights that most people assume the opposite. Bion's notion of "thoughts without a thinker" has fascinated me for some time. Where, I have asked myself, do these original thoughts come from? And how do we discover them? Furthermore, how do we create a space in psychoanalysis for thoughts to appear and a thinking mind to develop, especially if the person we are with has used their mind to defend against a terror of being alive?

When I combine this idea with another of Bion's (1962b), namely that somatic overwhelm attacks and destroys our capacity to think, I am reminded of the difficulty I experience when working with patients whose capacity to think has seemingly been destroyed and whose focus of attention is on the somatic. Although focused on the somatic, these patients are unable to be embodied or to use their bodies as a 'dream space'. Their capacity to think has been conscripted and redirected toward the more urgent task of dealing with the unbearable awareness of being alive and alone. Being alive includes an infinite array of somatic responses that are coupled with an emotional experience of aloneness, isolation, and dependency (Ogden, 1991).

The Body as Background Object

The body in health is a background object, much like Winnicott's environmental mother or Freud and Bollas' shadow of the object. The body in health is also a space essential for the growth and development of the mind. Just as Winnicott claims there is no such thing as a baby without a mother, I am saying there is no such thing as a mind without a body. Aside from the obvious, the mind needs the body in order to dream. The body is a dream space where sensory and emotional experience is transformed into representations that can be used to make personal meaning (Eekhoff, 2019). Psychic meaning-making involves bringing two things together to make a 'third' or that which can be symbolized. Representations in the body evolve into

DOI: 10.4324/9781003544470-3

symbolization in the mind. Symbolization evolves in union with the body, just as the body concretely evolves after the union of egg and sperm. The 'third', physically and psychically, emerges from the body of the mother and through the name of the father (Lacan, 1966).

The physical and psychic body is a space that enables a sense of going-on-being (Winnicott, 1949; 1960; 1963; Ogden 1986; 1989a; 1989b; 1991). A sense of going-on-being is necessary for psychic existence, psychic functioning, psychic elaboration, and creativity. Impingement (Winnicott, 1974) in infancy, or reality coming in too soon (Tustin, 1986), can be traumatic, interfering with going-on-being. Initially going-on-being occurs as a very subtle sense of a self that is bounded by tactile experience (Bick, 1968; 1986).

In addition to being a psychic space for a sense of going-on-being, the body also marks time, moving us continuously into the future. Of course, this is true concretely as aging developmentally from birth to death changes our psychic awareness of time. Marking time also occurs psychically via the body's processing of sensory experience in a cumulative manner. Accumulative experience involves memory and representation. For example, when a bodily experience is linked to an emotional experience and remembered, such as the smell of lilacs in Berlin, the present is linked to the past. This is more than just memory; it is a somatic link to an emotion that links with an unconscious phantasy. To mark psychic time and space effectively, the body communicates to the mind and to others who will listen. Such communication includes information of wellbeing as well as of pain and suffering, of pleasure and displeasure. Amongst other things, communication from the self to the self informs one where in time and space one is. When traumatized, the mind attempts to foreclose future experience and distorts time, getting one caught in either the moment or what Scarfone (2015) calls "the unpast".

Psychic equilibrium depends upon the integration of mind and body so that experience can be interpreted and creative transformation of experience can happen. When this occurs, new experience can be generated from the old, creating a structure that holds and evolves. New experience always disrupts psychic equilibrium, but if the body holds a sense of going-on-being this experience can be integrated into the past experience. The body does all this, as well as maintaining life. Most of this bodily communication is unconscious, but nonetheless informs and helps us find personal meaning via a dream process Bion (1962b) terms "alpha functioning". Our nighttime dreams do the same, linking body and mind.

If we accept that the body is a dream space, we have to ask ourselves, who is the dreamer who dreams the dream (Grotstein, 2000) and what actually is dreaming? Why should dreaming require an actual space and how is the concrete body essential for such a creative process to occur? How could such a space become both the container and the contained so as to make dreaming possible? Dreaming is a process of making meaning of experience by representing it. The process of representation evolves from the sensorium.

Pictograms and images evolve from the sensorium and their information is essential for the act of figurability (Botella and Botella, 2015; Aulagnier, 2001; Eekhoff, 2019). Figurability is a process of representation, which evolves out of bodymind experience.

In this manner, the body is a continual generator of experience and the source of subjectivity. Ogden (1989b) has named the earliest relationship between subject and object as the autistic contiguous position and recognizes the body as the foundation of all experience. Ogden (1989b, p. 129) says, "Sensory experience in an autistic-contiguous mode has a quality of rhythmicity that is becoming continuity of being; it has boundedness that is the beginning of the experience of a place where one feels, thinks and lives; it has shape, hardness, coldness, warmth, texture, etc. that are the beginnings of the qualities of who one is". Sensory experience is an aspect of relationship with both internal and external objects. Like the paranoid schizoid and the depression positions, the autistic contiguous position is present throughout life. The body is essential for all three positions, for the organization of emotional experience, and for the development of the mind. The body provides a "sensation matrix" for the mind (Ogden, 1991). Bleger views this earliest position slightly different than does Ogden and names it the glischro-caric position. I have named it the primal position.

I have used Joyce McDougall's (1989) words "the body as dream space" because I believe that the body becomes more than a storehouse for "memories in feelings" (Klein, 1961; 1975). In addition, the body serves as a container for "memories in sensorium" (Eekhoff, 2019). Memories in sensorium are memories that recall earliest pre- and post-natal experience, such as sensations, smells, or sounds that evoke feelings of wellbeing or even feelings of terror. Sometimes we view the word memory as static. Alternatively, I am using the word memory to describe a fluid process involved in making meaning out of experience. Memories in sensorium and memories in feelings are transformed in a very elemental form of dreaming which begins in the body. By dreaming, I am describing a process, delineated by Bion (1967; 1970), where sensate and perceptual experience is used by the mind to create personal meaning.

Think for a moment of your own experience of dreaming. Typically, what we call a dream is a story we remember when we awaken and tell ourselves or someone else our dream. This story is a transformation of other transformations of the actual dreaming process. A nighttime dream begins when the body is still and perceptions remain active. Tactile awareness during sleep – of the temperature of the air, the weight of the blankets on our skin, the ambient sound sensations, the sensations of our partner's presence – link with unconscious emotional associations to form new connections that further elaborate our waking lives. The sensorium's output evolves into pictograms or visual images that evolve into linked images forming 'movies' in the mind. These movies are then transformed into emotional narratives that include language so as to be memorable. This whole process, which Bion (1962b; 1970) calls "alpha function", goes on whether we are awake or asleep.

Such somatic emotional dreaming enables the person to find relationship and passionate connection to both self and other. I suggest this process is enhanced and deepened when shared with another. Moreover, the inter-subjective elaboration of dream thought begins at or before birth and continues for a lifetime. The body and the proximity of the other (Eekhoff, 2017) are a major container for the creative elaboration of meaning. Bion (1962b; 1965) describes this relational connection within and between others as Love (L), Hate (H), and Knowledge(K). These links, even when they are attacked (Bion, 1959), represent uniquely personal emotional thoughts that are simultaneously relational and universal. These individual and universal passions reflect the personal process of representation and symbolization. Somatic and perceptual experience is infinite, taking in immeasurable information. Thinking is called into existence to cope with the infinite. A thinker is called into existence to make use of thoughts.

The Body as Defense

Some patients defend against these overwhelming awarenesses by shutting down psychic space and attending to the concrete necessities of life. Rather than using their somatic, emotional experiences as communication, they use them as autistic defenses against overwhelming terror and persecution. I surmise that for these patients uncontained experience occurred first in utero or in the first few months after birth. In the absence of the containing reverie of their mothers, they have turned to their own bodies as mother substitutes. A patient told me his mother did not know she was pregnant with him until she arrived at the hospital emergency room in pain. His mother denied her pregnancy with him, believing even then that she was having an appendicitis attack. He often felt terrified and had repeated experiences of nameless dread, accompanied by panic attacks. He also frequently had no experience of my presence with him, stating he could see me, but he could not feel me. He always felt alone. To compensate, he turned to alcohol, telling me the feeling of being inebriated was one of being accompanied. When he drank, he no longer felt alone. I imagine that inebriated states recalled his prenatal hazy experiences in the womb. I further imagine that his mother's psychic abortion of him was repeated in his difficulty feeling me in the room.

Healthy sensuality is necessary for wellbeing; however, the sensual can also be a defense. The use of the sensual as a defense is difficult to notice in analysis because it is often silent (Eekhoff, 2015). The sensual defense is concrete and denies the separateness and reality of the other while using the other for the sensual support of a delusion of oneness. The patient appears to be thinking, speaking, and relating to the analyst, yet is using the processing in the hour to attach to the analyst in a sensual way. Only when the analyst becomes aware of this fixation and the intoxication it brings to both parties can this *psychosensual impasse* be addressed via language so that growth may resume.

The use of somatic responses to internal and external stimuli seems to serve as a distraction from a terrifying awareness of aloneness. It is more than only aloneness, however; it is also an awareness of infinity and its unbounded and uncontained nature. Somatic experience used defensively interferes with the body's capacity for making meaning from experience. Somatic responses can replace dreaming rather than aiding a person to dream. For example, this happens when an analyst and a patient get caught up in the concrete meaning of language, ignoring the emotional and unconscious function it serves. Some patients are attached to the sound and rhythm of speech, not the symbolic meaning. Links between mind and body are compromised when somatic responses are the primary focus of attention. Focusing on the sensory enables one to deny the gaps inherent in all relationships. Denying a gap forecloses the necessity of making a link. Without adequate linking, the minds' capacity to dream is also severely inhibited. Along with this difficulty, patients who use their bodies' responses defensively are unable to make use of their objects or sometimes even to relate to them (Winnicott, 1969).

Paradoxically, individuals who use their sensory experience defensively lack the capacity to accurately reflect upon and interpret bodily experience. They are often somatically overwhelmed and hypersensitive to sight, to sound, and to touch. They seem to use one sensation to block out others. In this way, although they retreat to the sensory, they do not experience themselves as embodied whole persons. Out of these observations, I have come to believe that the place where thoughts appear is in the body. In health, the body links us to the infinite experience of being human. In an analysis with primitive states, transformation occurs first in the body before it reaches the mind as an emotional experience (Damasio, 1999). This process of transformation or change, when it occurs in analysis, is evoked primarily but not exclusively via proximity to the analyst (Eekhoff, 2017).

Patients who have suffered early infantile traumas have difficulty using their bodies as a dream space for organizing and generating experience. Instead, they have turned to their bodies as a substitute for the containing other. Such patients reveal an awareness of an early uncontained and unmediated experience of being overwhelmed, while feeling all alone. Their memories of being overwhelmed are held in their sensorium. The overwhelming experience while feeling alone was impossible to bear in infancy and is now, when re-experienced in the transference, quite awful for both analyst and patient to bear.

Patients who have suffered early traumas feel alone and unfortunately are unable to experience the embodied presence of the analyst. The analyst feels alone also and is unable to reach them even though feeling present for them. The experience for both is of total isolation and terror in the face of immense need and vulnerability. In spite of being largely unmentalized, the competing needs and terrors are held in the body as implicit memories. A background ambience of blankness evolves as both a potential that was not realized and as a defense against overwhelming experience.

I used to think such patients maintained a delusional denial of otherness. Today I believe that such individuals have an internal place where they deny their own existence via a representation of a blank place (Green, 1999). Without a subjective experience of self, otherness is not a relevant experience. The loss of a subjective sense of self is relevant. This blank place or delusion of not existing is nonverbal and preverbal. It is experienced primarily somatically rather than psychically. Although the blank place may become represented (Green, 1999), the representation of an absence becomes a background object of pain (Eekhoff, 2018b; Bion, 1962b). I have described this elsewhere as present with patients whose mothers suffered trauma and passed the trauma unknowingly onto their children via their psychic absence and their preoccupation with their own pain. Infants and young children internalize their suffering mothers and identify with them. Identifying with a pain mother is corporeal, experienced as psychosomatic symptoms or as a void.

The delusion of not existing is paradoxical. One would expect that excessive attention to the somatic would confirm one's existence. One would also expect that a memory held in the body would counter the delusion of nonexistence rather than supporting it. However, paradoxical reversals and negative hallucinations are part of the delusional denial of otherness and the delusional denial of self. These reversals and negative hallucinations contribute to the difficulty in uncovering and treating this delusion.

Some individuals have access to early traumatic experiences because their psyche is called into existence too soon (Tustin, 1986) in order to cope with physical and psychic overwhelm. Awareness comes before repression is possible, before splitting and projection are sufficiently in place to deal with the intensity of the perceptual field. The awareness, which is clearly a mental activity, is held not in the mind so it can be thought, but in the bodymind, where it cannot be repressed or forgotten. Ada, the patient whose story I will later relate, describes it thus: "When my despair and terror destroy my conscious will, my body goes on. I feel at those times that my body betrays me. It just keeps going on". It is at such times that the thought of suicide comforts her. Perhaps for this reason most of us have long ago repressed our own awareness of such early experiences. To go there with our patients requires a great deal of us. We have to be able to access and tolerate our own experience of nothingness, meaninglessness, and the black hole (Grotstein, 1990). Unless we can do this, our patients won't be able to bring these experiences to us.

When the analyst speaks from her own bodily awareness it can form a bridge for clarification of a patient's relationship with his or her own body, thereby differentiating somatic delusion from somatic symptom and from somatic communication. This action of the analyst fosters in the patient a development of a deeper and lasting connection to him or herself and to others. Also, there is development in the somatic process, both moment to moment and over time. Our patients' relationship to their bodies changes considerably in analytic treatment, as does their capacity to tolerate affect and relationship to self and other.

Patients who use their bodies to defend against their emotional experiences deny relationship with others. Denial of emotional relationship with another may make discovering the transferential relationship to their analyst difficult. A silent transference exists (Eekhoff, 2015). Relational psychosensual processes with their own body and to the analyst's body may become a substitute for the emotional transferential relationship and is at once concrete and representational. Physical proximity is essential. The analyst's attention to somatic phenomena and painstaking efforts to recognize and name these processes over time provides the patient with a new experience of relatedness between two physically and psychologically separate persons. A new relationship to the body, namely an integrated psychosomatic embodiment that normally would be accomplished between a mother and her infant, may be achieved in the analysis. It is not that an old experience is recovered. Rather, a new experience of embodied relatedness is realized. After much time, patience, and constancy, the experience of being contained and held in body and in mind is internalized. This enables what Cassorla (2018) calls "dreams for two". Dreams for two require two people who are psychically separate, not fused as Ada was with me initially. As no two patients are alike and no patient is the same from day to day or from moment to moment, the process involves much trial and error.

A small number of patients are unable to dream. It is not only that they do not recall their dreams. Their concrete attachment to the sensorial bodily experience leaves no gap to be filled with processing the meaning of their sensations. Without the gap, there is also no psychic space between patient and analyst. Without space internally, there can be no dreams for two. They project weakly or their projections themselves are not communications, but are evacuations that contribute to this more primitive blank place.

In the case of Ada, who frequently said to me, "There is no there, there…", beneath her projections lay a more difficult non-projective defense; that is, a negative hallucination that fed the delusion that she herself did not exist. When her delusion of not existing, of nothingness inside, surfaced to awareness, she went from a feeling of emptiness to a feeling of fullness. The fullness felt terrible and terrifying. It made her feel claustrophobic in relation to her own sense of presence. It was not a welcome change and she retreated again from her own aliveness, creating an oscillation between full and empty, empty and full. Somatically, these experiences were expressed in various ways. A common one was through her breath and her pattern of breathing. Other physical symptoms such as difficulty swallowing, upset stomach, and feeling cold sent her again and again to her physician. She could not imagine that these physical symptoms were psychologically meaningful communications from her bodymind.

Before this oscillation and rhythm between empty and full is established inside the patient's bodymind, there may be reference to nothingness or talk of a void or a black hole. After the somatic defenses and mental use of the body and sensation are made conscious, a beginning experience of a self may evolve that is experienced as nothing but pain. This is not identification with a pain mother. The *nothing-but-pain* experience is a lifting of the defensive psychosensual defense and a coming alive. Coming alive includes feeling the emotional pain of their lives. For me, this is the most difficult point in the analysis. It is the point when my patients cry out to me, and Ada in particular said to me, "All I am is pain!" "Why?" "Why did you take me here?" "What good is it to know this?" At such moments, I needed to hold onto my own separateness, my own faith in the power of the life force and effectiveness of the psychoanalytic method. If not, the risk is that the analyst will be drawn into an enactment that destroys separateness and hinders development instead of viewing pain as communicating a specific need in the present moment.

Another way of saying this is that slowly over time, the hidden delusions of no self, no other, no time, and of no space or infinite space may give way. Slowly, the reality of something beyond the concrete – of meaning in emotional relatedness to somatic and psychic self as well as to bodily and mental otherness – is experienced. When this occurs, healthy projection and introjection becomes possible. This is, as I understand it, the embodied process of dreaming. In Bionian terms, somatic beta experience is being transformed into alpha experience. However, initially any emotional contact with either self or other may be felt as unbearable and defended against by a process that makes relationship concrete or sensate and superficial at best. Often the most ravaging and painful moments come after a brief momentary experience of emotional contact. This is because concrete experience is, like an iceberg, breaking up. There has been an experience of somatic and psychic separateness in the live emotionality between patient and analyst that is terrifying. The terrifying experience implies space and time and an unknown and unknowable future.

Patients who do not experience themselves existing are difficult to treat and feel at times that they are untreatable. Yet, I believe they are treatable. I hypothesize that those who heal are able to do so because they possess an innate capacity for unconsciously experiencing a container/contained relationship within their own bodies and in psychical proximity (Eekhoff, 2017) to the analyst's body and to the analytic consulting room. They have an innate Essence of Being (see Chapter 1). In my view, this essence is an expression of the life instinct and of the patient's capacity for utilizing "thoughts without a thinker" necessary for the patient learning to relate more fully and to living a multi-dimensional life. This capacity utilizing an embodied relationship may also emanate from the universal experience of being contained physically and psychically in the womb during gestation. This universal physical experience is present even when the mother's reverie has been inconsistent or hostile.

The capacity for making use of sensory experience has been described by Bion as alpha function. Cassorla (2018, p. 67) describes this ability as making up the "… mental representation of emotional experience, acquiring the quality of 'thinkability' without yet actually taking the form of thoughts. This stimulates the formation of an 'apparatus' for thinking them, which causes dream-thoughts, unconscious waking thinking, dreams, memories, ideas, and more complex thoughts". I am adding that the somatic experience of both the mother and the infant as well as the patient and the analyst is the foundation of the emotional link between body and mind.

Clinical Vignette

I have written about Ada previously (Eekhoff, 2019). She was 33 years old when I met her, and is the middle of three children. She came from an upper middle-class family with two working parents. She reported an unremarkable childhood. Purportedly, Ada was neither abused nor deprived physically, although she believed her parents were indifferent to her emotional needs. Reportedly, her mother was depressed both before and after her birth. Via construction using the transference relationship, I came to believe that her mother was not only indifferent, but perhaps was repelled by Ada's infantile demands. Ada says her mother told her that she never wanted children. She felt herself to be an unwelcome child (Ferenczi, 1929). When with her, I frequently had an image of a dying baby. Initially, I experienced her constant talking and angry demeanor as intrusive, leaving me little room for thinking and no space for dreaming. I contributed to the problem with my own attempts to speak. In speaking, I was contributing sound and action, not using reverie to find or make meaning. Ada herself reported no nighttime dreams in the first three years.

Her presenting problems in those first few sessions were:
"I'm in a new relationship and will need support when it fails".
"I am actively suicidal ten to twelve days a month".
"I think I have a border-line eating disorder as I binge and then think I am fat so I starve myself".
"I grew up in a House of Horrors".
"I'm panicked at work all the time, and I feel intruded upon if anyone talks to me".

What I am interested in describing in this vignette are the somatic expressions in Ada's analysis that mark internal empty places, a somatopsychic no-place, along with a no-thing or a no-object or a no-self. I agree with Tustin, Meltzer, Bick, Bleger, Mitrani, Ogden, Grotstein, Lopez-Corvo, and D. Rosenfeld, that these internal states of mind are pre-thought experiences as well as pre-splitting and pre-projecting states of being.

In other words, these selfless and objectless states exist in a time and space before the paranoid-schizoid and depressive positions. As I mentioned previously, Bleger (1967) calls this symbiotic state of normal undifferentiation the glischro-caric position. Ogden (1989b) calls it an autistic contiguous position that he views as non-pathological and part of our experience throughout life. I call it the primal position. However, these positions can become fixed (Lopez-Corvo, 2006; 2014) and part of a pathological organization. Meltzer (1975a; 1975b) has described somatic dismantling used as defense during post-autistic or post-psychotic states. Dismantling, the separation of one sense from another, is an attempt to stop overwhelming emotional experiences.

Ada told me that nothing could accumulate inside of her because her skin didn't hold her. She experienced herself as a sieve, whose contents were leaking out. As a result, she felt often that there was nothing inside of her; that she was a two-dimensional cartoon character. She also experienced me as not having an inside and being two-dimensional. This meant we were both sieves. Consequently, she could not rely on me or anyone else to contain her.

Perhaps her feeling of not existing and having nothing inside her was present in me in the first session as evidenced by my needing to speak more than usual. She expected answers from me and then interrupted any of my attempts to speak, foreclosing the possibility of my containing her. She herded me again and again towards her preconceived notions and attempted to get me to agree with her. For example, when I wondered if she might leave her boyfriend rather than be left by him, she ignored me. She was certain he would leave her. She seemed to have all the answers already. If she needed anything from me, it was as a filler of space. My experience was that the two of us conspired to fill the space with sound, leaving no room for emotions or dreams to arise.

In that first session Ada avoided eye contact. For her to look at me would have been to acknowledge our physical separation. As she healed, eye contact increased until she reached a point of being able to tolerate not seeing me, thus benefitting from using the couch. As the couch work deepened, the visual depravation became unbearable and she once again needed to sit up so that she could see me. At first, she needed this in order to "keep an eye on me", fearing I might hit her when she wasn't looking. I came to understand counter-transferentially that for Ada sitting up and seeing me involved a primitive experience of the danger of the other. To deny this, Ada looked at me and in looking became me. While lying down, she could in phantasy be inside of me thus becoming me and reducing her fear. She went up and down on the couch, preferring to sit up and see me when experiencing the greatest anxiety.

Ada's world as she described it to me was two-dimensional, consisting mostly of surfaces and at times sensorial in a way that was very concrete and non-symbolic. For symbols to form, for words to have meaning, there needed to be a recognition of my separateness from her, of a gap between us. She could not tolerate such a gap. She lacked a psychic space for dreaming. I did not at first recognize this. Ada was articulate and highly verbal. She had been in treatment for ten years before coming to me. She knew how to speak about herself, without being truly reflective. She could speak about feelings without having any. I erroneously assumed that her words had the same emotional meaning for her as to me. They did not.

Ada had an uncanny capacity to mimic me. She took my words and fed them back to me. For example, she believed that I was telling her what to do and how to feel and act. At first, I thought this meant she was internalizing our work. I was most impressed with how quickly she was changing. Later, with horror I recognized her mimicry and experienced her as nowhere to be found psychically in the room. Her physical presence remained, along with her imitative words. She did this everywhere she went, matching herself to others, leaving no difference, bumps, or protrusions that would interfere with what I came to understand as her desire for perfect fusion.

This transference/countertransference situation was also evident in how she related to her own body. I initially attempted to interpret a transference relationship that was silent (Eekhoff, 2015). In hindsight, it would have been better if I had been able to interpret her bodily experience. Eventually I was able to make this shift in how I spoke to Ada and in what I offered in the way of verbal interventions. This was helpful to her in that before analysis, Ada did not know when she was hungry or tired. She did not feel a need to urinate or defecate. She sought medical treatment fearing her various aches and pains indicated a lethal illness. Her sensory world, which kept me out of contact with her in the transference, actually did keep her unconsciously in contact with her own life force as it evolved in utero and in relationship with her mother and with me. Her obsessive use of exercise, while serving an evacuative function, simultaneously gave her an experience of her beating heart.

Ada severely restricted her food intake, but forced herself to eat so she did not become anorexic. Hers was a pre-pubescent body and she prided herself on wearing the same size clothing when I met her as she had worn in junior high school. Whenever she felt stressed by contact between us, she perceived herself as fat, looking into the mirror and actually seeing a fat torso. As her ability to tolerate fullness and dimensionality increased, she has come to feel herself to be and to look womanly.

Ada's sensory experience was initially used primarily as a defense against psychic overwhelm. Interestingly, her experience was that her sensory world provided a relational connection. Moreover, it felt to her like the only contact she had with her own or others' humanness. At the same time, her attempt to control and distort her body was a way of denying her own life force and her need of others. Still, her bodily connection to me kept her in the treatment when her mind was against it. That is, the sensorial aspects of the treatment served to hold her to me. At the same time, her mind was continually devising ways to rid herself of what I was saying and of me. She was stripping meaning from my words and emotion from my well-intentioned interactions. For example, she continually told me that she was quitting analysis. At the same time, she in fact did keep coming. She stuck to me in a most elemental way, adhesively via mimicry (Meltzer, 1974), trapped by her own sensate needs, while she denied any emotional relationship with me.

First and foremost, Ada developed an attachment to the frame. The constancy of her hour with me became important to her. This attachment included the physical space of my office; its sight and smell and the texture of the room, the softness of the couch, the quality of the light coming through my windows, and the changing colors of the leaves on the trees she could see outside. Also included in the frame was the rhythm and sound of my voice. These are the things she clung to, while ignoring my words and consciously denying my value. While she was telling me that I was useless, even bad for her, and I feared she would flee analysis at any moment, she was unconsciously burrowing in and hanging on to me for dear life. When I was feeling most battered, beaten, hopeless and useless, she was physically relating to me.

Whereas my awareness of what was happening in the analysis evolved overtime, I will try to demonstrate through her words how these clues came to me. I recognize the limitations as I need to use words to describe what I believe is a deeply unconscious and nonverbal continuous sensual experience that operates primarily at a somatic level. What I concluded as my own understanding evolved is that Ada's sensory experiences functioned as an umbilical connection to me and as a second skin (Bick, 1968; 1986).

Eventually she began to understand how she was going through the motions. She described a man whom she loved as "looking like a boyfriend, smelling like a boyfriend, feeling like a boyfriend and acting like a boyfriend, but [for her] not a boyfriend". A few weeks later she said the same about herself; that she was looking like, acting like, talking like a person but had been for many years not a person. She was horrified at realizing how she had in many respects not existed as a person. She simply wasn't home. Her words and actions were mostly mimicry.

How does one notice the presence of an absence? After years of analysis, Ada told me she sensed it in her body. She said she had "always known something was missing", or "It's comforting, I don't exist at all". Later she described a place seemingly at the cusp of this no-place that was quite horrific. "I feel devastated", she said, "like after the atom bomb, there is nothing left to experience. Is there? Nothing is left". She wondered if her experience was like what happens when matter and anti-matter come together. Poof! Nothing.

Towards the end of her analysis Ada said, "I am getting used to my body and to myself. Bodies have a cadence. I was always pushing other people, but I was pushing myself too. Now I am listening to my body, resting when I'm tired, eating when I'm hungry. Can you believe that I never knew until recently what it felt like to be hungry?"

Discussion

In *Elements of Psycho-Analysis*, Bion (1963) describes the use of the senses as a necessary component of thinking. He elaborates his description of the thinking process by linking the domain of the senses with the domains of myth and passion. He provides evidence of the body as a dream space. Ada came to me unable to dream in either her body or her mind. The work we did together required us both to experience our perceptual identities, the physical responses of our bodies as they responded to the proximity (Eekhoff, 2017) of each other. Proximity leads to primary identification via the psychosomatic resonance and reverberation between us. Eventually these sensory experiences could be noticed and named. Eventually her early experience that she had not registered could be experienced somatically and emotionally within the analytic hour.

The *motion of the senses* is essential to the development of the mind. Ada's rigidity and fear of any experience she could not control caused her to shut off her awareness of her body's responses. She preferred stasis to movement. In doing so she limited her emotional life and restricted her capacity to think. She was shut off and shut down. At the same time, she used her mind to tell her when it was necessary to urinate or defecate, eat or drink, sleep or waken. Her body's natural rhythms were lost to her. Lost too were any feelings of sensual pleasure or sexual desire.

Ada did not experience her own body as a container of her Self. As her primary experiences had not been represented first in her body and then in her mind, she was caught in agitation, irritation, and extreme anxiety that left her suicidal. She was hyper vigilant and hyper stimulated. In spite of this, she felt she did not exist. Ada did not repress because "It is not possible to repress something that has not yet been represented through some mental process" (Bergstein, 2019, p. 14). In Ada's case the process of representation and mentalization was short-circuited by the restrictions she placed on her somatic experience. Before her body could dream, sensually creating the sensate experience of her skin as a container and her eyes as the image-maker that could become movies in her mind, Ada shut down. In such a deadened state, psychic elaboration – the process of figurability (Botella and Botella, 2015) – could not flourish.

As painful and tumultuous as her analysis was, it awakened her body so she could experience herself as existing in the real world during this time. Only then was she to embody her experience and dream so as to develop her mind. Transformation replaced repetition and re-presenting. Finally, thus embodied, she was able to marry and have a child and experience her own body and mind as existing.

Conclusion

An analytic space is typically a space within the symbolic order. Openness enables a space for dreaming, which brings primitive sensory and emotional representations into the symbolic order. As analysts, we are privileged to encounter patients wherever they are in this dream space and dreaming process. When early experience is traumatic and the infant and child are not contained by the mother's reverie, the work is more difficult, since language itself may be borrowed rather than generated. Differentiating that which was beginning to form but was attacked internally or from without (Bion, 1959) from that which has never been realized is the task of a receptive and containing analyst. How difficult this differentiation is is, in my view, influenced by the internal make-up of both analyst and patient. The way in which the analyst matches and meets the flesh and blood person in the consulting room and the way in which the analysand processes information and feels understood, misunderstood, or not understood can contribute to or help ameliorate this difficulty.

Separating mind and body at this primordial level is purely an intellectual exercise. The emotional interaction of two people interacting in a continuous oscillation between container and contained involves body and mind or, more accurately, bodymind. The oscillation is movement and movement is a function of the dream.

Transformations in the bodymind of both analyst and analysand enable psychic transformations, some of which become symbolized. The psychic transformations happen via dreaming or alpha function. In my view, only a tiny minority of these transformations becomes organized into language. Most remain in the body as background and are present but not recognized. In either case, emotional transformations require a thinker to cope with them (Bion, 1970).

Some people with seemingly benign upbringings nevertheless struggle enormously with these somatic transformations. To bear their experiences, they must alter and distort them. Others with horrific reports from their childhoods manage to hold and contain and examine their experiences without excessively attacking themselves or the analyst in the transference. They are able to experience themselves without excessive distortion, as happens in the case of massive intrusive or evacuative projective identification.

Dreaming is a process of transformation that enables change. The analyst's maternal function and attention to the body as well as to the primitive bodymind states of the patient allow dreaming and change to happen outside of conscious awareness, outside of remembered dreaming, and in the body itself through a sensorial experience of the emotional contact. In analysis, both analyst and patient are involved in organizing these unconscious transformations. The analyst's experience of the emotional and perceptual contact, or lack of it in the here-and-now of the session, makes it possible for her to differentiate somatic delusion from somatic holding and the integrative or nonintegrative use of the body as a dream space.

Just as I believe it is the mother's responsibility to do all that is humanly possible to prevent reality from coming into the infant's awareness prematurely, so too is the analyst's responsibility to notice and protect patients from sensorial and psychic overwhelm to ensure a space for dreaming. In this way, experience that was once unable to be dreamt can be slowly brought into the analytic relationship and into the symbolic order.

References

Aulagnier, P. (2001). *The Violence of Interpretation: From Pictogram to Statement.* Sheridan, A. (Trans.). Hove and New York: Routledge, 1975.

Bergstein, A. (2019). *Bion and Meltzer's Expeditions into UnMapped Mental Life: Beyond the Spectrum in Psychoanalysis.* London and New York: Routledge.

Bick, E. (1968). The experience of skin in early object relations. *International Journal of Psycho-Analysis*, 49: 484–486.

Bick, E. (1986). Further considerations on the function of the skin in early object relations. *British Journal of Psychotherapy*, 2: 292–299.

Bion, W. R. (1959). Attacks on Linking. *International Journal of Psycho-Analysis*, 40: 308–315.

Bion, W. R. (1962a). A Psycho-Analytic Theory of Thinking. *International Journal of Psycho-Analysis*, 43: 306–310.

Bion, W. R. (1962b). *Learning from Experience.* London: Karnac Books.

Bion, W. R. (1963). *Elements of Psycho-Analysis* (pp. 1–104). London: Heinemann.

Bion, W. R. (1965). *Transformations.* London: Karnac Books.

Bion, W. R. (1967). *Second Thoughts: Selected Papers on Psychoanalysis.* New York: Jason Aronson.

Bion, W. R. (1970). *Attention and Interpretation.* London: Tavistock. [Reprinted London: Karnac, 1984.]

Bleger, J. (1967). *Symbiosis and Ambiguity: A psychoanalytic study.* Churcher, J. and Bleger, L. (Eds.); Rogers, S., Bleger, L., and Churcher, J. (Trans.). London and New York: Routledge, 2013.

Botella, C. and Botella, S. (2015). *The Work of Psychic Figurability: Mental States without Representation.* Weller, A. with the collaboration of Zerbib, M. (Trans.). Hove and New York: Brunner-Routledge.

Cassorla, R. M. S. (2018). *The Psychoanalyst, The Theatre of Dreams and the Clinic of Enactment.* London and New York: Routledge.

Damasio, A. R. (1999). *The Feeling of What Happens: Body and Emotion in the Making of Consciousness.* New York: Harcourt Brace.

Eekhoff, J. K. (2015). The Silent Transference: Clinical Reflections on Ferenczi, Klein, and Bion. *Canadian Journal of Psychoanalysis*, 23(1), Spring 2015.

Eekhoff, J. K. (2017). Finding a Center of Gravity via Proximity to the Analyst. In Levine, Howard and Powers, David (Eds.), *Engaging Primitive Anxieties of the Emerging Self.* London: Karnac Books.

Eekhoff, J. K. (2018a). Somatic Countertransference as Evidence of Adhesive Identification in a Severely Traumatized Woman. *American Journal Of Psychoanalysis*, 78(1): 63–73.

Eekhoff, J. K. (2018b). Terrified by Suffering, Tormented by Pain. *American Journal of Psychoanalysis*, 78(4): 350–369.

Eekhoff, J. K. (2019). *Trauma and Primitive Mental States: An Object Relations Perspective*. London and New York: Routledge.

Ferenczi, S. (1929). The unwelcome child and his death-instinct. In Balint, M. (Ed.), *Final Contributions to the Problems and Methods of Psycho-analysis* (pp. 102–107). New York: Basic Books, 1955.

Green, A. (1999). *The Work of the Negative*. Weller, Andrew (Trans.). London and New York: Free Association Books.

Grotstein, J. S. (1990) Nothingness, meaninglessness, chaos, and the "black hole". *Contemporary Psychoanalysis*, 26(3): 257–290.

Grotstein, J. S. (2000). *Who is the Dreamer Who Dreams the Dream? A Study of Psychic Presences*. Hillsdale, New Jersey, and London: The Analytic Press.

Klein, M. (1961). *Narrative of a Child Analysis: The Conduct of the Psycho-Analysis of Children as seen in the Treatment of a Ten-year-old Boy*. London: Hogarth Press.

Klein, M. (1975). Envy and Gratitude and Other Works 1946–1963. Masud, M. and Khan, R. (Eds.). *The International Psycho-Analytical Library*, 104: 1–346. London: The Hogarth Press and the Institute of Psycho-Analysis.

Lacan, J. (1966). *Écrits: A Selection*. Sheridan, Alan. (Trans.). New York: W.W. Norton & Co., 1977.

Lopez-Corvo, R. (2006). *Wild Thoughts Searching for a Thinker: A Clinical Application of W.R. Bion's Theories*. London: Karnac Books.

Lopez-Corvo, R. (2014). *Traumatised & Non-Traumatised States of the Personality: A Clinical Understanding Using Bion's Approach*. London: Karnac Books.

McDougall, J. (1989). *Theaters of the Body: A Psychoanalytic Approach to Psychosomatic Illness*. New York: Norton.

Meltzer, D. (1974). Adhesive identification. In Hahn, A. (Ed.), *Sincerity and Other Works: The Collected Papers of Donald Meltzer* (pp. 335–350). London: Karnac, 1994.

Meltzer, D., with Bremner, J., Hoxter, S., Weddell, D., and Wittenberg, I. (1975a). *Explorations in Autism: A Psychoanalytic Study*. Strath Tay, Perthshire: Clunie Press. [Reprinted for the Harris Meltzer Trust, London: Karnac, 2008.]

Meltzer, D. (1975b). The psychology of autistic states and of post-autistic mentality. In Meltzer, D., with Bremner, J., Hoxter, S., Weddell, D., and Wittenberg, L. *Explorations in Autism* (pp. 6–29). Strath Tay, Perthshire, UK: Clunie Press. [Reprinted for the Harris Meltzer Trust, London: Karnac, 2008.]

Ogden, T. H. (1986). *The Matrix of the Mind: Object Relations and the Psychoanalytic Dialogue*. Northvale, NJ: Jason Aronson.

Ogden, T. H. (1989a). *The Primitive Edge of Experience*. Northvale, NJ: Jason Aronson.

Ogden, T. H. (1989b). On the Concept of an Autistic-Contiguous Position. *International Journal of Psychoanalysis*, 70: 127–140.

Ogden, T. H. (1991). Some Theoretical Comments on Personal Isolation. *Psychoanalytic Dialogues*, 1(3): 377–390.

Scarfone, D. (2015). *The Unpast: The Actual Unconscious*. Bonnigal-Katz, D. (Trans.), with House, J. (Contrib.). New York: Unconscious in Translation.

Tustin, F. (1986). *Autistic Barriers in Neurotic Patients*. New Haven, CT: Yale University Press, 1987.

Winnicott, D. W. (1949). Mind and its relation to the psyche-soma. *British Journal of Medical Psychology*, 27: 201–209. [Reprinted in *Collected Papers – Through Paediatrics to Psychoanalysis*. New York: Basic Books, 1958.]

Winnicott, D. W. (1960). Ego distortion in terms of true and false self. In *Maturational Processes and the Facilitating Environment* (pp. 140–152). New York: International Universities Press, 1965.

Winnicott, D. W. (1963). Communicating and not communicating leading to a study of certain opposites. In *The Maturational Processes and The Facilitating Environment* (pp. 179–192). New York: International Universities Press, 1974.

Winnicott, D. W. (1969). The Use of an Object. *International Journal of Psychoanalysis*, 50: 711–716.

Winnicott, D. W. (1974). Fear of breakdown. *International Review of Psycho-Analysis*, 1: 103–107. [Reprinted in *Psychoanalytic Explorations* (pp. 87–95). Winnicott, C., Shepherd, R. and Davis, M. (Eds.). Cambridge, MA: Harvard University Press, 1989.]

Chapter 4

In Defense of Hope

Psychoanalytic theory has evolved since Freud, even as its foundation rests with him. Today, we analysts are treating patients with life-long suffering who bring us both defects and defenses (Alvarez, 1998). They come to us in despair and often see us as their last hope. Whereas in the early days of analysis, these patients were considered untreatable, today we analyze them. In order to do so, we see them longer, enabling us to analyze mental processes that are more and more primitive. Their suffering disrupts their pleasure, their relationships, and their abilities to know what is real. Their defenses do not protect them from their primary processes. Frequently, they are overwhelmed by what they perceive. These primal processes include disruptions in the perception and the processing of experience. They also include somatic defenses that incorporate auto-sensuous behaviors.

Today, we analyze not only defenses, but deficits in defenses arising from failures in a person's apparatus for thinking. An analysis of thought processes includes an analysis of the precursors to thought and thinking that includes the body. Body relations (Bleger, 1967; Eekhoff, 2021) and object relations create and re-create the Self. The apparatus for thinking, the organization of the body-mind, has become a focus of our attention. Such attention facilitates the strengthening of the apparatus for thinking and the birth of new thinking. Psychoanalysis itself is continually becoming.

"In Defense of Hope" may seem a strange title for a chapter on the living theory of analysis, but I believe hope is a neglected element of psychoanalysis. It is the living edge of growth and creativity. At the same time, it can be a defense against despair, which is hope's conscious manifestation. Furthermore, I am linking hope to a truth principle (Grotstein, 2004) that includes an instinctive drive to find personal truth. The drive for personal truth is also an instinct to procreate, to be creative and alive.

Analysis today needs hope, since we are in the midst of collective traumas affecting everyone. It is hard to remain hopeful even though we survived a pandemic, and are fighting climate change as it presents itself in floods, extreme heat, violent storms, and multiple destruction of environment and habitat, endangering many species of wildlife. There is increasing global

DOI: 10.4324/9781003544470-4

political turmoil, with war a horrific consequence in some instances. These external circumstances link with primal somatopsychic states to have very personal ramifications to our patients and to us.

Perhaps we analysts do not write about hope more frequently because we recognize it as a conscious defense against uncertainty and entropy. Perhaps this is so because hope <u>can</u> be a defense, an omnipotent bulwark against reality, rather than (as I also think of it) a primary affect, experienced in the body and a precursive aspect of representation and symbol formation, a precursor to desire and renewed life, which begin in the body. Hope is an element of the use of the senses via dreaming processes to create and recreate the mind (Monteiro, 2023). Hope is the Unthought Known (Bollas, 1987) behind every analytic intervention.

At the same time, hope is ineffable. You cannot taste hope, smell hope, or see hope. You can only sense it. Even if you sense hope, you cannot know hope. You cannot make yourself know or sense it by using positive psychology – affirmations or cognitive behavior therapy. You cannot create hope by using brain implants or anti-depressant medication. In analysis, you cannot create hope by suggestion (Freud, 1890; Caper, 2020) or induction (Blum et al. 2023). Artificial intelligence cannot generate hope. Nor can hope be generated by the manic denial of reality by either the patient or the analyst. Hope is ineffable, yet I am saying, it is in the body.

Meltzer (1986), speaking specifically of defenses that confuse fact and fiction and result in lies instead of truth, believes the true symbol cannot be destroyed. I believe he is talking about using pain and despair as a defense against reality. He says: "If this is the situation in the mind, that the true symbol cannot be destroyed, but only covered over, hope must exist that the truth will shine through, that it can 'dawn' on the benighted mind" (p. 104).

There are a number of ideas worth considering in Meltzer's statement. I would like us first to consider the idea that the true symbol cannot be destroyed. Implicit in this is that truth itself cannot be destroyed. As Bion (1962a; 1962b) says, it does not take a thinker for truth to exist. Truth is. Only lies require a thinker. Thoughts without a thinker are true thoughts.

Today we might say psychoanalysis is a search for the truth. Truth cannot die no matter the horror and disasters that occur around and amongst us. When we cannot bear to face the truth, we avert our eyes, block our ears, retreat to the womb in phantasy. Symbiotic attachment (Bleger, 1967) is a defense against truth, even as it is a normal aspect of our corporal relationships. Symbiotic attachment is also mutually beneficial. Bion's (1961) basic assumption, pairing, is a defense against truth. Such defensive efforts do not change the reality of that which we cannot face. Rather, these efforts distort our perceptions of reality, leaving us in a cycle of lies that creates corrosive doubt, erroneous assumptions, and false hopes.

Corrosive doubts and erroneous assumptions interfere with the birth of the new idea. They interfere with problem-solving and being able to act following thinking. They also interfere with the process of analysis. At the same time, there is a nagging realization somewhere in all of us that these lies are not the truth. Often that nagging takes the form of despair. Sometimes it takes the form of hope. Bion (1961) says the feeling of hope is a rationalization that is "itself both a precursor of sexuality and a part of it" (p. 151). As such the feeling of hope is a defense, as then also would be the feeling of despair. Hope is also the precursor of desire and a bastion against impotence.

Another point that Meltzer (1986) is making is that the truth gets covered over. Implicit in this statement is the idea that all humans are born with a capacity to recognize truth; it is only that all are not equally able to use it, to tolerate the frustration or the pain inevitable in reality. Bion (1962b) says that not every person develops a capacity for using thoughts. I would add, for facing truth. Freud intuited something like this when he moved away from the pleasure principle to the reality principle. However, pleasure and the comfort of the senses must not be forgotten. The body, as a representation of the mother, is the background object and the container for truth to be found. Thoughts may themselves be born in the body (Eekhoff, 2021; see Chapter 3.).

Finally, I bring our attention to Meltzer's phrase, "*hope* [italics mine] must exist that the truth will shine through, that it can 'dawn' on the benighted mind". It is this belief, that hope exists that the truth can be found, that I am considering here. Further a benighted mind is an unenlightened mind. The additional hope is for enlightenment. Here is the link between Bion and Meltzer's exploration of truth and hope. Both appear to be moving toward the direction of faith – a word that is unfortunately often considered the domain of religion. Hence hope is often linked to illusion or delusion, and a religious stance itself is seen as a defense (Freud, 1927). Green (1986) integrates these when he says:

> In *The future of an illusion*, Freud (1927) asserts, "the intention that man should be 'happy' is not contained in the plan of 'Creation'." The fragility of our bodies, external natural threats, and our relation to others are sources of misery. Hope, not unlike illusions and fantasies, is thus a mere palliative. These mental configurations bring to the fore the psyche's devices that are deployed to deal with our deepest fears.
>
> Hope joins ranks with illusions, fantasies, and religion in building a buffer against the silent awareness of despair—the most private of madness. Hope and despair may be regarded as two sides of a coin since the presence of one will necessarily evoke the other. The interconnection between hope and despair reveals an inherent paradox. This paradox is embedded in a logic that defies the logic of secondary process while accentuating the logic of primary process.
>
> (p. 241/2)

Indeed, some have accused psychoanalysis of being a religion. Perhaps this accusation comes out of our unspoken hope, embedded in our beliefs that psychoanalysis can alleviate suffering, stimulate the mind, and bring life to dead psyches. Bion reminds us, "There can be no genuine outcome [in an analysis] that is based on falsity. Therefore, the outcome depends on the closeness with which the interpretive appraisal approximates to truth" (Bion 1970, p. 28).

As an Object Relations analyst, each time I meet a patient I am exhibiting an Act of Faith. Each time I speak, I am exhibiting hope in analytic change. The act itself is a transformation of my emotional experience of the moment and a manifestation of my hope. Every silence is a measure of hope. Simultaneously, I am in the moment with the patient and in an unknowable but imagined future. This act is related to the pain of integration and the loss of omnipotence; it is not an element of omnipotence. Since I cannot know what will happen next, my Act of Faith holds me as reality, buffered by hope and despair, swirls around us.

Hope is primarily unconscious, found in the body and in primary process. Hope, against all odds, keeps us going. It signals the true symbol that cannot be destroyed, only covered over. I believe hope is an instinct, related as such to Panksepp's (1998) mammilian affects. Hope is an aspect of psychological deep structure (Ogden, 1984). It is an element of the epistemological instinct of Klein and Bion and of the representational imperative of Levine (2021). I also place it firmly within Klein's and Isaac's ideas about unconscious phantasy and Bion's ideas about preconceptions. Yet as analysts, we rarely write about or talk about hope. Mitchell (1993) wrote about hope and dread, from a relational perspective, seemingly from a more conscious perspective. I, with Green (1986; 1999) and Klein (1975), place hope in a more primal psychic position as an organizing element in the internal world.

Perhaps some analysts equate hope with desire, an innately sexual drive. As I stated previously, I believe it is a precursor to desire and sexuality (Bion, 1961). Others may equate hope with wish, although I do not. A wish is an aspect of the symbolic order, and primarily a secondary process, even when it is unconscious. I see hope as a precursor to the wish. Some may equate it with longing or expectations – other words that I believe are indicative of a more developed, more mental experience, than hope.

When I speak of hope, I am speaking of a primal somatic experience, which becomes symbolized and developed over time. I place hope in the body, even though I have said we cannot find hope with our senses. How can I place hope in relationship to intimate others, when I am speaking of a lost object? In the absence of loving and containing others, hope is visible by our reliance on strangers. We see this evidenced by the refugees of the world or the analysands in our offices. I place hope as an element of the Life Instinct.

When I remember Freud's assertion that an orgasm is related to the death instinct, I also say that hope is an element of the Death Instinct. No wonder so few people believe in the death instinct. Yet the sperm and the egg destroy themselves in order to create a conceptus. Bion writes about any true encounter with an 'other' as being catastrophic. This is true because when I truly meet you, what I once was, I am no longer. Change and transformation involve the death of what was.

That is not to say there are no cognitive manifestations of hope that might be found in systems of conscious or unconscious beliefs, as described by Figueiredo (2004). He describes both paranoid hope and depressive hope. He also links this to an Act of Faith. However, I am attempting to explore *primal hope* as is found in all humans and is ineffable and unknowable except as it is manifested in body relations (Bleger, 1967). As such, primal hope forms an element of the ontological vibrations in relationship. Simultaneously these ontological vibrations fuel the epistemophilic instinct and the representational imperative (Levine, 2012; 2021.

Perhaps in using Panksepp's (1998) research we would include it as an aspect of seeking, of care, and of a conative impulse rather than a cognitive one. As early as 1890, Freud said, "The contrary state of mind (of fearful expectation), in which expectation is coloured by hope and faith, is an effective force with which we have to reckon, strictly speaking, in *all* our attempts at treatment and cure" (p. 289). Here Freud is distinguishing hope from expectation and hinting at a force that inhibits as well as motivates.

When I speak about hope, I am describing a search for meaning that can only be found in relationship. I am also writing about an infant's expectation of care (Bion, 1962b; 1965; Anderson, 2016. Bion (1962b) describes this as the preconception of a breast. I am adding hope as an unconscious and instinctive element in these seeking activities. Boris (1979) says, "Hope resides in time and it is lost, therefore, both to the timelessness of eternity and the instantaneousness of the moment" (p. 149). He continues,

> These twin check-reins upon hope—eternity and the moment—reveal its paradoxical nature: hope is potential, and potentiality is lost both to actualization and to finality. As Bion (1961, pp. 151–2) puts it, 'Only by remaining a hope does hope persist'. The stayed moment, the static situation, the constant object—these are the conditions propitious for desire. But for hope they are too finite, too unambiguous. Hope flourishes in change, uncertainty and flux.
>
> (p. 149)

I would add that hope flourishes in becoming. This statement brings me back to my opening statement about the patients we treat today – patients who are in despair and come to us as their last hope.

The stayed moment and the static situation may become a defense against hope. The constant object is an illusion, a remnant of the prenatal state and the umbilical connection; and change, uncertainty, and flux are anathema to those who have been traumatized as young children. For traumatized patients, the concretization of material things, the patterns of synchrony and rhythmicity, and the self-soothing of sensations dominate. The fluid shifting between the primal, the paranoid schizoid, and the depressive positions, so essential for growth and creativity (Charles, 2001) is impeded. And therefore hope, which exists both in the moment and in infinity, falters. Hope lives in motion and time.

Clinical Evidence

Perhaps I could speak of any case as evidence of hope. I am differentiating belief from hope and our more neurotic patients demonstrate an evolution of hope that is symbolic. The cases I think of are people seeking analysis out of desperation. They are the people who say to us, "What is the point? Why bother?" Often, they are suicidal, seemingly without hope. Nothing reaches them. Patients in such states of despair are outside of time. To exist in time – have a past, a present, and a future – forces an awareness of reality and for these patients, reality is unbearable as is pleasure.

One such person was a man named Dennis. Dennis was a 74-year-old man, who came to me "because my cat died". He appeared an attractive well-groomed man who looked composed and confident. Yet, even in the first meeting, I sensed a deep depression and anger. He looked at me guardedly, yet with longing. He told me my office was "too far away" and asked for a referral, which I gave him. A month later, he called again, saying he did not want to see the person to whom I had sent him. He wanted to see me. Years later, I leaned that he had called me several times in the years before I met him, listened to my voice, and decided it was "too deep" and so did not leave a message.

Dennis had discovered psychoanalysis by reading Karen Horney. Since then, he had subscribed to an analytic journal, bought analytic books of mostly relational theorists, and read and re-read them. He had been in an analytic psychotherapy group for over 12 years, which ended when the analyst died. He had been in a committed relationship for ten years with a man who died of AIDS. He initially described this as a "bad relationship". After which, he had had a nine-year analysis with a gay analyst "whom I should have left, but I was too passive. I did what he said, like use the couch". Clearly, from his conscious perspective, no one could help him. Everybody died or failed him.

Initially, I was impressed by his articulate descriptions of his early life and attributed this to a successful first analysis. He appeared insightful, self-observant, and self-reflective, although clearly ambivalent and wary. His stories were matter-of-fact, lacking in emotion. My object relations manner felt non-analytic to him. I talked too much. When I interpreted the transference, he would sometimes say, "This is not about you". But he stayed, claiming he liked my office. He said he didn't really trust or like women, so he did not want to use the couch.

Purportedly, Dennis's mother rejected him at birth, wanting to have a girl, this in spite of having two boys and a girl already. The nurses in the hospital had been fearful to let her take the baby home as, upon seeing he was a boy, she had thrust him back at the nurse saying, "Ugh...you keep him". In those first months, mostly what I heard were childhood stories of abuse from both parents. Any interpretation I made was met with a childhood story of cruelty and violence. He said he couldn't invite his friends to his home because his house was a house of horrors.

Interpreting the transference and his experience of me as intrusive and rejecting angered him. He denied any interpretation I made. Frequently he would tell me he was a very concrete person and didn't understand what I was getting at. Yet, he came faithfully, always dressed beautifully. Once, I interpreted his wish that I find him attractive. He accused me of seducing him. He said he dressed like he did for himself. Years later, he told me he was attracted to me on the first day and found that confusing.

After several months at twice a week, I told him I felt something was missing in our work together, *interpreting to the atmosphere*, instead of the transference directly. Another story followed about an insight he had after running away from home at 15 following a beating from his father. He accidentally saw his mother outside a grocery store. Later he told me he felt his soul leave his body then. He'd had a moment of fright that ended with the thought, "There is something missing in me". It didn't particularly bother him. It just was true. I told him he had been trying to let me know what was missing since his first call to my answering machine. I told him I felt like he was missing. He added, "in action".

I realized then, that each time I spoke, he dissociated. He could keep talking but was in fact missing. Slowly I begin to speak to these observations of deep somato-psychic dissociations. If I was silent, he was "gone". When I spoke, I could see a flash of him, but then he would go missing again. He would flash on and off, like Christmas lights. I could not understand what kept him coming, since the analytic process was so painful. It was also painful to me. Soon, he asked to come more often.

Back to Hope

I want to say something about his constant telling and re-telling of his childhood stories. This was not life review as we see with older patients, nor was it working through. The stories were sounds he made and auto-sensuous repetitions of the tongue in his mouth and the movement of his lips. The stories were mostly – but not always – an autistic defense against intimacy. I soon learned that what appeared to be insight was mimicry of his former analysts or snatches of articles he had read – including mine. Penetrating his wall of sound and gathering the wordless infantile transference was difficult because the adult man with me was bright, articulate, and silently, unconsciously desperate and hoping to be found.

Dennis did not use the word hope, nor did he use the word despair as many such patients might have done. He was too out-of-touch to do so. I feared the analytic work more than he did, fearing that analysis at his age would only make him miserable. He would die before getting any benefit. But it was not mine to choose. He wanted analysis; he did not know why. It was not about his cat. It was something about a death, but one that had already happened to him. And as surprised as we both were, he wanted to see me, a woman. As the work deepened, he began to feel and to grieve. It was awful for us both, but his dissociation in the hour lessened. He was able to tolerate more and more connection between us and hate it.

At first, he was perplexed by this, fearing his whole life had been a lie and that he could have married and had children. Then he grieved the years he'd spent before coming out; then he grieved his common-law marriage saying they had loved each other but he had been too broken. His partner had told him this again and again. He began to recognize that his first analysis had been good for him.

I am making this sound easy. It was not, there was so much pain and more awful stories from his childhood, some of them about incest. Through it all, Dennis remained, what now in retrospect, I would call hopeful. He suffered so, and increased his sessions, continued to work hard, bringing me his dreams. He told me that every time, just in the half hour before his analysis, he felt dread and a "kind of anxiousness" in his chest.

I want to tell you only one dream that came near the end of his analysis: Dennis tells me that he had his usual before-analysis night of dreaming, but this time his dream was silly. He says,

> The one I remember did not amount to much. I was in bed with a woman and she was upset with me for coming to bed late. We lay there, back-to-back, tense. Then the phone rings, and I get up to answer it. I say hello and there is silence. I feel irritated and say, "Who is this?" A man says, "Dennis". Now I am more irritated. "I'm Dennis! You are not Dennis". I slam down the phone on him. Then I wake up.

I was silent after he told me this dream, a little stunned perhaps, and feeling very moved. I didn't say anything. Dennis finally says, "Phew. Guess I was wrong. What a dream. That was me". He goes on to elaborate and associate to his dream. At the end of it, he says, "I mostly do not feel like anything is missing in me anymore. I have found my missing piece. There are still some things I cannot face though. No offense, but I still dread this work, but more and more I feel I have come alive".

Discussion

Hope is related to the mystery of life, to the passion of two people and to the reality and truth that we need a concrete real other to be born, physically and psychologically. Enlightenment and embodiment come from emotional intimacy. Psychoanalysis offers intimacy, if both analyst and analysand can face the catastrophic truth of life and death that contact brings.

I want to emphasize here that I am not advocating a symbiotic transference, but attempting to analyze one. Bion describes two people experiencing the same thing, but not in same way. Otherness is important to remember. The isolation of personal experience (Ogden, 1991; Bion, 1963) is a reality not to be denied. Even at birth, newborns are able to differentiate themselves from their mothers at times. They also have moments of undifferentiation. Both moments enable differentiation and individuation. Shifting states of body and mind elicit similar but not equal experiences in others. Hope unrealized may be experienced as dread by the patient while the analyst experiences hope. Sometimes both analyst and patient experience a nameless dread before a new experience can be had.

I have come to believe that Dennis' dread, and the nameless dread that other patients bring, is related to the early loss of a receiving and containing mother or father. It is related to infantile trauma, whatever might be the cause – defect or defense. It is related to what Bion (1958) calls the obstructive object. However, it is also related to an inability to hold onto the good in relationship. It is related to what Dennis once said, "I do not believe I have a receptor for love".

Dread includes the fear of hope. For this reason, I do not believe that just being a caring receptive mother analyst is particularly helpful. Such care cannot be received and introjected unless the obstructive internal object is realized and interpreted. That is not pleasant. For patients like Dennis, it is a slow and gentle process, but it none-the-less involves interpreting rage that has been turned back against their own body-mind, causing dissociation at all levels of his self, body and mind. Dennis shifted rapidly between *organizational positions* – from the primal to the paranoid-schizoid to the depressive positions – and used different kinds of dissociation depending upon his position.

Through it all, he maintained hope – never as a concept, but by his actions. He didn't think about hope or talk about hope. He demonstrated hope, by overriding his doubts about a female analyst, his fear of an attacking analyst, and finally his love for and gratitude that he could be with me just as he was. In spite of my interpretations of his self-attacks and attacks on me, he felt that I also saw his goodness and his love and named them.

Today, Dennis has both male and female friends. One such friend is a younger heterosexual man with a wife and children. They are very emotionally intimate and Dennis is sometimes amazed at his capacity for openness, trust, and love.

Analysis with an older person involves some life review, but what we did together was much more than that. More, it was an in-depth engagement and intimacy that comes in any true analysis. It was also a lesson in surviving hope, as painful as it was. He tells me, "Now, something new has happened. I used to know with my mind what happened to me as a child. Now I feel what I would have felt then when those things happened. I couldn't feel anything then. It is so amazing. I feel in my body all that I could not. I feel every-thing – sad, angry, hurt, hate, but I also feel love. I love my father and my mother. I never felt that before".

Conclusion

This chapter has suggested that hope is a basic element of psychoanalysis, originating in the body. Hope is an element of any analysis and a primary affect. Furthermore, I have described hope as not only a defense, but as a primal aspect of our innate expectation of care. This primal experience of the expectation of care is present even when the object has gone missing. The impetus of the search for the lost object may be hope. Hope is the impetus behind every expression, the movement behind the sense, then the perception, then the expression of a future. Hope is intimately connected to both time and timelessness (Boris, 1976). Hope is found in every breath we take.

Hope underlies our faith in the transformative power of a two-person ana-lytic relationship where unrepresented and poorly represented states of mind can become symbolized and represented – not only in words but in deeply experienced body affects and somato-psychic emotions that enhance and develop an apparatus for thinking. This involves not only being able to think, but being able to use the thoughts one has. Such deep internal organization enables the birth of new ideas that can be tolerated and used for change. Those changes happen individually in relationship, but they also happen institutionally in groups, even in psychoanalytic groups.

References

Alvarez, A. (1998). Failures to Link: Attacks of Defects? *Journal of Child Psychotherapy*, 24(2): 213–231.

Anderson, M. K. (2016). *The Wisdom of Lived Experience*. London: Karnac.

Bion, W.R. (1958). On Arrogance. *International Journal of Psycho-Analysis*, 39: 144–146.

Bion, W. R. (1961). *Experiences in Groups and Other Papers*, 6: 1–191. London and New York: Routledge, 2014.

Bion, W. R. (1962a). A psycho-analytic theory of thinking. *International Journal of Psycho-Analysis*, 43: 306–310. [Reprinted as "A theory of thinking", in Bion, W. R., *Second Thoughts* (pp. 110–119). London: Karnac, 1984.]

Bion, W. R. (1962b). *Learning from Experience*. London: Heinemann. [Reprinted London: Karnac, 1984.]

Bion, W. R. (1963). *Elements of Psycho-Analysis*. London: Heinemann. [Reprinted London: Karnac, 1984.]

Bion, W. R. (1965). *Transformations*. London: Heinemann. [Reprinted London: Karnac, 1984.]

Bion, W. R. (1970). *Attention and Interpretation*. London: Tavistock. [Reprinted London: Karnac, 1984.]

Bleger, J. (1967). *Symbiosis and Ambiguity: A psychoanalytic study*. Churcher, J. and Bleger, L. (Eds.); Rogers, S., Bleger, L., and Churcher, J. (Trans.). London and New York: Routledge, 2013.

Blum, A., Goldberg, P., and Levin, M. (2023). *Here I am Alive*. New York:Columbia University Press, pp. 1–304.

Bollas, C, (1987). *The Shadow of the Object: Psychoanalysis of the Unthought Known*. London: Free Association Books.

Boris, H. N. (1976). On Hope: Its Nature and Psychotherapy. *International Review of Psychoanalysis*, 3: 139–150.

Boris, H. N. (1994). *Envy*. Lanham: Jason Aronson, Inc.

Caper, R. (2020). *Bion and Thoughts Too Deep for Words*. London. Routledge.

Charles, M. (2001). Auto-Sensuous Shapes: Prototypes for Creative Forms. *The American Journal of Psychoanalysis*, 61(3): 239–269.

Eekhoff, J. K. (2021). Body as Dream Space. In Harrang, C., Tillotson, D., and Winters, N. (Eds.), *Body as Psychoanalytic Object: Clinical Applications from Winnicott, Bion and Beyond*. London and New York: Routledge.

Figueiredo, L. C. (2004). Belief, hope and faith. *International Journal of Psychoanalysis*, 85: 1439–1453.

Freud, S. (1890). Psychical (or Mental) Treatment. *The Standard Edition of the Complete Psychological Works of Sigmund Freud*, 7: 281–302.

Freud, S. (1927). *The Future of an Illusion*. New York: W. W. Norton & Company, 1989.

Green, A. (1986). *On Private Madness*. London: Karnac.

Green, A. (1999). *The Work of the Negative*. Weller, A. (Trans.). London: Free Association.

Grotstein, J. S. (2004). The seventh servant: The implications of a truth drive in Bion's theory of 'O'. *International Journal of Psychoanalysis*, 85: 1081–1101.

Klein, M. (1975). Envy and Gratitude and Other Works 1946–1963. Masud, M. and Khan, R. (Eds.). *The International Psycho-Analytical Library*, 104: 1–346. London: The Hogarth Press and the Institute of Psycho-Analysis.

Levine, H. B. (2012). The colourless canvas: Representation, therapeutic action and the creation of mind. *International Journal of Psycho-Analysis*, 93: 607–629.

Levine, H. (2021). *Affect, Representation and Language: Between the Silence and the Cry*. London: Routledge.

Meltzer, D. (1986). *Studies in Extended Metapsychology: Clinical Applications of Bion's Ideas*. London: Clunie Press for The Roland Harris Educational Trust.

Mitchell, S. A. (1993). *Hope and Dread in Psychoanalysis*. New York. Basic Books.

Monteiro, J. S. (2023). *Bion's Theory of Dreams: A Visionary Model of the Mind*. London and New York: Routledge.

Ogden, T. H. (1984). Instinct, phantasy, and psychological deep structure: A reinterpretation of aspects of the work of Melanie Klein. *Contemporary Psychoanalysis*, 20: 500–525.

Ogden, T. H. (1991). Some theoretical comments on personal isolation. *Psychoanalytic Dialogues*, 1(3): 377–390.

Panksepp, J. (1998). *Affective Neuroscience: The Foundations of Human and Animal Emotions*. New York: Oxford University Press.

Chapter 5

Premonition
Hope and Dread in the Analytic Hour

Since Freud's brilliant *The Interpretation of Dreams* (1900), we analysts have explored the role of images in the development of thought. When we pay attention to the images evoked in any analytic session, we participate in an intimate communication with our patients and with ourselves. We have learned that images, our own as well as our patients', bring us closer to an emotional truth in relationship. They emerge from reverie and premonition. Meltzer (2005, p. 155) and Bergstein (2013; 2019) have called the analyst's images counter-dreaming and described counter-dreaming as an element of intuition. Intuitive understanding may or may not result in images and eventually in language, but I believe intuitive imagery and analytic understanding always include premonition. Together, intuition and premonition form a continual interactive process that elaborates meaning in relationship, without the medium of language.

Today many psychoanalysts have begun to explore interactive processes that promote transformations, which lead to change and development. Using Bion's (1963) ideas about the psychoanalytic object as extension in the domains of sense, myth, and passion, these analysts seek to provide a setting in which both analyst and analysand are engaged in a process of being and becoming (Bion, 1965; 1970). No longer are many of us primarily focusing on history and the uncovering of repressed phantasies (see Levine, 2022). Instead, we are interested in the ontological and epistemological processes of generation and re-generation as it occurs in the session and within the analytic relationship. Whereas the history is not forgotten, it is no longer a primary focus. We do not seek to make what is unconscious conscious or to provide opportunities for insight into past experience, even though that is inevitable in the intimate relationship we have with our patients. Instead, we notice what is emerging in the here-and-now of the session. What we notice is determined by our premonitions and intuitions.

Sensate Vertex

In this pursuit some analysts have begun to observe and explore the precursors to imagery and intuition. In this chapter, I am exploring our analytic use of what Bion (1961; 1963) has named *premonition*. Premonitions are

DOI: 10.4324/9781003544470-5

precursors of images and precursors of conceptions. Bion (1963) uses this word not as it is traditionally used, that is signifying a forewarning, but rather describes premonition as an awareness of emotional links. Premonitions are somatic presentations that anticipate the future. We might say they anticipate representation. Sensations and the rhythmic pulsing of heartbeat and breath are bodily manifestations of object relations, what Bleger (1967) calls bodily relations. Premonitions primarily utilize sensation and sensuality instead of preconceptions and conceptions, as does intuition. Sensations, smells, and sounds help create the multidimensional imagery of dreaming and counter-dreaming.

Sensation and sensuality permeate infantile sexuality (Abel-Hirsch, 2004). Indeed, they permeate all infantile experience and continue to always be of primary importance to us as adults. Since early experience remains with us all our lives, Bion's vertex of the sensual underlies premonition, which is an element of intuition. As precursors of images, they are elements of dream life.

When I say *precursors of intuition and emotion*, I do not mean cause and effect. Rather, I believe Bion is speaking of proto-mental experiences that are multi-determined, not determined by one factor or one sense. Proto-mental experience is body experience that is a precursor to mentalization; however, the relationship is more circular than linear, with each element interacting with every other and enhancing and building internal objects as representations. Premonitions are always present, but usually are unregistered consciously. They are a foundation of awareness. At the center of both perception and cognition, premonishing enables us to have a subjective experience of ourselves in relationship. The process builds mutual rapport and, via introjection, enables experience and relationship to accumulate meaningfully.

Premonition provides a center of gravity which grounds us in reality. Premonition also links affects which are instinctual and emotions which are a bridge between psyche and soma (Eekhoff, 2019). Premonitions are the center of ongoing transformation and development. A small example occurs each time we greet a patient. Without words, both analyst and analysand unconsciously sense something in the other. Emotional adjustments are made on the basis of this sixth sense, without thought or observation of physical expression entering in. This sixth sense includes premonition and intuition.

Premonition as an Aspect of Embodiment

Premonition organizes affective and emotional experience and helps to build internal structure. As precursor of our emotional responses to experience, premonition builds pluricausal psychic dimensionality. The multi-determined dimensionality premonition brings serves to simultaneously ground experience in a predictable form and provide a function that enables a subjective sense of self. The processes of premonition and intuition and the movement between them form the basis of embodiment and bodymind unity so necessary for the elaboration of consciousness and subjectivity. Mind and body unity is not a given. Bion (1976) says, "The individual has to live in his own body, and his body has to put up with a mind living in it" (p. 10).

Being in the body with a mind living in it is embodiment. Embodiment assures balanced body relations and object relations. Embodiment enables learning from experience and the accumulation of experience into meaningful patterns. This realm of the sensual – sounds, smells, and sensations – provides a primal organization of relational experience, enabling two people to know one another in an intimate, creative, psychically and physically pleasuring way, without images or words. Embodiment enables passion and Bion (1963, p. 13) tells us that passion is always about two people. Premonitions, coming as they do from the body, imply emotions and relationships, without being them. Perhaps premonitions are the psychic integration of the sensual and the emotional.

At-one-ment, Awareness, and Attention

The analyst's at-one-ment with self and other, which includes open receptivity to premonitions in relationship, joins with the analysand's wish and innate expectations to be met. As analysts, we too share this unconscious expectation to be met. These innate expectations are somatic and an aspect of the survival instinct. Together, in a private and uniquely personal manner, sensuality and sexuality meet in an intimate psychic analytic encounter that celebrates life. Premonitions of sex create hope (Bion, 1961). Hope, as an expression of the life instinct, allows both analysand and analyst to be patient and secure (Bion, 1970) until out of the infinite chaos of sensate experience, "a pattern evolves" (p. 123). Something new is anticipated and created. Openness to the new experience enables curiosity to blossom and doubt to be creative, not persecutory. A space for *reverie*, what Bion (1962) has named the means by which a mother shows her love, opens.

Analysts' and analysands' sensory perceptions of each other are the bodily source of premonition and intuition – the awareness of which are two essential outcomes of analytic reverie. Their myths, which evolve from imagination, use these premonitions and intuitions to find images and words for that which has never been verbalized. But long before emotions and words, there is a primal sensorial arena of connection – a premonition. This soon-to-be emotional arena is the origin of consciousness – awareness emerges from both the presence (Meltzer, 1984) and the absence (Bion, 1962; 1970; Green, 1993; Eekhoff, 2021c; Levine, 2021) of the other. Awareness is dependent upon the introjection and assimilation of the senses (Bion, 1957; 1970).

Further, premonition emerges as the *attractor of attention*. Premonition, as the forerunner and the outcome of intuition, happens in relationship. It is a two-person event. Intuition links premonition with a preconception to create a *hunch* or a feeling outside of language. An approximation of the feeling can sometimes be verbalized. Bion (1963) says, "The counterpart of the pre-conception is the *premonition*. Directly observed emotional states are significant only as premonitions" (p. 75, emphasis in original). I would add that premonitions imply a future.

Premonition and intuition are significant. While grounded in the body, they ultimately bring us into contact with the non-sensual, the arena that is the heart of analytic mutative relationship. Non-sensual links make up the atmosphere of the psychic union and include all emotions with love and hate and curiosity being the most prominent (Bion, 1963; 1965; 1970). Premonitions are elements of any love relationship and include passion – the 'O' of raw unmediated relational experience. They are presentments waiting to be sensed, noticed, and imaged. When realized, they might become, via imagination and myth, representations of the future. As such, they are elements of Faith (Bion, 1970).

Premonition is not only related to the sensuality and sexuality of the infant. As I have said, it is related to the infant in the adult or to the *infantile* origination of a thought. The intuitive thought brings together a preconception with a realization. Premonitive senses occur on the outer edges of inner space (Eekhoff, 2022b) bringing together sensation with affect that becomes emotion. The outer edge of an internal psychic place is where mind and body meet via emotional responses to experiences that bring significance, consciousness, and ultimately memory. These outer edges of awareness are barely discernable since they are not yet fully organized by the mind, but if perceived, are organized by the body (Eekhoff, 2019; 2021c). Further, these premonitions expand the containers that are our minds. They put us in touch with the finite and the infinite.

Often, in order to work deeply in these primal arenas, an analyst will have to learn to recognize these barely noticed bodily sensations and then to value them as significant information. Doing so involves a radical openness to one's own and the other's bodily experience. These eventually become emotional responses in relationship. Discovered first as premonitions, they are organizers of experience and reduce the chaos of the unmediated perceptual experience of infinite sensuality. They are integral to the ongoing unintegration, disintegration, integration process that serves to create a subjective sense of self. Included in this process are undifferentiated states of at-one-ment (Bion, 1970) and symbiosis (Bleger, 1967). At-one-ment "*resembles* possession and sensuous fulfilment" (Bion, 1970, p. 33, emphasis in original) without being it, enabling a constellation to emerge that increases the possibility of 'O' moving to 'K'. Symbiosis provides a constant background of safety that offers security and comfort.

Without the analysand's integration of these somatic sensations with emotional connection and unnamable or not-yet-named understanding, analytic premonition and intuition may unwittingly be used to prick the patient. Then what can be used for good – for growth and development emerging out of an immediate experience of emotional truth and empathic understanding – is accidentally used to harm. No matter the analyst's good intentions, the insightful descriptions derived from premonition and intuition can be too much, too soon for the patient and evoke the fight or flight impulse. Patients say, "Do not harm me. Do not hurt me" because they too have a premonition of just how painful their own personal truth in relationship can be. Sometimes, the actual concrete experience of being sensed or seen is averted, being too much and causing embarrassment or shame. The relationship illuminates what has been hidden and this can be unbearable for both analysand and analyst.

Integration is painful. Separation and individuation, as well as fusion and merger (Eekhoff, 2021c), facilitate integrative movements. However, there is another reason that truth may be avoided and analysands say "Do not harm me". The actual presence of the analyst may be difficult to tolerate. The sense of the analyst, the image of the analyst, evokes both boundless hope and nameless dread. Meltzer (1984) describes how the apprehension of the beauty of the mother (analyst) can evoke fear and dread. Too much emotional contact also can blot out the emergence of the subjective self of the patient and the nascent self remains hidden or does not evolve. Transformations in 'O' cannot happen.

Reverie, when one is working without memory and desire and understanding, occurs by being on the edge of the paranoid-schizoid and the depressive positions (Bion, 1970). I would include being on the edge of the primal position (Eekhoff, 2021c). The primal position is not unconscious, coming as it does from the body. Nor is it an aspect of primary process (Aulagnier, 1975). Rather the primal position is the origin of consciousness. Working without memory and desire does not preclude the senses but includes them as an *immediate experience*. Being in the immediate experience, the perpetual moment of the session may be extremely difficult. Even though we often speak of reverie as being a product of our analytic wisdom and discipline, it is not a given, especially since it is achieved via the integration of *sense, myth, and passion* (Bion, 1963).

Like transformations in 'O', reverie can be elusive. Once achieved, it can be rich with sensation and imagery, reflecting relationship, although fleetingly. This occurs before the paranoid-schizoid position in the primal position where at-one-ment is possible. These sensations and images, what Aulagnier (1975) calls pictograms, may then become verbalizable as we move from and between the primal connection of symbiosis (Bleger, 1967; Eekhoff, 2021, 2022b) to a differently organized connection that includes emotional intimacy and language. We might say we shift from one vertex to another, changing our perspective, and thereby enhancing our psychic depth and breadth.

Bion describes this as a movement from 'O' to 'K'. If we analysts are present with care and concern, with compassion and kindness, that is, speaking only from the depressive position instead of the paranoid-schizoid position or the primal position (which we also must embody in order to find an intimate link), then the emotional truth of the moment can be gently experienced and perhaps named. Bion (1967) says, "a sense of truth is experienced if the view of an object which is hated can be conjoined to a view of the same object when it is loved and the conjunction confirms that the object experienced by different emotions is the same object. A correlation is established" (p. 119). This requires a transformation from premonition and intuition and an integration of seemingly conflicting emotion. With transformation, an interpretation can be given that may minimize the sting that truth evokes (Bion, 1970).

Clinical Considerations

Clinically, premonition occurs as an anticipation – not a wish – of a future. Perhaps we might include it in the realm of Faith. Faith in a future is not a given. Since many of our traumatized patients seem to live in the unpast (Scarfone, 2015) or the *perpetual present* (Eekhoff, 2021c), without awareness of the future, the analysts' somatic and emotional awarenesses and valuing of their own premonitions can be an essential element in the ongoing transformation of premonition and intuition into *emotional resonance* with the patient. Personal and relational at-one-ment and symbiosis in a body-relations connection enables movement. Movement in time suggests a future.

Analytic resonance and rapport enable experience to be recognized, named, and imagined within a context of time and space and relationship. Resonance, however, is an in-the-moment experience that includes premonition and intuition. Bleger (1967) calls this *symbiosis*. Nissen (2015; 2022) calls this the *presence moment*. Eshel (2019) names this *presencing*. Reis (2021) calls this resonance *being with*.

The *perpetual present* is filled with emotional resonance, even when it may appear that the patient is devoid of feeling and unconnected with the analyst. The reverberation of the emotional contact is always there, even when it cannot be consciously found. This reverberation originates from the premonitive and intuitive link between analyst and patient. Bion described this contact as essential for transformation in 'O' and the birth of consciousness (Bion, 1965; 1967; 1970). It is also what he called the *Seventh Servant*. Grotstein (2004) links this to a truth drive.

Clinically, a premonition in the analyst may be experienced as a hope even as it is experienced by the analysand as a dread. Both are emotional experiences of time. I believe it is more accurate to speak of premonishing and intuiting. Whereas some may describe this as a split or the reception of projective identifications – which in fact they can be – I am more interested in these as expressions of emotional resonance. I believe emotional resonance is more primal than splitting and projective identification. It arises as an aspect of normal symbiosis (Bleger, 1967; Eekhoff, 2022b) and is an aspect of the primal position (Eekhoff, 2021c).

The primal position is a relational vertex and is present both pre- and post-natally. It includes states of undifferentiation and barely differentiated relationship with live others as well as unconscious phantasized undifferentiated, and barely differentiated, object and body relations. Emotional resonance occurs before empathy and is experienced as *somatopsychic equivalency*. Premonitions originate in the body and in the affective union between two people. As an aspect of body relations, premonitions are the precursors and the result of emotion. As a bridge between raw somatic experience and personal emotion, they are elements of both beta function (Goldberg, 2017; 2022; also see Sheehy, 2023) and alpha function (Bion, 1963). Both facilitate at-one-ment.

Premonishing and intuiting are powerful processes for apprehending dynamic unconscious communication. They are the subliminal background in any intimate relationship. In analysis, they are a mute aspect of the frame and the setting (Bleger, 1967; Moguillansky and Levine, 2022). In addition, premonitions are an unconscious means of organizing experience normally outside of awareness, which perhaps are present as a trace or an impression. The premonition of an emotion acts as a notation, enabling a trace of recognition of an experience. These traces are on the edge of our ability to notice them, at the outer reaches of inner space (Eekhoff, 2022a). In our consulting rooms, premonition plays a key role enabling the emergence of a selected fact from the infinite chaos of sensate and emotional experience. Premonition and intuition are carriers of emotional truth and of transformative relationship.

I want to emphasize that both premonition and intuition are aspects of psychological deep structure (Ogden, 1984; 1989). They are not states, although present in fluid states of psyche and soma. They are aspects of healthy, normal symbiosis (Bleger, 1967). They are about being and becoming and are intimately connected with unconscious phantasy and what Freud (1900) called *perceptual identity*. Information coming from these deep perceptual structures become awarenesses that take the form of premonitions and intuitions. Accessing premonitions, via reverie during moments of at-one-ment, enables both analyst and analysand to listen deeply to what is emerging psychically between them in the presence moment (Nissen, 2015)

However, writing about their appearance is not easy. Verbalizations from our premonitions and intuitions are already transformations of other transformations. Also, both premonition and intuition are ways of knowing that are *not* directly supported or maintained by sensuous experience. Sensuous experience is mostly conscious. Therefore, we can describe premonitions and intuitions only in their derivative forms. Perhaps premonitions and intuitions are the derivatives themselves. Our eventual descriptions are the shadows on the cave wall. They are a bridge between the innate mammilian affects and human emotion (Eekhoff, 2019; 2021c). Emotion, which cannot be seen, tasted, or touched, is the means by which we humans learn from experience (Damasio, 1999). Premonition is to emotion what preconception is to concept. Intuition links them.

Hope and Dread

I recognize that my attempt to describe premonishing is inadequate. I am attempting to demonstrate the ineffable primal link between two people. I am also attempting to write about premonishing as a neutral somatopsychic event. I want to try. Perhaps my attempts will enable others to track this mostly ineffable process. As I have said, premonishing is not about forewarning when used as Bion used it. Any affective charge comes later. I believe that premonition and intuition in relationship are made visible by the experience of hope and dread.

I will attempt to describe premonition by tracking these two key emotional responses common to all analyses, but particularly common when working with traumatized individuals. Boundless hope and nameless dread, both of which for most people usually appear first on the edges of consciousness, are central for our most difficult-to-reach patients, many of whom suffered early infantile trauma. I believe hope and dread originate in the body as premonitions – bodily manifestations of affects that both torment and inform. They are forms that imply a future that might portend either good or bad experiences.

As I explained in Chapter 2, I differentiate affects from emotions, seeing affects as the bodily expression of mammalian instincts, and emotions as their unique and personal transformation by the individual mind (Eekhoff, 2019). As such emotion links body and mind and is an aspect of embodiment. Since many trauma survivors believe they do not exist and therefore do not have potential, or as we might say, a future, premonitions found via the body facilitate analytic movement. They are also a source of pain and suffering for they are not well mediated by the higher order defenses. Without the mediation of symbolic representation, they may interfere with psychic equilibrium, which magnifies the pain. To quote a former patient, Ada, whom I also quoted in Chapter 3, "When I give up, my body just keeps going on" (Eekhoff, 2021c).

Hope and dread are two relationally-stimulated emotions that I believe are vestiges of preverbal and nonverbal premonition, while simultaneously forecasting a future emotional emergence. They mark both a beginning premonition and a realization of one. Like preconceptions that once realized become new preconceptions, premonitions once realized become new premonitions. In this way internal structure, representation, and symbolization accumulate via the emotions that premonitions foster. Premonitions are at once the beginning and the end of a process of embodiment and of an ongoing continual accumulation of a subjective sense of self and of multiple selves in relationship. They also may be derivatives of the life and death instincts. As such, boundless hope and nameless dread are one-person experiences made manifest in two-person expressions. Hope and dread are transformations of premonitions. Both indicate infinite possibility and hence are overwhelming. Both require intuitive comprehension by both analyst and analysand.

Clinical Case

The analysand, whom I will call Gloria, is similar to others I have known. Gloria, who first came to see me when she was 37, was in four times a week on-the-couch analysis for many years before I was able to sense, identify, and notice significance in premonitions and sensory movement in a session. I was initially impressed with her observations about herself and her body, not recognizing the radical dissociation between her body and her mind. As a massage therapist, Gloria spoke the language of the body. Her articulate speech distracted me, as now I assume it was meant to do. She was bright and eloquent, some of which was an aspect of her precocious mental development, particularly a precocious super-ego (Klein, 1928; 1932; Bion, 1963; 1970; Eekhoff, 2021a; 2021c), again something I did not originally recognize, preferring to believe she was more embodied – integrated – than she was. Her initial presenting reason for seeking analysis was the break-up of a relationship and the loss of what she described as "blissful moments of union" with a partner.

Gloria was the middle of five children, two boys who were older and two girls who were younger, in a family suffering from poverty, substance abuse, and alienation from community. They lived on the margins of society. She herself had purportedly been physically and sexually abused by both her parents and her older siblings. She had never married nor wanted children. She proclaimed to love touching and being touched, something her profession gave her. She told me she was inspired to seek analysis by a client who was a psychoanalyst. This client, who rarely spoke, used Gloria's touch differently than many others did. She received it. Once, her client had thanked her as she left saying, "You have wonderful hands. Your fingers heal me and bring me back to myself". Gloria instinctively knew that as much as she needed to be touched and sought it, she did not use touch to find herself. She used it to escape herself. The co-opting of sensation and sensuality to use as a defense against relationship, something we might name an autistic defense, seemed to take Gloria out of her subjective sense of herself and kept her emotionally isolated from herself and her objects. She was vaguely aware of this.

Gloria realized that, contrary to her previous belief, she herself was unable to receive touch, even though she often had massages as an aspect of training courses she took. This made her wonder whether she liked being touched in theory but not in reality. She assumed her abusive childhood history prevented her from getting full benefit from a massage or even sexual intercourse. As a member of a group called the Body Electric, she engaged in erotic touch with other group members. With all of her experimentation of touching and in spite of her purported love of touching, she had never had an orgasm, except with masturbation. Mutual touch, as she described it, was sensual not sexual. This was true whether her partner was male or female.

This description, although spoken without feeling, deeply moved me. Looking back, I am sure it contributed to my being distracted by her words for many months. I thought she felt what she was saying. I assumed she understood what she was telling me. I was incorrect. As is common with patients like Gloria, her descriptions did not include insight based upon personal emotional truth. What she spoke was not remembered or even integrated into her personality so that the understanding could accumulate and be used for modifying frustrations or problem solving.

In retrospect, I believe Gloria profoundly dissociated her body and her mind. Hence, she could not remember what she said nor learn from her experience. Rather, she needed to be held and remembered by me until her experience could come alive, have meaning, and function as a component of her growth. My awareness of this process occurred outside of the content of the sessions. The content seduced me away from a premonition of deep confusion. Today I would say this confusion arose from a boundaryless place of undifferentiation within and between us. Initially I experienced it as disorienting and unsettling. Only later, outside the hour, could I begin to intuit that something was 'there'. In the session, I experienced what Bion (1965) calls a no-thing, which is the absence of something. I also experienced only fleetingly being a no-object. These were not solid represented experiences in that they were extremely difficult to perceive and remember.

Gloria told me she was always depressed, "for no reason". She frequently felt wounded by interactions with friends and lovers, causing her to withdraw and isolate. She then felt persecuted by their indifference to her, not recognizing her withdrawal as impetus for what she perceived as rejection. She said she had very much hoped to escape her childhood home but leaving home had not meant leaving the pain behind. She felt that loving and being loved was a myth – "a lie people tell themselves".

In spite of this desperation, I found Gloria an engaging and likable person. Only later, did I come to realize that the woman she brought to me was someone she thought I would like. She anticipated me, I now believe via her premonition, and became me. My narcissism was gratified by her response of becoming me. Slowly over time, when I was with her, I noticed a split between my own mind and body. This reached my consciousness as an impasse in the analysis occurred. She began each session with an ongoing repetition – a litany of complaints about her friends and her family. Although she insisted this was not true with me, I began to dread our sessions, something that I had not done before. The dread took me out of the no-thing and the no-object experience which was an assault to my narcissism. However, the presence of dread pointed to an absence that I could begin to intuitively imagine.

Gloria, on the other hand, said she always looked forward to our sessions, hoping to gain new insights. She idealized me as "the best" and described driving home from sessions "blissed out". Today, I recognize that these oceanic experiences were an aspect of more primal defenses, where she became me. I was unknowingly colluding with her need to deny reality. The at-one-ment we experienced evoked memories and desire, "with impulses of possessiveness and sensuous greed" (Bion, 1970, p. 33). We were caught in an impasse.

Only later, after I was able to identify a certain heaviness in my body and a deadness in my skin, was I able to recall those sensations as present before the dread. I also noticed that my mind was very active, something I have learned to recognize as a response to anxiety. Later, perhaps a month or more, as I felt my body's responses to my patient and my mind's responses to my own anxiety, again in the hour, I was able to speak of what I called a *missing resonance*. In that moment, it seemed almost as if one of us were missing. Gloria agreed and was able to tell me she was holding her breath. She said she often did and associated it with always feeling cold in my office. She felt her skin tighten and, in her words, "become a shield against the cold". She said her tight skin made it difficult to breathe. It also helped her disappear. This confused me as I imagined, although did not say, that a tight skin would give her a sense of herself as present, serving as a second skin (Bick, 1968; 1985). This was not her experience. My escape to theory signaled something far more ominous.

This session initiated an exploration that lasted for many months on the nature of her skin and the use she made of sensation to stay out of relationship with both herself and me. Touch had become a means of dissociation. Sometimes, while lying on the couch she would sensuously run her fingers along the pattern on the rug hanging on the wall beside the couch. When she did this, I experienced her as absent. Touch had become an autistic defense against relationship. Although as I report it now, our discussion seems an overly-intellectual exploration, at the time it felt very emotionally alive. Out of this exploration came her awareness that she did not think of herself as empty or hollow or even as solid or full. To have an inside she would need to exist. She thought of herself as not existing. She clarified that this was different than being invisible, which was a consequence of not existing. She did not know who she was and feared that she had somehow died before being born.

Perhaps the reason these explorations felt alive was that they were accompanied by physical manifestations of seemingly intense anxiety. She would stiffen and arch her back on the couch. Her hands and fingers would become distorted and rigid. Sometimes she would shake. At others she would jerk away from the edge of the couch and put up her hands to block something she saw but could not name. She did not speak, but at times, would moan. During these times, I would mostly be silent, with an absence of images or thoughts. Occasionally, I would describe her body movements without attributing meaning to them. I merely wanted her to know I was there with her. Then she would be able to speak again.

Theoretical Considerations

The phenomenon of premonition is similar for everyone, but more notice-able with borderline or psychotic functioning, due to the hyper-sensitivity and hyper-vigilance such functioning contains. As Bion (1967) says, the mystic and the schizophrenic are in touch with the same phenomena, however, the mystic can manage the experience and make use of it, whereas the schizophrenic becomes overwhelmed with the awareness. It may also be that the bodymind dissociation (see Chapter 8) peculiar to early infantile trauma requires us analysts to become aware of the slightest alteration in relationship so as to stay attuned to the dynamic unfolding in the hour.

This phenomenon is an aspect of what Botella and Botella (2003) have named *psychic figurability*. They describe the process of representation, as do Aulagnier (1975) and Levine (2022). In exploring the representational processes, we are exploring the human ability to become aware of a self, experiencing its Self. This awareness marks sensate and psychic transfor-mations enabling the birth of a mind as well as ongoing transformations which elaborate our consciousness and deepen our emotional intimacy with others.

I want to speak again of premonition – the sensory precursor to emotion. I believe, with Bion (1967), Meltzer (1984), and Tustin (1990), that this bodily subliminal awareness occurs outside of the projective and introjective processes. In the clinical example I have given, a secondary expression of premonition was found in the tightness Gloria experienced in her skin. This second skin phenomena seemed to be used to create a cohesive sense of self, binding the unbearable emotion that was beginning to present itself as an aspect of her unconsciously denied relationship to me.

What makes patients like Gloria treatable is the symbiotic bodily con-nection (Bleger, 1967) to others, including their analysts. Symbiosis is a normal life-long response to intimate relations. Elsewhere, I have placed hope in treatability to the experience of being contained within the mother's body, again with the skin functioning to experience the amniotic fluid and the placental sac. The primal sensory experience cannot be named. Even if you spoke every language in the world, the sensory world of symbiosis and the emotional world of at-one-ment that evolves from it, could not be fully expressed in language. It is experienced and gains sig-nificance, via premonition and intuition, in the non-sensory world of emotion and feelings, which we name. Once named, the representations gain significance and can be elaborated. Premonitions and premonishing are central to the processes of representation. Premonition belongs to the oneiric realm of experience and the use of the body as dream space (Chapter 3; Eekhoff, 2022c).

Back to Gloria

After many months, Gloria confessed she dreaded her sessions, telling me she predictably felt dread as she drove to my office and then, as she walked toward the office door, her whole body felt tense. Sometimes her dread manifested in her inability to remember the code that let her into the waiting room. Sometimes she couldn't breathe or felt a tightness in her throat. Always, the dread was accompanied by a blank mind. No matter how many different interpretations I tried, they just didn't resonate with her. The reality of a sense of dread could not be named. It was not about knowing; it was about being. Rather, in her experience it was about *not* being (Eekhoff, 2021b). She described her whole being as nothingness.

As she felt dread, I experienced hope. Gloria sensed this and wished I would stop trying to name her experience of nothingness. She said my words were too much for her and added to her deadness. Silence too was unbearable. She felt my silence "put my lack of existence in my face". Her perceived deadness and lack of existence obliterated her being. Knowing about it made it worse. Nameless dread had appeared as a phantom in the room. It would neither be contained nor limited by having a name. I silently felt this dread was a hopeful sign; perhaps her delusion of not existing was breaking up and she was terrified. At the same time, her nameless dread was a torment and a defense.

I struggled to find words and waited for her to find hers. Gloria found both actions – my struggle for words and my waiting for her – unbearable. I soon noticed myself paying as much attention to my own bodily responses as I was to Gloria's breathing. I also listened carefully to the sound and rhythm of her moans, groans, and speech. Now, in retrospect, I believe I was attempting to calm myself enough to find a space of reverie. I was linking with her physically, in the realm of premonition, intuiting the atmosphere between us. When successful, I would experience a different kind of quiet alert awareness. Sometimes we breathed together, taking in air at the same time, releasing it also together.

Included in this awareness of premonition and intuition that slowly accumulated were emotions that belonged to both of us, originating in the space between us. This was a manifestation of our symbiosis and our private as well as shared at-one-ment. Bion calls this the shared 'O' of the session. These primal emotions were often accompanied by my own vivid images of her. One such image was of her as a fetus, scratching at the uterine wall. Another was of an unborn fetus clinging to the walls and not wanting to be born. Often it took many weeks or months before I was able to name the emotions these images evoked. During that time, I paid attention to the precursors of those images, trying to find Gloria in her sensate forms and my bodily responses to our experience.

Gloria's nameless dread was undifferentiated and to her always the same. She felt it could not change because she could not change. She was it. It was her. She had no future as a psyche that did not exist. Her body tormented her by its presence, as did mine. My words were mere sounds. Even then, I imagined that they were also markers. They served to create a mutual experience of discovery of something new. Gloria met this experience openly, sometimes with disbelief that I simply did not get what it was like to not exist. She told me that not existing meant there was no hope, and I seemed unable to comprehend her nothingness. Words implied hope. At other times, she was horrified as she watched her indifference to me and felt sorry that I had to work so hard in my attempts to reach her. As for me, I could not understand how nothingness could include dread and hopelessness. If she did not exist, who was registering these feelings? Usually, these were my unspoken thoughts, hopeful counters to the despair in the room.

The process was far from peaceful, as it evolved eventually into rage and outcries that I feared would destroy the analysis. Her despair at having no future was expressed also in frequent suicidal thoughts and even in dangerous accidents. She fell while hiking and broke her leg; she ran a stop sign and totaled her car, giving herself a head injury; and, finally, she broke off several important close relationships with lovers and friends. Sometimes she did not get out of bed for days, cancelling clients or simply not showing up at her office or at mine.

With the arrival of COVID-19, remote analysis at first suited her fine since she no longer felt her dread when walking to my door. Only later did she come to hate working remotely, recognizing that she couldn't feel me on a flat screen. I agreed and when we resumed in-person sessions, it was as if the *body electric* were present in our sessions. Gloria's movements, her intense perusal of my face as she entered the room and went to the couch, highlighted her sensuality and her sexuality in relation to me. She had begun to exist, as had I, and the relationship felt terrifying and exciting at the same time.

She was in love and in hate with me and the passion brought new forms of hope and dread. Whereas previously she had been dependent upon me and angry that she needed to come in order not to kill herself, now she felt the passion of our connection. She became curious about me, looking for clues about me on the internet. Sometimes, she drove past my office in hopes of seeing me. Previously she had often told me her experience had nothing to do with me. Transference interpretations went nowhere. Now, she feels the truth or falsity in them.

When in-person sessions resumed, she seemed to experience me as present. This ability to experience me marked her own capacity to exist psychically, in both body and mind. Gloria no longer maintained her delusion of not existing. She began to have full body experiences of herself, of me, and of us. Hating me and loving me made it possible for her to change. Ordinary dread was now accompanied by ordinary hope. To experience them both, seemingly simultaneously, confused and angered her. However, neither were limitless as they once had seemed. Over time, her love and hate of me transformed into an acceptance of my humanness. She began to date both men and women. Eventually she found someone whom she called a soul mate and married him.

Discussion

My patient Gloria could be discussed from many different vertices, each with valuable aspects. I have chosen to look at the role premonition and intuition played in her treatment. From a vertex of the primal position, the *presence moment* (Nissen, 2015) was the focus of my attention in my analytic relationship with her, as it evolved in the sensory bodily relationship between Gloria and myself. There were, of course, other vertices that I also used.

Bion (1967) deliberately chose the word *vertex* rather than point of view in order to include all of the senses in the apprehension of and organization of experience (Eekhoff, 2022a). He felt that *point of view* was too narrow in that it implied a visual frame. Images arising in a session were already further developed than the sensory experiences, especially those of sound, smell, and sensation. Also, I infer that Bion's preference of *vertex* over *point of view* arose due to the experience that the expression *point of view* restricted the field of perception. The word *vertex* expands our area of observation. It also reminds us that there are many different vertices, often occurring simultaneously. If we are looking for precursors to distortions in a sense of reality, as Bion did, we might include the sensate vertex. By paying attention to experiences of the body, the analyst may understand precursors to images and to language. Together analyst and analysand may begin to uncover the origin of symptoms and defenses.

Bion understood that primal sensory experiences could overwhelm the psyche were it not for their organization via alpha function into premonitions, intuitions, images, dreams, and thought. In that way, paying attention to premonition means that we are noticing the origin of a subjective sense of self. Being and becoming become the focus of our analytic relationships from a primal vertex. This was especially important in the analytic relationship with Gloria. It was not that we did not also explore processes that were of a higher order. However, I believe that Gloria's use of language was primarily borrowed from the culture around her and from the people she associated with, including me. It was not that she did not have some ability to represent her experience symbolically. However, she had large internal areas of unrepresented or poorly represented experiences. Being with her symbiotically, which included premonition, intuition, and finding words, provided her with new experience that could become introjected and assimilated.

Conclusion

In this chapter, I have defined premonition following Bion's exploration of that which can be experienced but not known. The essence of a person and the atmosphere created when two people meet is ripe with unknowable potential. I have described premonition as the bodily manifestation of that which is affectively and emotionally arising in the moment of encounter with another person. Premonition, as sensual manifestation of relationship, links with intuition to create an illusion of knowing. This healthy illusion provides order and cohesion, enabling the patient and analyst to find a center of gravity and a floor for experience. Further, I have differentiated premonitions, which originate in the body, from preconceptions, which are ideational.

I have asserted that this realm of the sensual (Bion, 1965), is the basis of both the function and the form of meaning-making (Meltzer, 1984). The realm of the sensual is the foundation of dreaming and counter-dreaming. The body becomes a dream space where new symbols are formed (Eekhoff, 2022c; Chapter 3). This is the process Bion (1962) has named alpha working on beta.

In this chapter, I have used the clinical experience of Gloria to demonstrate the transformation via relationship of primal experience of bodily instincts into psychic emotional representations of hope and dread. In this way, her dreamwork alpha was enlivened. She became able to integrate her body and her mind – her soma and her psyche. I could imagine her alive, not dead or nonexistent and eventually, she too came alive. Gloria moved from feeling she did not exist to a place of psychic existence and emotional turmoil inevitable in her deeply personal relationship with herself and with me, her analyst. She began to imagine a future where she would experience both good and bad things and be able to manage them.

I have described premonition as a primal psychic phenomenon arising from sensations, sounds, and smells evoked in proximity to an alive other. Premonitions are presentments that predict. As such they are elements of the representational imperative (Levine, 2012) and key to what makes us human.

Acknowledgement

This article was published in German, under Eekhoff, J. K. (2023). Die Vorahnung Hoffnung und Grauen in der analytischen Stunde. [Premonition: Hope and Dread in the Analytic Hour]. *Jahrbuchder Psychoanalyse*, *64(2)*: 41–67. Nissen, B. (Ed.). Berlin, Germany.

References

Abel-Hirsch, N. (2004). Lust for life: Pleasure under the reality principle and growth in eros. *British Journal of Psychotherapy*, 20(4): 473–483.

Aulagnier, P. (1975). *The Violence of Interpretation: From Pictogram to Statement.* Sheridan, A. (Trans.). London and New York: Routledge, 2001.

Bergstein, A. (2013). Transcending the caesura: Reverie, dreaming and counter-dreaming. *International Journal of Psycho-Analysis*, 94(4): 621–644.

Bergstein, A. (2019). *Bion and Meltzer's Expeditions into Unmapped Mental Life. Beyond the Spectrum in Psychoanalysis.* London and New York: Routledge.

Bion, W. R. (1957). The differentiation of the psychotic from the non-psychotic personalities. *International Journal of Psycho-Analysis*, 38, 266–275. [Reprinted in *Second Thoughts* (pp. 43–64). London: Karnac, 1984.]

Bion, W. R. (1961). *Experiences in Groups and Other Papers*. London: Tavistock.

Bion, W. R. (1962). *Learning from Experience*. London: Karnac, 1984.

Bion, W. R. (1963). *Elements of Psycho-analysis*. London: Karnac, 1984.

Bion, W. R. (1965). *Transformations*. London: Karnac, 1984.

Bion, W. R. (1967). *Second Thoughts: Selected Papers on Psychoanalysis*. London: Karnac, 1984.

Bion, W. R. (1970). *Attention and Interpretation*. London: Karnac, 1984.

Bion, W. R. (1976). *The Tavistock Seminars*. London: Karnac, 2005.

Bick, E. (1968). The experience of the skin in early object-relations. *International Journal of Psycho-Analysis*, 49(2–3): 484–486.

Bick, E. (1985). Further considerations on the function of the skin in early object relations: Findings from infant observation integrated into child and adult analysis. *British Journal of Psychotherapy*, 2(4): 292–299.

Bleger, J. (1967). *Symbiosis and Ambiguity: A Psychoanalytic Study*. Churcher, J. and Bleger, L. (Eds.); Rogers, S., Bleger, L., and Churcher, J. (Trans.). London and New York: Routledge, 2013.

Botella, C. and Botella, S. (2003). *The Work of Psychic Figurability: Mental States without Representation*. Weller, A., with Zerbib, M. (Trans.). London and New York: Brunner-Routledge, 2005.

Damasio, A. R. (1999). *The Feeling of What Happens: Body and Emotion in the Making of Consciousness*. San Diego: Harcourt Brace.

Eekhoff, J. K. (2019). Affective bridges between body and mind. In *Trauma and Primitive Mental States: An Object Relations Perspective* (pp. 15–28). London and New York: Routledge.

Eekhoff, J. K. (2021a). *In Defense of Hope*. Paper presented at Living Theory Conference, Free Association (November, 2021). Lisbon, Portugal. (Online). A revised version of this paper is now Chapter 4 in this book.

Eekhoff, J. K. (2021b). Body relations and the Black Hole. *International Forum of Psychoanalysis*, 30: 139–148.

Eekhoff, J. K. (2021c). *Bion and Primitive Mental States: Trauma and the Symbiotic Link*. London and New York: Routledge.

Eekhoff, J. K. (2022a). *The Outer Reaches of Inner Space*. Unpublished manuscript presented at the Regional Bion Conference, (May, 15th, 2022), Los Angeles, CA. (Online).

Eekhoff, J. K. (2022b). Psychic equivalency as an aspect of symbiosis. In Levine, H. and Moguillansky, C. (Eds.), *Psychoanalysis of the Psychoanalytic Frame Revisited. A New Look at José Bleger's Classical Work* (pp. 57–79). London and New York: Routledge.

Eekhoff, J. K. (2022c). Body as dream space. In Harrang, C., Tillotson, D., and Winters, N. C. (Eds.), *Body as Psychoanalytic Object: Clinical Applications from Winnicott, Bion and Beyond* (pp. 50–65). London and New York: Routledge.

Eekhoff, J. K. (2025). Receptivity and unrepresented states. In Power, D. and Power, N. (Eds.), *The Somato-psychic Realm: Analytic Receptivity and Resonance*. London and New York: Routledge.

Eshel, O. (2019). *The Emergence of Analytic Oneness: Into the Heart of Psychoanalysis*. London and New York: Routledge.

Freud, S. (1900). The interpretation of dreams. *Standard Edition, Vols. 4–5* (pp. 1–626). Richmond: Hogarth Press.

Goldberg, P. (2017). Reconfiguring the frame as a dynamic structure. In Tylim, I. and Harris, A. (Eds.), *Reconsidering the Moveable Frame in Psychoanalysis: Its Function and Structure in Contemporary Psychoanalytic Theory* (pp. 92–110). London and New York: Routledge.

Goldberg, P. (2022). Embodiment, dissociation, rhythm. In Harrang, C., Tillotson, D. and Winters, N. C. (Eds.), *Body as Psychoanalytic Object: Clinical Applications from Winnicott to Bion and Beyond* (pp. 116–133). London and New York: Routledge.

Green, A. (1993). *The Work of the Negative.* Weller, A. (Trans.). London: Free Association, 1999.

Grotstein, J. S. (2004). The seventh servant: The implications of a truth drive in Bion's theory of 'O'. *International Journal of Psychoanalysis*, 85(5): 1081–1101.

Klein, M. (1928). Early stages of the Oedipus conflict. *International Journal of Psychoanalysis*, 9: 167–180.

Klein, M. (1932). The psychoanalysis of children. Strachey, A. (Trans.). *International Psycho-Analytic Library*, 22: 1–379. Richmond: Hogarth Press.

Levine, H. B. (2012). The colourless canvas: Representation, therapeutic action and the creation of mind. *International Journal of Psychoanalysis*, 93(3): 607–629.

Levine, H. B. (2021). *Affect, Representation and Language: Between the Silence and the Cry.* The International Psychoanalytical Association Psychoanalytic Ideas and Applications Series. London and New York: Routledge.

Meltzer, D. (1984). *Dream-life: A Re-examination of the Psychoanalytic Theory and Technique.* Perthshire: Clunie Press.

Meltzer, D. (2005). Creativity and the countertransference. In Williams, M. H. (Foreword and Chapter 8 by Meltzer, D.), *The Vale of Soulmaking: The Post-Kleinian Model of the Mind and its Poetic Origins* (pp. 175–182). London and New York: Routledge, 2019.

Moguillansky, C. and Levine, H. (Eds.). (2022). *Psychoanalysis of the Psychoanalytic Frame Revisited. A New Look at José Bleger's Classical Work.* London and New York: Routledge.

Nissen, B. (2015). Faith (F) and presence moment (O) in analytic processes: An example of a narcissistic disorder. *International Journal of Psychoanalysis*, 96(5): 1261–1281.

Nissen, B. (2022). Understanding early experiences: Bleger's contribution to the undifferentiation of early stages. In Levine, H. and Moguillansky, C. (Eds.), *Psychoanalysis of the Psychoanalytic Frame Revisited. A New Look at José Bleger's Classical Work* (pp. 127–147). London and New York: Routledge.

Ogden, T. H. (1984). Instinct, phantasy, and psychological deep structure: A reinterpretation of aspects of the work of Melanie Klein. *Contemporary Psychoanalysis*, 20: 500–525.

Ogden, T. H. (1989). *The Primitive Edge of Experience.* Lanham: Jason Aronson.

Reis, B. (2021). The analyst's listening: For, to, with. *International Journal of Psychoanalysis* 102(2): 219–235.

Scarfone, D. (2015). *The Unpast: The Actual Unconscious.* Bonnigal-Katz, D. (Trans.), with House, J. (Contrib.). New York: Unconscious in Translation.

Sheehy, J. (2023). Book Review. Body as psychoanalytic object: Clinical applications from Winnicott to Bion and beyond. Harrang, Caron, Tillotson, Drew, and Winters, Nancy C. (Eds.). *American Journal of Psychoanalysis*, 83(2): 281–286.

Tustin, F. (1990). *The Protective Shell in Children and Adults*. London: Karnac.

Chapter 6

Psychic Equivalency as an Aspect of Symbiosis

Just as there is something gained when anything is translated from one language to another, there is hopefully also something gained in the transformation of ideas from one person to the next. Of course, in each instance there is always something lost. My gratitude to Jose Bleger contains appreciation for what he gives us and for the inspiration he fosters. My hope is to convey respect for his wisdom and to expand on his ideas that remain relevant to us today.

Bleger's understanding of a psychic organization prior to the paranoid-schizoid position enables analysts today to work more deeply and effectively with unrepresented states as they appear in the consulting room. He describes symbiosis and ambiguity as being a function of undifferentiation. Bleger wrote at a time when prominent analysts, he included, believed there was an infantile stage of primary autism. He knew and studied Mahler's work. Years after Bleger's untimely death, Mahler and Tustin (1991; 1994) reversed their professional opinions on primary autism. Infant research taught them that infants at birth were able to differentiate themselves from their parents. Pre-natal research finds that the infant also has a primal sense of the other and intentionality. Fetal observation via ultrasound (Maiello, 1995; 2012; Pion-telli, 1985; 1987) indicates the fetus is capable of agency, of dreaming, and of responding to sensory stimuli such as sensation, sound, and sight. Already in utero, infants' personality is discernable. The fetus also feels pain. In other words, the fetus experiences multiple states of being, other than states of undifferentiation. It follows that so does the infant. However, undifferentiated states are present from before birth and remain forever in the psyche.

Like adults, infants experience many states of mind and body. These states mark different degrees of psychic organization. Undifferentiation as one of multiple infantile states remains a psychic phenomenon that organizes experience from infancy onward. Under normal circumstances, the molten undifferentiated core in all of us remains as a background. When it emerges in adulthood, it becomes a symptom of overwhelming affect. Bleger (1967) calls the undifferentiation magma (p. 106). Magma is an undifferentiated material mass. Magma is an aspect of the molten core of the self where differentiation

DOI: 10.4324/9781003544470-6

and discrimination are lacking. Whereas magma might pulsate and bubble, magma is not alive, although it does adhere to surfaces.

Understanding symbiosis and undifferentiation enables us to deeply understand our patients who have survived childhood trauma. Symbiosis, according to Bion, is a primal linkage where both members of the dyad benefit. Undifferentiation informs and can comfort, even though we are unaware of it. It can be a pleasant sensory respite from a busy world and influences creative discoveries in every field. As a bodily experience, it may be an aspect of the background of safety we all need and share in order to function. States of undifferentiation also unconsciously contribute to communication with an actual other via the senses. Body relations communicate to others, and the undifferentiated state is intimately connected to the body.

Bleger understands the primitive nature of the defensive use of undifferentiated states and autistic protections evoked when necessary for psychic survival. Using different language, he explores what Bick (1968; 1986), Tustin (1986; 1990), and Meltzer (1974; 1975a; 1975b) call adhesive identification and adhesive equivalency. He explores the psychotic aspects of our personalities, as does Bion (1957; 1958; 1959). His knowledge and understanding enables us to work deeply with patients whose poor psychic filters keep them in constant turmoil and whose primitive autistic defenses keep them psychologically isolated and alone.

I am particularly interested in applying his ideas about body relations to patients who have been traumatized as children and who use mimicry as a means of functioning. These individuals often lack a subjective sense of self and suffer from weakened projective and introjective identification processes. Their weakened processes of projective and introjective identification alternate with massive fragmentation, atomization, and leakage. These are not projective identifications.

I, like Klein and Bion, believe the infant is born object related, with a primal capacity for differentiating self from other. Moments of undifferentiation that occur during breast feeding or falling asleep come from a primal trust in the care of the other. These moments are not perceived as persecutory but as blissful sensual oneness with the mother. These are not defensive but restorative. On the other hand, moments of undifferentiation that occur following a shock are defensive and include immobilization and dismantling the senses. They include a withdrawal from awareness of the other. The senses themselves are then used defensively (Bion, 1957) and separated one from the other, resulting in a psychic collapse (Meltzer, 1974). It is as if the person's attention itself were suspended. Infants in a state of psychic collapse are inconsolable and unreachable. They physically shake. Adults suffering from a history of trauma can also seem inconsolable and unreachable when their autistic defenses block the analytic process. Frequently they describe their collapses as *Black Holes* (Tustin; 1981; 1986; 1990; Eekhoff, 2021b; 2022).

Using Bleger's understanding of these primal experiences enables us to analyze psychotic and autistic processes of protection from overwhelming states of body and mind. These organizational processes persist long after trauma has ceased. Further, his descriptions of these processes enable analysts today to understand and work productively with patients who have psychic delusions that they do not exist. Patients who believe they do not exist suffer from a lack of differentiation from their objects even as they appear isolated and alone. When they come for analysis, the analytic situation becomes a container or depository for the exploration of their suspensions of the Self.

Bleger's brilliance lies in his ability to understand the multiple and simultaneous presence of psychic processes in all body relations and object relations. In this, he is speaking of actual two body relationships and the concretization inherent in all relations. Reality and relationship with an external other are essential for development. His glischro-caric position occurs beneath the paranoid-schizoid position and resembles what Bion (1957; 1958, 1963) calls the psychotic part of the personality. Ogden (1989a; 1989b) names it the autistic-contiguous position. I have called this earliest position the primal position (Eekhoff, 2021c). All of these authors recognize these states as normal. Normalizing autistic psychotic experience and accepting the chaotic unmediated sensory involvement within our perceptual identities enables us as analysts to work effectively with our severely disturbed adult patients. It also enables us to work deeper with our neurotic patients. Primary process and *perceptual identity* (Freud, 1900) underlie all creative endeavors; but without the containment of the symbolic and the continual processes of representation, these organizational states persecute.

Many aspects of Bleger's work deserve further consideration, but in this chapter, I am exploring primal adhesive defenses against primitive agonies and the symbiotic connection to the analyst that keeps those patterns in place. These defenses are concrete in nature and rely on the body of the analyst as external scaffolding of the weak ego and *meta-ego*. The body of the analyst becomes an aspect of the analytic situation as part of the setting (Bleger, 1967, p. 228–241). I believe it can also be part of the process (Eekhoff, 2017). This blurring of setting and process contributes to the difficulties we analysts face in the analysis of symbiosis. The healthy concretization of the analytic relation involves the bodily relation of interdependence. Patients who have ongoing access to their undifferentiated aspects vehemently deny dependence upon anyone. The analyst needs to be patient and secure and have faith in the analytic process (Bion, 1970). Further, I hope to expand on Bleger's understanding of ways in which the projective and introjective identification processes, which fuel representation, can be inhibited.

The ego functions on three (or more) levels of organization and always includes an observer. The psyche also includes areas that are non-ego and areas that cannot be represented. The primal position, Bleger's glischro-caric position, is one organizational aspect of our inner world. The paranoid-schizoid and depressive positions exist simultaneously with it. Bleger (1967) says,

Symbiosis is established and operates first and foremost in the area of the body and the external world. *The mental area is severely dissociated or split off* from the other two and is present as a spectator at the events and vicissitudes of symbiosis, unable to intervene in them or channel them.

(p. 35)

Bleger suggests that the mental is present even in undifferentiation, however it is split-off and projected into the universe. I believe that this point of being a spectator, a witness of oneself, is a position out of which the self evolves when reality is bearable. The analyst must find ways to gather the bits and pieces of the spectator. Seeing and being seen enables differentiation. Primal experiences of sensation, sound, and smell inform the observing participant and enable learning from experience (Bion, 1962b).

When reality is too much to bear being a spectator to one's life involves "standing beside oneself" (Ferenczi, 1988) and already implies some degree of differentiation and development. Although Bleger believes in an original state of psychic undifferentiation, he acknowledges the witness as present. When the analyst can engage the witness (Eekhoff, 2017), analytic progress is possible. The use of undifferentiation as a defense results in *psychic equivalency* that is maintained by the psychic processes of *adhesive identification* and *adhesive equivalency*. Psychic equivalency requires a lack of differentiation and is an infantile defense against premature awareness of separation between an infant and his or her mother (Tustin, 1980; 1986). Psychic equivalency is a normal part of development (Fonagy and Target, 1996). In other words, instead of being a primary state of undifferentiation that is only one of many states the infant has, undifferentiation can become a defense against awareness of premature separation from the caregiver. As a defense, psychic equivalency blocks other infantile states that are creative and helpful. It interferes with ongoing development.

Disturbance of infantile undifferentiated states shocks the undefended infant and can be traumatic. When infancy and childhood include continual intrusions that violate the child's physical and psychic boundaries, symbiosis in the form of objectless sensation (Ferenczi, 1920–1932, p. 261) foregrounds to provide safety. Klein (1975) asserts that narcissism is not primary but secondary and arises out of trauma. Childhood abuse of any kind includes psychic annihilation of the child's need. When a child loses a primary object, he or she automatically also loses a subjective sense of self. Parental intrusion via projective identification into the child and psychic threat via lack of receptivity damages a child's capacity to make meaning out of experience. Such intrusion also evokes attacks on linking (Bion, 1959). The same reaction occurs when the analyst prematurely highlights a patient's psychic separateness, focusing on differences and hence implying psychic distinctiveness. When such interpretations occur too early in the analytic process of patients who have a history of abuse, they can re-traumatize.

Psychic Equivalency

Equivalency is present not only as a deficit in development but also as a protection against threat. Prolonged use of equivalency as a defense results in encapsulated emotional areas of the self that do not develop along with other developmental physical and cognitive abilities. Tustin (1981; 1986; 1990) would call these *autistic encapsulations*. Some patients describe these pockets as voids; others call them black holes. I believe the void and the black hole are differing manifestations of the loss of a subjective sense of self. Deficit and defense interact, maintaining each other. Psychic equivalency is not a regression to infancy but a position and vertex of organization of reality that persists to a greater or lesser degree in everyone. Usually, in analysis, symbiosis and psychic equivalency are mute as an aspect of the setting (Bleger, 1967). Its defensive use originates from a primitive attempt to survive in the face of massive threat to psychic life. Psychic equivalency is both the body memory of undifferentiated states and a defense against manifestation in the here-and-now of a threat of otherness. Psychic equivalency protects against awareness of dependency upon an unreliable other by a delusion of being the other.

Psychic equivalency is an aspect of Bleger's symbiosis. It is accomplished via the psychic phantasies of adhesive identification (Bick, 1968; 1986; Meltzer, 1974; 1975a) and adhesive equivalence (Tustin, 1986; 1990). Bick observed that disintegration occurred when the psychic skin failed. Adhesive identification is a defensive state of mind that protects the psyche from disintegration. It provides a delusional shape and form. "In adhesive identification, the experience of space between two individuals is denied and replaced with a delusion of oneness" (Eekhoff, 2019, p. 42). A delusion of oneness holds the self together by forming a sensual boundary to prevent leaking, spilling, dissolving, and evaporating. A severely abused child clings to the senses as a second skin. For example, an adult diagnosed by previous therapists as dissociative identity disorder says he chooses which "skin suit" to wear depending upon his circumstances. His skin suits enable him to symbiotically become the other and feel safe. They include mimicry.

Adhesive identification involves the introjection and projection of sensation and originates from the glischro-caric position. "Adhesive identification is the unconscious sensory use of hearing, seeing, smelling and touching to take in and fuse with the other" (Eekhoff, 2019, p. 43). It is also communication from the agglutinated nucleus of the patient and identification with a warm live body. Adhesive identification creates a seamless symbiotic link with the analyst, although there may seem to be no relationship at all. In doing so, it denies the reality of inner psychic space. Meltzer (1975b), like Bleger, uses the word "agglutinate" in writing about work with autistic children. In describing the slow analytic process, he says:

In this sea of meaninglessness there were little items of meaningful experience that gradually began to agglutinate, gradually filled up the Wednesdays, filled up the middle of the week or the middle of the term, as it were. These children turned out to have incredible intolerance to separation.

(p. 199)

Adhesive identification and adhesive equivalency protect against the unbearable reality of psychic separateness.

Tustin (1986; 1990) preferred the term adhesive equation to adhesive identification. I believe these are two distinct forms of body and object relations that are revealed in an analytic process via somatic counter-transference. Adhesive equation may appear to be a one-body experience; and yet I believe that even at this primal level of contact with the *other-as-thing*, there is communication, hence separateness. Separateness is necessary for the uninterrupted flow of projective identifications. As Bion (1957) says, the nonpsychotic part of the personality is always present. Primitive mentalization is found as bodily sensation and is not yet namable. Some of it may never become nameable or ever be experienced as a differentiated emotional communication of body to self or body to other.

During adhesive equivalency, both members of the dyad will not be able to differentiate who is who. As the patient appears calm and un-impacted by the analytic encounter, the analyst becomes a sensor, like a tuning fork or seismograph. The unperceivable action is knowable outside the patient in the body of the analyst. Some analysts may find this extremely uncomfortable and resist the reception of such primitive and intrusive communication, yet I believe it is inevitable, whether recognized or not. Working with traumatized patients includes the analyst's body as well as his or her mind. These *somatic communications* can be recognized and translated into language.

At the level of symbiotic body relations, where, potentially, the projective and introjective identifications are weak or failing, the link can even be one of shared rhythm, of reverberation, resonance, and at-one-ment (Bion, 1970). This is a relational intersubjective state of adhesive equivalence, even more primal than adhesive identification. It is a symbiotic link. This shared state requires that the analyst be sensitive without superimposing his or her experience onto the patient. Doing so is to reenact the original trauma. The same is true of prematurely naming somatic experience as an emotional experience. At the symbiotic level, emotions have not yet emerged or differentiated themselves from affects. Naming emotions prematurely focuses attention on a higher order of development linking body and mind. Premature naming evokes mimicry.

Adhesive identification and adhesive equation involve a lack of awareness of a subjective self. The primal ego becomes another. The agglutinated nucleus can only pulse with energy and life, with seemingly no internal space. Inside and outside appear to be the same. Perhaps the inside also is, in phantasy, denied and projected via the senses, hence the term adhesive, which is to surfaces. In his paper, "On Hallucination," Bion (1958) writes about a psychotic patient who demonstrates adhesion via movement that is attuned to the analyst's movement:

> So closely do his movements seem to be geared with mine that the inception of my movement to sit appears to release a spring in him. As I lower myself into my seat he turns left about, slowly, evenly, as if something would be spilled, or perhaps fractured, were he to be betrayed into a precipitate movement. As I sit the turning movement stops as if we were both parts of the same clockwork toy.
>
> (p. 341)

Patients who use primal symbiotic process as a defense have a fascination with the sensual, which turns them into an inanimate machine with interlocking gears. It is a defense against life, against existence. Their identifications are with the surface of things and with movement. The subsequent use of sensorial experience seems to blot out the awareness of the other, but this is the result of blotting out awareness of the self – the self that has collapsed and imploded into a black hole or exploded into a universe without a depository to contain it, leaving a void where the self would be (Eekhoff, 2021c, 2021d , 2025; Chapter 11) In addition, the senses are not linked in the usual way but are often separated from one another. In my attempts to understand a somatic and sensate experience in the hour, I have recognized that there is information about my patient within my own somatic counter-transference. Paying attention to these body relations while also noticing higher levels of organization is an aspect of the deposited and depository process described by Bleger. Since all these levels of organization are simultaneously present in every analytic encounter, the analyst pays attention to the level that seems most urgent to the patient.

The body is not separable from the mind. The psychic skin (Bick, 1968; 1986) holds the body together, enabling containment of affect and emotion and the mobilization of agency. The psychic skin-to-skin of analysand and analyst may never be interpreted, but it is present and impactful as a mute aspect of the setting. Body-to-body proximity functions as a primal container in the growth of the mind, enabling us to find our centers of gravity even when the senses are being used in reverse and hallucinations are present. Bion (1958) says:

> Hallucinations and the fantasy of the senses as ejecting as well as receiving, point to the severity of the disorder from which the patient is suffering, but I must indicate a benign quality in the symptom which was certainly not present earlier. Splitting, evacuatory use of the senses, and hallucinations were all being employed in the service of an ambition to be cured, and may therefore be supposed to be creative activities.
>
> (p. 342)

Here Bion's understanding provides hope for the difficult analytic work.

Using Bleger and Bion's theoretical and clinical formulations, I am exploring deficits in cognitive functioning of extremely bright and functional people as defenses against separation. These cognitive impairments show up in our offices as deficits in the capacity to classify and subordinate information. Form and content are not discriminated (Bleger, 1967, p. 35). In the absence of differentiation and discrimination, ambiguity dominates. As Bleger so brilliantly demonstrates, patients can function by using their abilities to observe and mimic. Underneath the mimicry is a lack of discrimination that means all facts are of equal weight and value. One fact cannot be subordinate to another. This failure to discriminate form and content contributes to immobilization and what looks like passivity and poor decision-making. If everything is of equal weight, discriminations necessary for decision-making are lacking. The failure to classify and subordinate information further contributes to deficits in emotional development.

Deficits require defenses. Defenses become deficits. These protections do not arise from an internal experience of conflict. They arise from an inability to perceive the other as different from oneself and arise out of being psychically overwhelmed early in their lives. Object relations suffer. Anger and aggression, and conflict and doubt, arise from differentiation. Psychic equivalency is found in patients who seem to be passive and calm. Such patients can look normal (Meltzer, 1974; Bick, 1968; 1986; McDougall, 1989). However, what looks like calm is in fact an inability to discriminate and differentiate. *Psychic immobilization*, one aspect of which is the inability to make decisions, looks like withdrawal and cannot result in learning from experience (Bion, 1962b). Whole "undrawn" (Alvarez, 1992; 2010; 2012) areas of psyche are left undifferentiated, unformed, unclassified, and unsubordinated, while other areas develop, sometimes precociously.

Arnie

My patient, whom I will call Arnie, tells me that when I speak, even when I use his own words, I "...change the subject. If I follow you, all my gears grind and the machine that is me, freezes up and cannot move". Arnie's relationship with me is primarily bodily relations. We are, in his phantasy, fused and undifferentiated. I am he and he is me. We are one person. When I speak, I threaten the undifferentiated symbiotic phantasy he needs in order to function. When I use his words, it is more difficult for him to lose himself in the sound of my voice and the rhythms of my speech. My tone intrudes. I have drawn attention to our separateness. This is partially because in the moments between his speaking and my repetition of his words, he has moved on. He has moved on because he lives in the perpetual moment, where each moment is unique to itself and not related to the one before or the one after. I have not moved on. He responds with anger. When I do not speak, however, he dissociates and describes himself as "gone".

This dissociation is not the dissociative repression of the depressive position, nor the dissociative divisions of the paranoid-schizoid position where splitting and projecting maintain psychic equilibrium. Primal dissociation is the dissociation of psychic equivalency – an autistic defense that includes dismantling his senses (Meltzer, 1975a) and becoming one with his object. Becoming one with the object involves a collapse of his self, that I have inadvertently supported by remaining silent. He has imploded into the black hole of himself. When I do speak, his delusion of oneness with me, which is paradoxically also a defense against his collapse, is lost for him. His delusion of autonomy and safety is disrupted by my presence. He protects his sense of reality with anger.

For example, after 30 minutes of listening patiently and carefully to Arnie's concrete and detailed description of an event that has troubled him, he lapses into silence. I recognize this silence as different from a productive creative search for associations. It feels dense and impenetrable. I wait only briefly, fearing that the silence marks a psychic collapse, a black hole. When I speak, I am too late. Arnie is in despair, telling me, "there is no there, there. You act like there is something there inside of me. There is nothing". I try to reach him, speaking just for the sake of my tone and sound and rhythm. But he is gone. I fail to reach him.

The next day he returns as if the previous day had not happened. Again, he begins with a monologue and presents a story of what has happened to him since we met. After some time, I finally come to an interpretation. I attempt to tie my words to his words so as to make a link with him. In fact, I even use his words to show that I have been listening and how I reached my thinking. I am then surprised by the immediate anger and the intense push back I receive. This time, he tells me I am blaming him, telling him it is his fault. I am not helping him. I am making it worse. In re-examining myself, I do not find my own tone judgmental, not that it never is. I try again to reach him. I cannot, as somehow the damage has been done. We cannot have an exchange. He cannot take in my attempt to understand him.

In fact, perhaps in that moment my unrecognized assumption that we could work together, which would imply our differentiation, missed his symbiotic relationship to me. I erroneously thought he might be able to use what I have noticed. Instead, my interpretation left him feeling like a "bug under a microscope, pinned and examined". I have heard this before from him when I use his words and add to them in order to explain my thinking. Yet, at other times, he is able to work with me. Not today.

Once again, I have forgotten in this state, he is in the moment. It is not that he is in the here-and-now, because to be here would involve having a subjective sense of himself in the moment. He is in 'the now'. He experiences 'now' in a bodily way. In that primal state, he lacks a sense of "going-on-being" (Winnicott, 1960; 1965). He is not aware of past or future in that his memory is impaired. In being in time, I also am different than he. I become 'The Authority' and my observations become moral judgements. It will take much effort on both our parts to re-connect, and often re-connection is not possible in the session.

In this particular example, I feel I have been patient and neutral – non-judgmental and not all knowing. I have merely described an observation of something happening in the moment between us. He tells me I am talking about something that is over. This too has happened before. Sometimes he denies having said what I remember. At other times, he remembers but says he said those words five minutes ago. They are no longer accurate. From his perspective, this is true. I am speaking from within a framework of time and space. I am speaking from within the symbolic order. When I do that I am not speaking from his immediate framework of the senses and the body. I have disrupted the adhesive equivalency between us, by having a separate mind and making an observation. This separateness is ultimately necessary for growth to occur, but I have brought the reality of his dependency upon me into the session too soon. Dependency is counter to a phantasy of oneness.

Making myself different from him just by speaking an observation of our process is disturbing. I must slow down since such differentiation is disruptive. I must have patience and accept it will take time. As Bleger (1967) says, "... the symbiotic relationship is a highly condensed relation with very complex and contradictory aspects that need to be 'broken up' in order to be introjected and worked through by degrees" (p. 24). Arnie was in analysis long enough to recognize the risk he faced in analysis. Breaking up feels like breaking down. Of course, he is upset because the breaking up of his symbiosis confuses him and feels dangerous.

Theoretical Discussion of Psychic Equivalence

In the above vignettes, I have shown two ways of being with Arnie; one in being silent and the other in speaking. In each, the symbiotic fusion is present and challenged by my physical existence. Silence leaves Arnie with no center of gravity, which normally he has placed in me. He cannot sense my proximity and collapses into the black hole of himself, which sucks life and hope away. It is a collapse of space, a sucking place of undifferentiation. Anything said can only be 'as if' he existed. Furthermore, everything is destroyed as it enters the psychic event horizon, including his relationship with me. No wonder he becomes claustrophobic, then experiencing me as the black hole.

In the second instance, my attempt to show Arnie the origin of my thinking implied the passing of time. Time passing is dangerous and must be defended against as it moves Arnie into a different internal psychic organization. Bleger says, "Time stops when the paralyzing of projection-introjection becomes necessary to control the confusion" (p. 54). When I challenge this by speaking, I am changing the vertex from which to witness our interaction. This has the potential of re-instating the projective and introjective cycle so necessary for learning. However, the cycle is not re-instated in this instance. Instead from Arnie's point of view, I have been violent and attacking. Quickly, I have become bad and then as suddenly, good and all knowing.

From the new vertex, I am good and he is bad. I am superior and he is inferior. Arnie feels I have pronounced judgement upon him, told him that he is evil and condemned to Hell. To him, my comment was not a neutral observation. Rather it highlighted the truth about how hopeless the situation is and how bad he is. My words concretely make it so. He is what I said and cannot be otherwise. This concretization is another result of psychic adhesion. It too often ends with a psychic collapse and retreat into a black hole of despair.

In this case, his anger suggests projective identification processes that leave him drained and empty, with a void. And yet, if this can be tolerated, and we can speak of the process, it can mark a potential movement from the glischrocaric position where the Black Hole wipes out all distinctions, to the paranoid-schizoid position where the void leaves him depleted and empty.

No wonder he rages at me. No wonder he is angry. My speaking my opinion of a truth about him, even though he told me about it, is humiliating and condemning, even when I carefully include how what he has just said informed me. He has forgotten that I am an ally attempting to help him. He cannot experience my voicing an observation as simply my opinion. In a symbiotic link, relationship is a concrete experience. My interpretation is understood as a concrete unchangeable fact and he seems to "...feel betrayed *(by my interpretation)*, since if she *(he)* had already said it once why would I repeat it to her *(him)*? What is the point? [italics mine]" (Bleger, 1967, p. 97).

In a world of signification and meaning, there is a point. Time and space work together to provide a context for personal meaning within a relational context. Experience accumulates. Time moves on as evidence of change. In the concrete world of psychic equivalency, nothing accumulates. There is no time. Stopping time prevents change. It also prevents confusion. Words that were spoken are the final say, are not to be added to or altered in any way. They do not need to be repeated. What is, is. This concretization, where living things do not evolve and people become things and words become law, is a means of blurring distinctions. Without distinctions there is a *delusion of safety*. This is very different from the background of safety a good enough mother provides for every infant.

Lack of distinctions and differentiations provide a feeling of being invisible. One means of being invisible is to blend concretely with whoever one is in contact. Blending concretely is the symbiotic link of adhesive equivalency. Visibility is only possible with distinctions. To see and be seen signifies difference. Difference means there is a space between us. Any hint of discrimination and differentiation becomes dangerous so it follows that a gap is dangerous in that it leaves a space to be filled by the other. Otherness raises an awareness of separateness and is dangerous, hence bad. A pounding concrete experience of difference hints at badness. Being different equals being bad.

Briefly, concretization as a defense focuses attention on the material world of the senses. In the consulting room, the body of the analyst as an aspect of the setting becomes used as a vehicle for psychic equivalence and symbiosis. Bleger confirms this: "Symbiosis functions and is stabilized on the concrete level" (p. 50).

Back to Arnie

Arnie despairs of being understood. He says he always longs for understanding from me and is disappointed not to get it. I have come to understand in such moments, I am not demonstrating understanding to him. My definition of understanding is different from his. Instead of demonstrating that I am with him in his pain, I am demonstrating that I am not he. This is a failure on my part to maintain the symbiosis long enough to be able to speak to it. My empathy comes as a shock, an intrusion into him. My understanding becomes an attack. My reflection of his words back to him plus a few of my own intrudes because it breaks an unconscious delusion of oneness. I am asserting my difference and my separateness. In doing so, I am responding to him from a different level of organization. I am not supporting his phantasy that I am the same as he and that we exist in a *forever now*. Instead I have become a threat to breaking up his concrete world. I have given him a glimpse of his dependency upon me, which he cannot tolerate knowing. In a world of time, there is separation and loss. Life and death become possible.

Arnie began to feel immeasurable dread each day before a session. One day he was able to name it. In this excerpt, I am primarily silent, letting him name his discoveries and even demonstrate them by losing his ability to put words together to form meaningful sentences. He says: "I am jittery. It has to be about being here, because it started on the drive over. I don't know what it is about".

He is silent several minutes.

Hmm. The words "breaking down" just came to me. Like my basement re-model. The contractor is jackhammering the concrete, breaking it up. You have to break things down before you can build again. It's violent.

He begins to speak very haltingly with much space between his words. His sentences are incomplete, and I am very tempted to fill in the blank spaces. I know this would be fusing with him. I feel so much pressure. Yet this may be evidence of a breakage of old patterns.

I am not functioning very well...but...uh...sunk in...stationary...hmmm. It is violent again. Ugh... [He sighs, rolls to face wall] ...not it...Hmmm. [He is silent for several minutes]. There is some...ah...I don't know if this is real or imaginary. Violence...of the process...of...breaking down. My...rigid...beliefs are together. Hmm.

He is silent for several minutes, but physically agitated. He tosses and turns on the couch, moves his toes up and down and wiggles his fingers. He is in constant motion. He starts to speak and stops. I feel tense in my body and a constriction in my throat. I feel like coughing. I want to speak. In this instance, I sense that he is working something out in the silence. His silence is not dead. After five minutes, he continues.

> Maybe that is due to the part of me that doesn't give up easily. Hmmm. Why don't you just change your mind? [He is silent]. To what? [He is silent for another two or three minutes]. It is not like there is a new belief system to just slip into place [He trails off, making little sounds, but without words].

Many months after the above example, he was able to articulate something very important. He said, "When I complain you do not understand, I think I am complaining that we are not merged. You are not me. I hate you for that". His hatred is a good sign in that his indifference is breaking up and his delusion of not existing is being threatened. I exist as separate from him, who therefore may also exist. Perhaps we have moved temporarily from the adhesive equivalency of a fixed symbiotic place where existence is questionable to a black and white world of existing, but where survival is threatened. His sucking black hole, which marks an implosion, is becoming more explosive – hence projective. When he says, "It is not like there is a new belief system to just slip into place", he is recognizing the absence of something inside of him, a void that has been created not just by his massive projections, but also from the deficit that exists from his previous collapses.

Psychic Equivalency – Theory

Patients who have been traumatized early in their natural growth – perhaps the first three years of life before becoming verbal – bring us phantasies from all stages of their organizational development. They have access to primitive mental states that ordinarily would be repressed. These individuals perceive their worlds from differing vertexes (Bion, 1962a; 1965) or positions (Klein, 1946) depending upon their state of mind. These organizations of experience shift continuously and often are present simultaneously. They alter perspective. Bleger (1967) brings our attention to an early position of undifferentiation, of symbiosis, which is normal, in all of us, and only becomes a difficulty when it is accessed persistently and excessively. He says,

> Furthermore, this state of primitive undifferentiation is a *particular organization of the ego and of the world,* so that we are obliged to make an effort and face a new injury to our narcissism, as Freud put it, which occurs with each scientific advance: that *our* identity and *our* sense of reality are not *the* identity and sense of reality but only one of many possible organizations.
>
> (p. 4)

He goes on to describe this organization as being one of *bodily relations* (p. 5). Bodily relations of this primitive undifferentiated position are only vaguely related to object relations.

Psychic equivalency uses the senses of the body to create a delusion of oneness, where self and other are undifferentiated. Adhesive equivalency in phantasy agglutinates the two physical bodies into one body. Two bodies are psychically necessary for one person to exist (McDougall, 1989). Present in the room is a symbiotic attachment to the surface of things that uses sensation, smell, sound, and sight to achieve the symbiosis. The adhesion is as much to the actual office as it is to the actual body of the analyst. The same is true even when working remotely. Discrimination and differentiation require space, as does identification. Psychic equivalency is *symbiotic oneness* where space and time are absent. In this place the projective and introjective processes are minimal. Identification itself is of sensation.

When I break the delusion of psychic equivalency with an interpretation or even with a descriptive comment, patients similar to Arnie, maintain the symbiosis by switching the phantasy. They do not exist, but I do. There is room in such a psychic world for only one person at a time. It is not the fight or flight of the paranoid-schizoid position. It is rather the symbiotic world of the glischro-caric position and the agglutinated nucleus where one person is subsumed by the other, and each is necessary for existence itself. The two cannot be separated, but one or the other may foreground. One woman told me: "We are Siamese twins, joined at the head". Later she told me she had changed her mind – we had one body and two heads. If we were to separate, both of us would die.

The action in the hour is passive in its subtlety since the subjective sense of self is subsumed by the sounds and rhythms, smells, and colors and textures of the context of the work. These include my body: my sounds, my smell, my appearance, and the tone and rhythms of my voice. It matters little whether Arnie or I am foregrounded, since in his phantasy, we are the same. When I forget that we are one and behave as if he is functioning at a neurotic symbolic level, I am doing to him what he does to me. He does not exist as himself to me but as someone more like me. This is not projective identification because I am not finding myself via identification in him. Rather I am resonating and vibrating with the bodily relations he conveys.

As much as I attempt to meet my patient without memory, desire, or understanding, I find it difficult to comprehend that from my patient's point of view, there are times we are the same. My error from his perspective is in behaving as if there were a psychic space between us that would enable a productive to and fro. Existence involves being and becoming. Not existing psychically, except as me in the moment, keeps everything the same. Equivalency concretizes and immobilizes the psyche by using bodily sensations to fuse.

In this sense, my interpretations, from his point of view, do not respect his need for me to be him or him to be me. Whereas he may be responding to the sound of my words and the tone and rhythm of my speech, I am behaving as if he is responding to my meaning. When I deviate from his words by adding to them, I am asserting a gap between us. Worse still, I am behaving as if the past moment is not the same as the current moment, while my patient remains in the *forever now*. There is no space for true collaboration and connection, and no time for discovery, since I am always out of his time. Our synchronicity and rhythm are broken. I believe with Bleger, that to work effectively with patients who have ongoing access to the glischro-caric or primal position, we must allow ourselves to be used as an extension of the patient. When we fail by prematurely naming that which should not yet be named; we become dangerous. At the same time, such 'failure' may be an essential element in the breaking up of the symbiosis.

I have come to realize that when I become too big by asserting myself too soon with an interpretation, my patient perceives me as the Old Testament God, speaking Truth. There is no room for a dialogue to come together for a back and forth of conversation and elaboration where a personal truth can be found. Such discrimination is not possible in symbiotic union. Instead, God – the God of Judgment – has spoken. Like the command to not look back at the burning Sodom and Gomorrah, if we turn to look behind to bid goodbye to all that we have loved God will turn us both into Pillars of Salt, solid and inanimate. For what we have loved is other than God, other than Truth. What we have loved is absolute oneness – in other words, psychic equivalency and symbiosis. We have loved the concrete material world of the senses. In the realm of body turned to salt, pleasure is sacrificed and pain is evidence of existence.

Another Biblical story comes to mind: the people of Israel decided to build a tower to reach God, to become one with God. God interrupted their efforts by changing each one's language so they no longer could be one in search of union, but became many: distinct and unable to communicate. God facilitated separateness and the symbolic order rather than the concrete material oneness of being God. Sometimes Arnie reacted by becoming God, or in the hour, becoming big like me. He would assert that he already knew whatever I said and how could I insult him by telling him what he already knew. When he did so, his hatred of the reality of separateness and the reality of his need of me became equivalent to a hatred of life itself.

Lizzy

Here is another example of a patient who is moving out of symbiosis into a two-body relationship that involves an increasing awareness of space: Lizzy tells me a story of panicking in the night as she awakens. Her whole body is buzzing with affect. It is impossible to return to sleep. She remembers a comment I made last night in her session about how chatty we were and not so analytic.

I reply that my comment about chatty seemed to indicate a change in our relationship, one where the two of us had more space between us. It seemed to pick up on the feeling I had had that she was getting ready to leave. Perhaps in the night she could feel our differences and our separateness. She agreed. I feel close to her, recognizing and empathizing with her panic. When she describes it, I listen, feeling moved. I then repeat what she said to me. When I do, I feel her withdrawal and speak to it.

She says,

> It is like we are together in an emotional place. I tell you and then you tell me what I have said. My mind knows you are doing that to show me you are with me and that you were listening. But when you do that it is as if you become the "other" and are coming from a different location than the one I am in.

I say, "A location different than the location we were both in previously". She agrees. When I become the 'other', Lizzy feels agitated and irritated. My reflection, which has included the words "both of us", refers to a symbiosis. Saying it changes it. She becomes aware of separateness and difference. We are not equal. We are not the same. I am her analyst whom she needs and we come together from separate locations.

This vignette involving psychic space demonstrates the rapid shifting between simultaneous states of body and mind. As my patient has spent many years learning to identify and discriminate, when she brings me her panic, we are able to find words for it. Such is not the case in the beginning years of working with symbiosis and ambiguity, when dependency and need are denied and hidden in the symbiosis.

Discussion

In bringing to Bleger's brilliant work on symbiosis and ambiguity a contemporary understanding of autistic defenses, I am asserting that somatic responses are used defensively and inadvertently create deficits in cognitive and emotional processing. To interpret conflict or interpret aggression prematurely is to be on a different psychic organizational level than the patient. Bleger (1967, p. 85) asserts that working to shore up the ego is necessary before being able to address these more primal areas of functioning. I believe this is true because what is presented is always the deepest anxiety of the moment. When psychic equivalency is evoked via adhesive identification and adhesive equivalency, the anxiety is hard to find. Once found, the anxiety that is present is about existence itself. It is not about survival. Bion (1970) says, "Non-existence, immediately becomes an object that is immensely hostile, and filled with murderous envy towards the quality of function of 'existence,' wherever it is to be found" (p. 103). No wonder undifferentiated states of symbiosis are needed.

In symbiosis, anxiety is seemingly lacking, hence too is aggression, because the somatic fusion with the analyst keeps it at bay. Immobilization keeps the patient passive and agreeable. As mobilization begins, irritability, agitation, and anger emerge. These serve to maintain bodily relations. They also mark the hatred of existence. Bleger (1967) says, "...aggression is an attempt to control and restore the boundaries of her body, configuring them anew through abrupt contact with external objects" (p. 28).

As the analysis of the setting begins to impact the patient's ability to discriminate and differentiate one thing from another, insight develops. Some of this is mimicry of the analyst, but some of it is mobilization of the life instinct and the innate predisposition to grow. The epistemophilic instinct and love of knowledge is re-discovered. Both Arnie and Lizzy began slowly over time to realize those around them were confused by their actions and their words. Although they themselves did not feel confused by holding seemingly contradictory points of view simultaneously, they eventually could notice others' bafflement, including mine. They found this frustrating and at times infuriating. They felt their ability to hold contradictory views made them superior to others and me. They did not understand that ambiguity was not ambivalence.

Lizzy eventually could name this. She said she felt that everything she perceived existed on an equal level with everything else. Things were "side by side, not really touching each other". She felt this meant that her experience of things was chaotic since they didn't seem to impact each other. She noticed for example that people were pretty much interchangeable to her, not having distinguishing features. Mostly this did not bother her, but she began to see that it bothered other people, myself included. She said, "I know with my mind that these things must have some kind of relationship to each other. Other people act like they do. I am trying to figure it all out, but my mind fails me". This is stated as a fact, not to be questioned or pondered. It was not upsetting. She merely changed the focus of her attention to what was concretely happening at the moment. She felt her ability to change her focus was a strength she had. She did not perceive that changing her focus inhibited her learning and sometimes confused her objects.

A growing awareness of distinctions begins in the setting of the analysis and via my attempts to name, not interpret, somatic responses to the setting, which included my own body's response to both Arnie and Lizzy. My somatic counter-senses were often all I had to go on. I listened to the vibrations and resonances within my own body and paid attention to the rhythm of our speech more than the content of what we said. I focused on process, not content. Sometimes I would notice this aloud, knowing that when I did, I broke the rhythm. Lizzy noticed my attempts to clarify what she was saying. When she could eventually tolerate the frustration of difference – that of not being wordlessly and seamlessly understood – she was better able to think. She could also tolerate a bit of psychic space between and within us. Her experience of being understood changed from requiring fusion to wanting empathy. With this change came an increased capacity to tolerate frustration. I no longer had to get it right every time. I could be human and so could she. This happened slowly over many years.

Our patients often teach us about psychic equivalency by describing it. Their descriptions are accurate. Simultaneously, they do not listen to or understand and remember their own descriptions. We become the depository where the words accumulate and have meaning. They only understand what they were telling us months and sometimes years later. Then we can bring their words back to them. Better still, they will tell us that they did not understand what we were saying when we used their words to reflect themselves back to them, but now they feel the significance of them in their bodies.

How are we as analysts who are used to operating from a symbolic order able to recognize psychic equivalency? If our patients' use of language is as if the words were concrete things instead of symbols, how are we to know? I suggest the concrete use of 'words as things' is felt in our bodies. Words are a bodily relation that uses speech as sound and rhythm. Patients use the unconscious phantasies of adhesive identification and adhesive equivalency in order to maintain body relations with the analyst. These unconscious phantasies are the bridge between the body and mind. Body relations give them a sense of existing as a live human being, not as an inanimate thing.

The body relationship, which is dependent upon proximity, uses the senses to inform, not about safety as in the paranoid-schizoid position or about concern for the other as in the depressive position, but about existence itself. Existence is a function of the glischro-caric position. Adhesive defenses provide the person with a shape. Molded by the analyst's form, the person is able to function 'as if' being contained by the mind. The containment is the most primal possible, going back to early prenatal experiences of the amniotic fluid on the skin and the pulsing of blood through the placenta and umbilical cord. Whereas the fetus may not have an experience of time, it does have an experience of being contained in the amniotic sack and in the womb. This provides an experience of space and a very primal awareness of otherness – the maternal object. Maiello (1995) has called this first awareness of the object *the sound object*. This is the first experience of the other but also of the self.

Enactments with traumatized patients are frequent but do not provide the same benefit in moving the analytic work forward because the patient has difficulty with the projective and introjective processes. If the analyst and the patient are in two separate locations in space, two differing organizational levels, meeting in order to collaborate is not possible. An enactment may reveal this to the analyst; but to the patient it will only elicit a defense against the breach. Bion (1962b) says some patients have difficulty learning from experience. Without internalization via introjection, learning from experience falters. Without projection into an object, the healthy to and fro of projective identification cannot occur. The depository remains without a deposited.

Instead, the enactment becomes an impasse that cannot be used for learning. It becomes a means of adhering to each other. No amount of explanation will break up the symbiosis of enactment. What breaks it up is slowly over time the understanding of the analyst is communicated, not only in words, but also in the emotions and actions of the hour. These are the actions of being a depository or container that makes use of what it receives and allows accumulation to occur. These actions within the analyst are eventually introjected, breaking up the concrete autistic and psychotic protections. The process can then be internalized as a structure for processing experience.

Some patients only relate symbiotically to those to whom they are closest. With most people, they are able to maintain a healthier boundary and differentiation. However, some patients persist in using symbiosis as a defense with whomever they know. In becoming another, they develop what Bleger (1967) calls factic personality traits (pp. xxxv, 223, 227). These are similar to what Deutcsh named "as if" personalities. They use mimicry (Eekhoff, 2019; 2022) as a means of molding themselves to the surface of the other by adapting movements, dress patterns, speech patterns, and other physical traits. My patient Kay (Eekhoff, 2019) was a masterful mimic. Near the end of her analysis, she said, "I have a life. I do not know if I have ever before had my own life. Maybe. Sometimes. If ever I had one, it should be now".

Bleger says, "The function of psychoanalytic treatment is to provide a symbiosis that was lacking or distorted. This function is fulfilled fundamentally by the setting, which undoubtedly includes the role of the analyst" (p. 209). He advocates a tight analytic frame while at the same time a *flexibility of technique* in order that the psychotic aspects of the personality may be analyzed. He says, "…the analyst needs to accept the setting brought by the patient (which is the patient's 'meta-ego'), because within it will be found in summary form the primitive unresolved symbiosis" (p. 240). In accepting the patient's setting, the psychic equivalency is gradually revealed. The symbiosis is invisible until minute psychic separation creates confusion and reveals entanglement.

Sometimes the entanglement and the fusion in the patient create confusion in the analyst. This confusion is a message – a message that tells us that we are being drawn to adopt the roles assigned by the patient. However, confusion may also signal movement out of symbiosis. Usually confusion comes when there are massive projections; and in fact, may indicate that the patient's projections have begun to gather into the object of the analyst, instead of into the infinite universe of outer space or compacted via implosion into a psychic black hole.

With the primarily neurotic patient, projection and introjection into and onto the analyst are more easily gathered into the transference. Transference interpretations work. Patients who have difficulty representing their experience project massively into the universe around them, even into outer space, and gathering the transference is difficult. They become their analysts in phantasy and any action on the part of the analyst that denies this symbiotic unity is a threat to their whole being. This occurs on the level of the body, not the mind, and in an arena of sensuous experience. Yet the mind is always functioning, even when it is split off and projected into the analyst. Sensation and sound vibrate and move around the analytic dyad. I say dyad but the word itself is misleading in that it is a dyad in the analyst's mind, but only concretely a dyad in these moments of psychic fusion and symbiosis in the patient's mind. The patient accepts and knows there are two people in the room physically. For the patient, in these moments of deep work, it takes two physical bodies to make one person. Psychically there is only one person present.

Conclusion

In this chapter, I have described Bleger's understanding of bodily relations in the earliest organizational levels of the mind. I have focused on a particular process of symbiosis – psychic equivalency – as a means of maintaining a fused relationship with the analyst. Further, I have maintained that in adulthood, ongoing access to psychic equivalency is both a deficit and a defense arising from early trauma. I suggest that trauma derails the normal course of development and impacts the creative and necessary flow of projective and introjective identifications. In a deep analysis, the concrete bodily relation with the analyst enables that which has been concretized and immobile to become free, fluid, and differentiated. This requires us to accept the setting the patient brings while interpreting the separation between the process and the setting as well as the separation between the analyst and the analysand.

I have described a process of fusion and symbiosis that occurs when patients have too much access to their own deep levels of personality. Such access is overwhelming. In order to organize their experience, these individuals become so fused with their analysts as to make transference and counter-transference experience indistinguishable. In certain moments, who is who is lost. In those times, hopefully, it is the analyst who gathers him or herself and holds what can be represented until the patient is able to bear the re-introjected aspects of the self. The analyst must maintain the separateness of a depository even when the patient cannot. This process takes many months of empathy and careful interpretation, during which intellectual description of the process can frequently result in negative therapeutic reactions or enactments of the most devastating kind. These too are helpful however, in that often they mark impasses that can only then be understood and worked through – made sensible via action.

I have described how in finding words for experience that has not been represented verbally, bodily relations are internalized and accumulate into a richly dimensional inner world of time and space. The analyst's recognition of the situation from the patient's point of view enables the symbiosis to be broken up. We know that these states of symbiosis are not only primal, but also can be defensive and persist as foreground throughout life. As Bleger teaches us, psychoanalytic treatment can successfully occur if the pathological symbiosis is broken up. The patient and the analyst begin to be able to repair the broken links. Object relations can then be re-instated and the patient gains a subjective sense of self.

References

Alvarez, A. (1992). *Live Company*. London: Routledge.

Alvarez, A. (2010). Levels of analytic work and levels of pathology: The work of calibration. *International Journal of Psycho-Analysis*, 91: 859–878.

Alvarez, A. (2012). *The Thinking Heart*. London: Routledge.

Bick, E. (1968). The experience of skin in early object relations. *International Journal of Psycho-Analysis*, 49: 484–486.

Bick, E. (1986). Further considerations on the function of the skin in early object relations. *British Journal of Psychotherapy*, 2(4): 292–299.

Bion, W. R. (1957). The differentiation of the psychotic from the non-psychotic personalities. *International Journal of Psychoanalysis*, 38: 266–275. [Reprinted London: Heinemann, 1967; London: Karnac, 1984, pp. 43–64.]

Bion, W. R. (1958). On hallucination. *International Journal of Psycho-Analysis*, 39: 341–349.

Bion, W. R. (1959). Attacks on linking. *International Journal of Psycho-Analysis*, 40: 308–315.

Bion, W. R. (1962a). A psycho-analytic theory of thinking. *International Journal of Psycho-Analysis*, 43: 306–310. [Reprinted as "A theory of thinking", in Bion, W. R., *Second Thoughts* (pp. 110–119). London: Karnac, 1984.]

Bion, W. R. (1962b). *Learning from Experience*. London: Heinemann. [Reprinted London: Karnac, 1984.]

Bion, W. R. (1963). *Elements of Psycho-Analysis*. London: Heinemann. [Reprinted London: Karnac, 1984.]

Bion, W. R. (1965). *Transformations*. London: Heinemann. [Reprinted London: Karnac, 1984.]

Bion, W. R. (1967). *Second Thoughts: Selected Papers on Psychoanalysis*. London: Heinemann. [Reprinted London: Karnac, 1984.]

Bion, W. R. (1970). *Attention and Interpretation*. London: Tavistock. [Reprinted London: Karnac, 1984.]

Bleger, J. (1967). *Symbiosis and Ambiguity: A psychoanalytic study*. Churcher, J. and Bleger, L. (Eds.); Rogers, S., Bleger, L., and Churcher, J. (Trans.). London and New York: Routledge, 2013.

Eekhoff, J. K. (2017). Finding a center of gravity via proximity with the analyst. In Levine, H. B. and Powers, D. G. (Eds.), *Engaging Primitive Anxieties of the Emerging Self: The Legacy of Francis Tustin* (pp. 1–19). London: Karnac, 2017.

Eekhoff, J. K. (2019). *Trauma and Primitive Mental States, An Object Relations Perspective*. London and New York: Routledge.

Eekhoff, J. K. (2021a). Body as Dream Space. In Harrang, C., Tillotson, D., and Winters, N. (Eds.), *Body as Psychoanalytic Object: Clinical Applications from Winnicott, Bion and Beyond*. London and New York: Routledge.

Eekhoff, J. K. (2021b). Body Relations and the black hole. *International Forum of Psychoanalysis*, 30(2021): 3.

Eekhoff, J. K. (2021c). *Bion and Primitive Mental States: Trauma and the Symbiotic Link*. London and New York: Routledge.

Eekhoff, J. K. (2021d). Body Relations and the black hole. *International Forum of Psychoanalysis*, 30(2021): 3.

Eekhoff, J. K. (2025). Perceptual Identification as analytic receptivity of unrepresented and dissociative states. In Power, D. and Power, J. (Eds.), *The Somatic-Psychic Realm (Bion)*. London and New York: Routledge.

Ferenczi, S. (1920–1932). Notes and fragments. In *Final Contributions to the Problems and Methods of Psycho-Analysis* (pp. 216–279). London: Karnac, 1955. [Reprinted London: Karnac, 1994.]

Ferenczi, S. (1988). *The Clinical Diary of Sándor Ferenczi*. Dupont, J. (Ed.); Balint, M. and Jackson, N. Z. (Trans.). Cambridge, MA: Harvard University Press.

Freud, S. (1900). The Interpretation of Dreams. *S. E. Volume 4*: ix–625. London: Hogarth. [Trans. by Crick, J. Oxford, UK: Oxford University Press, 1999.]

Fonagy P. and Target, M. (1996). Playing with reality, 1: Theory of mind and a normal development of psychic reality. *International Journal of Psychoanalysis*, 77: 217–233.

Klein, M. (1946). Notes on some schizoid mechanisms. *International Journal of Psycho-Analysis*, 27: 99–100.

Klein, M. (1975). *The Writings of Melanie Klein*. London: Hogarth Press.

Maiello, S. (1995). The Sound-Object: A Hypothesis about Prenatal Auditory Experience and Memory1. *Journal of Child Psychotherapy*, 21(1): 23–41.

Maiello, S. (2012). Prenatal experiences of containment in the light of Bion's model of container/contained. *Journal of Child Psychotherapy*, 38(3): 250–267.

McDougall, J. (1989). *Theaters of the Body: A Psychoanalytic Approach to Psychosomatic Illness*. New York: Norton.

Meltzer, D. (1974). Adhesive identification. In: Hahn, A. (Ed.), *Sincerity and Other Works: The Collected Papers of Donald Meltzer* (pp. 335–350). London: Karnac, 1994.

Meltzer, D., with Bremner, J., Hoxter, S., Weddell, D., and Wittenberg, I. (1975a). *Explorations in Autism: A Psychoanalytic Study*. Strath Tay, Perthshire: Clunie Press. [Reprinted for the Harris Meltzer Trust, London: Karnac, 2008.]

Meltzer, D. (1975b). The psychology of autistic states and of post-autistic mentality. In Meltzer, D., with Bremner, J., Hoxter, S., Weddell, D., and Wittenberg, L. *Explorations in Autism* (pp. 6–29). Strath Tay, Perthshire, UK: Clunie Press. [Reprinted for the Harris Meltzer Trust, London: Karnac, 2008.]

Ogden, T. H. (1989a). *The Primitive Edge of Experience*. Northvale, NJ: Jason Aronson.

Ogden, T. H. (1989b). On the concept of an autistic-contiguous position. *International Journal of Psychoanalysis*, 70: 127–140.

Piontelli, A. (1985). *Backwards in Time: A Study in Infant Observation by the Method of Esther Bick*. London: Karnac Books Ltd.

Piontelli, A. (1987). Infant Observation from Before Birth. *International Journal of Psychoanalysis*, 68: 453–463.

Tustin, F. (1980). Autistic objects. *International Review of Psycho-Analysis*, 7: 27–40.

Tustin, F. (1981). *Autistic States in Children*. Boston: Routledge & Kegan Paul.

Tustin, F. (1986). *Autistic Barriers in Neurotic Patients*. New Haven, CT: Yale University Press, 1987.

Tustin, F. (1990). *The Protective Shell in Children and Adults*. London: Karnac.

Tustin, F. (1991). Revised understandings of psychogenic autism. *International Review of Psychoanalysis*, 72(4): 585–592.

Tustin, F. (1994). The Perpetuation of an Error. *Journal of Child Psychotherapy*, 20(1): 3–23.

Winnicott, D. W. (1960). The Theory of the Parent-Infant Relationship. *International Journal of Psycho-Analysis*, 41: 585–595.

Winnicott, D. W. (1965). The Maturational Processes and the Facilitating Environment. *Int. Psycho-Anal. Lib.*, 64: 1–276. London: The Hogarth Press and the Institute of Psycho-Analysis.

Chapter 7

The Primordial Symphony of Life
Truth and the Body

This chapter explores how truth or lie emerges in the emotional relationship between two or more people. It describes how emotions link body and the mind, serving as they do to promote symbolization. Emotions are the symphony of life. They are the invisible and mysterious link between soma and psyche as well as between self and other. Emotions create harmony amongst the sights, sounds, and sensations of experience. Further, the chapter asserts that emotions are evoked in relationship. They link us with each other. They unite imagination with reality. The symphony of life is in the beauty of the world and the emotional atmosphere engendered intrapsychically and intersubjectively. The emotional capacity for passion: to truly love, hate, or know another person is to register their individuality with our hearts and bodies. In registering their individuality, we also find our truth.

"It's just the truth," says my patient, Gina. When she says this, I have no comment. What can I say or do when this is her emotional reality? What can I say or do when her certainty in essence denies not only my credibility, but my very presence as a factor in her experience? I cannot debate her certainty that she knows the truth. I do not like my powerlessness in the face of her certainty nor do I like what she asserts, because this time what she means by truth is that she is forever broken and irreparable. Nothing can change. There is no hope for her. There is no meaning in anything she does. Underneath that certainty is an unconscious belief she does not exist. How can there be meaning without existence? She feels forever broken and irreparable. It just is. She does not differentiate her thinking from her feeling or her doing. When she thinks of a future, there is "nothing".

I am careful to not attempt to talk her out of her certainty. I am trying to be with her in her experience, but it is hard for me. To do so is to accept that for her, at least in this moment, I do not exist either. She seems a very long way from her emotions, from herself, describing her 'truth' in a very matter-of-fact tone. She is also distant from me. We are very far away from each

DOI: 10.4324/9781003544470-7

other psychically, united only by the simultaneity of our physical presences and the music of our voices.

Gina's truth is in direct opposition to my truth. I believe in psychoanalysis. I believe in what we are doing. I feel like she has changed. She does not. When I wonder why she comes, she replies, "It's in my schedule. It's part of my day". Her schedule and my schedule meet an hour a day, four days a week. We concretely share a time and space. Presumably, we share an experience in our meetings. I say presumably because I have learned that in spite of our shared time and space, our experience of being together differs radically. She tells me that she might have had a glimmer of hope when first she came to me, but mostly she came because it was that or be hospitalized. She also could have killed herself. She didn't want either of those and so she chose analysis. Notice, she says nothing about me. In this moment, I am not a person to her, but I do have a function.

A function separated from the person providing that role, is not an emotional experience of intimacy. A person-less function is not using an object, but relating to an object (Winnicott, 1969) as if the object were a no-object. She relates to me as if I were some 'thing' or some 'one' other than me. Sometimes, that relationship is one of being the other. She is me; I am her. Machines have functions and do not need to be alive in order to perform them. They also are interchangeable. People are neither interchangeable nor replaceable. My function as a thing is hard for me to comprehend because I experience myself as a person. She tells me she is not a person but a function too. Functions do not have emotions. You do not need to think about them or have an emotional relationship with them. Emotions without thought are forms of a lie (Meltzer, 1986b).

What are emotions? Where do they originate? Why are they important? Are infants born with them? Are they invoked? Evoked? Learned through social interaction? Are my emotions yours? Your emotions mine? These questions are important because what we believe about emotions affects the psychoanalytic process that emerges in our consulting rooms. Bion (1962b) says emotions are links and that they cannot be experienced except in relationship with internal or external others. He says the same about passion, that it is a two-person experience, which puts us in touch with truth. Truth, according to Bion (1962b), nurtures the mind like food nurtures our bodies. I agree with him, but facing truth is not easy. The emotions that arise in the face of truth are difficult. Life itself is difficult. In extreme circumstances, our desperate patients manage to rid themselves of emotions, thereby producing thoughts that are a lie that provide relief. Even those thoughts are functions.

If my patient has an unconscious negative hallucination that she does not exist or that I do not exist, an emotional link between us is not possible. Not existing defends against the violence of emotions. Emotions are violent (Bion, 1962b; Civitarese, 2013; Bergstein, 2019; 2020) and cruel in that truth, as I have said, is often difficult to bear (Eekhoff, 2020). The intensity of love is as cruel as the intensity of hate (Civitarese, 2013; Eekhoff, 2022). Love includes a genuine wish to know the other person and a curiosity about what that person feels or thinks. Certainty destroys curiosity. Love also requires two separate people who need each other and are vulnerable to each other. In analysis, facing a reality of the painful truth of separateness and potential loss of the other is present in every interpretation. It is one reason interpretations are violent (Aulagnier, 1975).

The emotional ferocity of need and vulnerability can shatter links just as a talented opera singer can shatter a crystal glass with her voice. Intense passionate love and hate also bring attention to boundaries, again – for good and for ill. In doing so, new possibilities emerge by opening up new areas for our attention and curiosity. In uniting love and hate with knowledge or curiosity and the desire to know another (Bion, 1962b), harmony and discord enable links where truth can be found.

Truth and beauty are inseparable in the symphonic rhythms of the body and music of the voice. However, truth is always in transit (Bergstein, 2020) and beauty too is transitory. They both are forever changing. Hence, both truth and beauty bring with them an awareness of vulnerability to loss. Certainty attempts to stop time and in doing so destroys a potential for truth to be found. As with my patient Gina, certainty also collapses space. With the stoppage of time and the collapse of space, communication falters. Need and vulnerability are destroyed as is the intimacy of communication.

The discovery of personal truth is a mysterious process. Truths or lies emerge intersubjectively. They also emerge intrapsychically in our subjective interpretations of sensate responses to the internal and external environment. Further, emotional links serve to promote symbolization by using the sensate somatic experiences of the body to hold and contain the psyche in the face of awful truths. Passionate connection destroys and creates simultaneously. The result is catastrophic change (Bion, 1965; 1970) and sustenance for a vital life.

Embodiment and Emotional Links

Somatic experience itself enables order to develop within us a configuration of form and a patterning of sensations that embody who we are. *Memories in feelings* (Klein, 1961; 1975) contribute to a sense of being and to a *continuity-of-being* (Winnicott, 1945; 1949) that is communicated unconsciously. When Ferenczi (1909) speaks of the "primordial symphony of life" and "music of the instincts" (p. 62), he is describing a background experience of being contained and held by the body. He is asserting that unconscious communication of instincts and affects has the potential to become organized as sounds, sensations, and images of emotional connections. These may never be put into language and need not be. Yet they drive and organize a representational imperative (Levine, 2012) and the instinctive need to communicate (Bergstein, 2015).

Emotional links are communications that foster intimacy. Intimacy does not mean agreement or compliance. Intimacy is complex and multifaceted, bringing discord as well as harmony. Fostering intimacy includes fostering a development of the self. The development of personal depth and dimensionality enables the profound accumulation of relationship that requires separateness and individuality for true connection. Emotional communications are relational, even in phantasy. *Embodied communication* with either self or other requires an ordering of somatic experience that is processed and made meaningful via these unconscious emotional connections.

Love, hate, and curiosity are also communicated consciously. Bion (1962b) says,

> Alpha-function operates on the sense impressions, whatever they are, and the emotions, whatever they are, of which the patient is aware. In so far as alpha-function is successful alpha elements are produced and these elements are suited to storage and the requirements of dream thoughts.
>
> (p. 6)

Bion is speaking of conscious awareness here and the truth that emerges when sense impressions are 'played upon' by the ordering dreaming of the mind. This process of embodiment is the process of representation.

Physical sounds and sensations become representations of emotion. Simultaneously, emotions themselves are derived from sounds and sensations emanating from the body and are embodied signs of unconscious and conscious experience (Eekhoff, 2019a). Implicit memories are stored in the body and remembered outside of language as traces or impressions. As *memories-in-sensorium* (Eekhoff, 2019b), sounds and sensations transform into images which signal meaning via the emotions evoked. As memories-in-feelings (Klein, 1961; 1975), emotions build psychic structure.

Emotional mobility enables the registration of experience and evokes dynamic meaning. It is not that we find meaning somewhere outside of us. What is signified in any situation is personal. Meaning and truth are constantly evolving. We discover meaning via the organizational structures we use in order to manage the intensity of sounds and sensations as well as affects and emotions (see Chapter 2). All of this is both intrapsychic and intersubjective.

Again, this is an infinite, dynamic process. Psychological grounding – having one's feet on the ground, or being in touch with common sense as generated in community – gives a floor for experience (Ogden, 1991; Eaton, 2005) and provides a center of gravity (Eekhoff, 2017; 2019c). In somatopsychic experience, a center of gravity originates in relationship and is necessary for representational processes to evolve. Our senses ground us in reality, enabling significance to arise from relational experience.

The senses are animate, taking in and giving out. Sounds and sensations are transient, an infinitely alive experience. The ongoing vibrant nature of the somatic, the breathing in and out, creates an experience of going-on-being no matter the pain. To psychically and physically shift and change, to move, fluctuate, and sway, to swing and rock, is to be fully alive. These form the music of the universe. These words – shift, fluctuate, sway, swing, and rock, also have violent synonyms. They can signify power, control, mastery, force, blow, and shock.

Organizing these intense experiences is an innate aspect of the human mind. Boundaries provide security and give shape and form to experience. Boundaries imply twoness, and when any two people meet, the meeting can evoke catastrophic change (Bion, 1965; 1970). This is the ontological process of being and becoming where emotional links are created not uncovered, and in the process, potentials are realized. The ontological process is one of figurability (Botella and Botella, 2005; Botella, 2014). Figurability as evoked by emotions of love, hate, and knowledge is dancing to the music of life. The symphony of life is the music of being and embodiment.

Pictograms or Pictographs

Typically, analysts have explored visual images as pictograms or pictographs on the road to symbolization. Italian field theory focuses on pictograms as precursors to narrations (Ferro, 2005; Civitarese, 2016). Ferro (2005) suggests that image formation and transforming them into narrations are the main focuses of psychoanalysis today (p. 101). Aulagnier (1975) describes the process of moving from pictogram to statement, highlighting the violence emotional linking entails.

Bion (1973) says, "The dominance of the ocular senses, both real and imagined, is such that it affects our capacity for thought" (p. 8). And later, he adds, "The verbal formulation of a visual image is more comprehensible and probably more false" (p. 9). Transformations serve to both mediate the affective charges and symbolize them. A transformation is not the thing-in-itself. Bion is exploring the pathway the senses take enroute to making meaning of emotional experience. He is also highlighting the original experience as true.

When falsity enters, because reality is too much to bear, the transformations may become dissociated from the body. Then, the body's registration of experience becomes untrustworthy. It is then that we especially need emotional intimacy with a trusted other to help us find our balance and our emotional truth. Visual images, such are found in reverie and in night dreams, provide information that has meaning. They are communications. Unfortunately, when trauma disrupts this meaning-making process, even visual images, in the form of positive or negative hallucinations, fail to bring satisfaction or relief. The result is a breakdown in the transformations of sound and sensation into imagery. The breakdown interferes with embodiment.

Such a breakdown results in the reality that many traumatized patients have a paucity of images, whether or not they recall their dreams. They focus on concrete facts of life in order to reduce their emotional vulnerability and to create a sense of continuity-of-being (Winnicott, 1945; 1949). Focusing on the concrete provides an illusion of certainty. Their certainty of knowing the absolute truth, as my patient Gina asserted, is an aspect of that concreteness. Their images, such as they have them, and their narrations, which are by-products of trauma, serve a defensive function via the somatic expressions they illicit. These are necessary protections. Both images and narrations may be borrowed or mimicked rather than arising out of the process of figurability on the road to representation and symbolization. Signs and signals are more evident than symbols.

Sounds and Sensations: Signs and Signals

When working with patients who were traumatized as children and are diffi-cult to reach, I find that the process of figurability has broken down. Also, frequently the patient has withdrawn to an undrawn state (Alvarez, 2006; 2010; 2012). In that state, relationship with self and other is disrupted, whe-ther defensively or due to a deficit that developed following the trauma. Levine (2012) describes this unrepresented area as a "colorless canvas". The emotional relational process, which is the foundation of all learning (Bion, 1962a), seems to have been disrupted prior to the imaging process (Eekhoff, 2023a). This disruption interferes with the capacity to dream whether awake or asleep (Bion, 1962a; 1962b; 1965).

This disruption contributes to my difficulty in reaching them. In order to engage meaningfully with patients whose imaging processes are weak or absent, I seek to discover the precursor to the disruption. This has led me to the somatopsychic realm of sounds and sensations. "Primal processes use the sensory modalities as precursors of the visual imagery that leads to language" (Eekhoff, 2022, p. 4). In discovering the precursors, or at least in believing that I have, I can sometimes reach patients who previously have seemed unreachable to me. Often patients who are difficult to reach (Joseph, 1975) have severely restricted emotional ranges, such as Gina whom I described earlier. That which seems to be emotion is the action of released raw affects (see Chapter 2 for a discussion of the difference between affects, emotions, and feelings). These actions often are expressed in rageful outbursts. The action disperses the *figurability potential*. Emotions themselves have been inhibited and dulled and can seem nonexistent.

Our patients who have experienced childhood trauma describe sensations of falling, liquefying, spilling out, and vaporizing when they do not have a *psy-chic skin* to contain them. Without a psychic skin (Bick, 1968; 1986), con-tinuity-of-being is lost. Second skin formations such as obsessiveness, mimicry, adhesion to objects, and radical splits between body and mind serve as boundaries to hold the fragile self. The cataloguing of experience begins sensorily even before birth (Winnicott, 1945). Winnicott imagines that even

cataloguing can be used defensively. Visual images are sensual memories organized and catalogued so as to be significant and remembered. They arise as
expressions of figurability (Botella and Botella, 2005) and can also be used
defensively when they are precocious mental development in response to trauma.

The sensory organs – eyes, ears, nose, mouth, and skin – serve at least two
functions. First they are receptors of the environment and as such provide
stimulus for learning. The sensory experiences they register link reality and
pleasure, providing comfort, solace, appreciation, and beauty. Sounds, smells,
and sensations become background objects that recall the earliest relationship
with the mother's breast. They provide a primordial sense of order within the
infinite chaos of our senses. They are also linked to experiences of satisfaction, where that which was lacking (e.g., milk; mother's love or hate or curiosity) has been received via the physical contact of mouth and nipple, of milk
and mouth, of cheek and breast, of being skin to skin. The infants' own sensual body becomes the body of the mother.

The research of Maiello (1995) and Piontelli (1987) suggests that sounds
already impact the fetus in utero. These are phenomenological experiences
and hypothesized as *sound objects* (Aulagnier, 1975; Maiello, 1995). Perhaps
so too do the sensations of amniotic fluid on skin. These sound objects and
sensation objects begin to form prenatally. Postnatally, these contribute to the
fusion and undifferentiated states with the mother. They also contribute to the
development of a self via reciprocal merger, which I differentiate from fusion
(Eekhoff, 2016; 2021). In merger, there is movement, a psychic entering and
leaving the other. The psychic melding enhances the self just as differentiating
from the other does. Fusion which is more fixed interferes with reciprocity
because in a negative hallucinatory state, the other does not exist. A*esthetic
reciprocity* (Meltzer, 1983) between mother and infant results in love-at-first
sight. Such reciprocal sensorial states, which I believe come and go from birth
onwards, are the source of all creativity. They are proto-mental (Bion, 1970)
and they are emotional. As reciprocal sensorial states harmonize with each
other and the world, they create the unique individuals each of us become.

In a similar manner, the setting of the analysis serves as a symbiotic
undifferentiated body relationship of the analysand with the analyst (Bleger,
2013/1967). It is not a process, but a constant that provides a background of
safety (Sandler, 1960). Psychoanalytic respect for the setting and the frame
recognizes the silent *somatic transference* found in the physical relationship of
the analytic dyad that often goes unnoticed and uninterpreted. Sounds and
sensations in the consulting room come to be equated with the mother's body:
the room is the womb or the couch is the lap. The analyst is, in the analysand's phantasy, the analysand. This is not pathological. It is creative. If we
stay with our musical metaphor: it moves into the realm of jazz and
improvisation. Nor is this symbiotic merger aggressive or a manic take-over.
Those can occur, but they are at a symbolic level, not at this level of Being.
Holding tight the setting and the frame enables these somatopsychic realities

to be registered, recognized, and remembered, enabling them to enter the realm of figurability. Extra-analytic relations cover over this symbiotic and undifferentiated relationship creating a pseudo-analysis (Bleger, 1967, p. 240) that inhibits figurability.

Secondly, the sensory organs evolutionarily serve a function of determining when there is danger. When the violence or intensity of emotions overwhelms the receptors and overstimulates the mind, such as happens with trauma, the sense organs respond defensively to provide containment. If this occurs too early for an infant or too often, the senses themselves become co-opted as defenses. Sensory receptors can become used for blotting out emotion and hence the link to the mind. Figurability is halted. The capacity for learning from experience (Bion, 1962a) is compromised. Relationships with others, instead of being used as validation of truth, become dangerous.

This process is related to but different than the use of the sensory organs to evacuate instead of take in. When the senses are used in reverse, there is release of pressure. A fixation on the sensation itself that eliminates the link with the object does not necessarily rid the psyche of the pressure of over-whelming emotions. It blocks them. In both cases, the object is unreachable. Without the interaction with either an internal or external object, the subject cannot find emotional truth. Delusions and distortions abound.

Fixation on sensation occurs when higher orders of defense such as repression and/or splitting and projecting or introjecting have either insuffi-ciently developed or have failed. When this happens, the person has retreated from the object and may even have lost a sense of having a *containing shape* (Korbivcher, 2017). It is not a violent attack on linking but a passive atomi-zation (Ferenczi, 1933) or liquifying (Levine and Powers, 2017; Eekhoff, 2017; 2019c). Loewald (1980) suggests that when this occurs projection and intro-jection, inside and outside, cannot be distinguished from each other: "the two terms signify different directions of the same process rather than two different processes" (p. 18). In those circumstances, emotions which are aspects of ego formation do not evolve, nor does a subjective sense of self or other. The adhesive *sensory fixation* results in mimicry that can be very difficult to notice. The end result is a fixation on the concrete and an unconscious fusion with the object.

Objects of Sense

Emotions in the form of love, hate, and curiosity are outside of the senses even as they are "objects of sense" (Bion, 1962b, p. 6). Whereas emotions are the link between soma and psyche (Eekhoff, 2019a; 2022; 2023), they also attach themselves to sounds and sensations, thereby giving meaning to them. *Memories-in-sensorium* (Eekhoff, 2019a) aid in the development of a sub-jective sense of self. Body relations and object relations cannot be separated (Bleger, 1967; Eekhoff, 2022; 2023). The somatopsychic movement is also a psychosomatic movement. The dynamic process occurs in both directions: Sounds and Sensations > < Love, Hate, and Curiosity. There is a double arrow between them. I am describing circumstances of forever-changing evolving processes that do not proceed linearly through developmental stages. These processes of figurability occur throughout the lifespan and are the background – the facilitating environment – of all human life.

Concreteness

Focusing on the concrete facts of life becomes a means of containing and sometimes eradicating overwhelming sensations and unmediated affect. Focusing on sounds and sensations builds a *perceptual container* that see-mingly erases emotions. Perceptual identity is removed from thought identity rather than nourishing it. The *"sound object"* (Maiello, 1995) and the *skin ego* (Bick, 1968; 1986; Anzeiu, 1985; 1990a; 1990b) become means of holding the self together, of having a continuity-of-being (Winnicott, 1949) at the expense of differentiation. *Sensation objects* serve to decrease the awareness of other-ness. Unfortunately, the concrete can interrupt the process of figurability even as it supports it.

Affects, the biological instinctive expression of our animal natures, are less easily encrypted. They can appear frozen, as we will see with my patient Linda. However, often rage appears seemingly unconnected to events. These primal affects are the hope for the resurrection of the symphony of life. They embody the "music of the instincts" (Ferenczi, 1909). When emotions are blocked, primitive instinctive affects remain. The resurrection of the symph-ony would allow for the somatopsychic figurability to function, bringing emotions with them. The primal affects link us with each other, when emo-tions have been frozen, time has stopped, and space has collapsed.

Since we know from Bion that emotions are the source of all growth in the psyche (Bion, 1962b, p. 94), encapsulating and encrypting emotions inhibits growth and interferes with relationshiaps with objects. Often, the encapsula-tion has succeeded because the somatic defenses have built a 'wall of sound' or a 'wall of sensation' around imaging and emotion, encapsulating nascent emotional experience and interfering with the experience of having a sub-jective sense of self. This results in being a lie and being unable to find truth even in relationship. Living a lie or being a lie makes truth inaccessible and the mind is not fed, but starved.

Clinical Applications

Sounds and sensations are invisible elements of the *psychoanalytic situation* (Bleger, 1967) and so the body of the analyst as well as the physical setting plays an essential part in establishing a frame. So too do the sounds of the analyst: voice, breathing, moving. A story of a patient I worked with many years ago, prior to becoming an analyst, comes to mind. I have never forgotten her but clearly the details escape me, and hence the story is a fictional narrative I tell myself. I believe my story includes emotional truth. The reality that my memory of her stays with me and that I am writing of Linda (a pseudonym) now speaks to the symbiotic relationship we had. It seems that what was helpful to her was primarily the setting and the frame of our work together. I also believe that my physicality – my actual body – served to inform me about her and to communicate safety to her. I met her more than 40 years ago when I was a psychologist.

Child Protective Services removed Linda and her two older sisters from her parents when she was two. Her sisters were three and four. Purportedly, the children had been physically and sexually abused. They lived in filth and often did not have food since their drug-addicted parents were incapable of holding them in mind. The children were placed in the same foster home and eventually put up for adoption. Linda's older sisters were adopted. She was not. Her foster mother told me that although she was a very easy child, her failure to be adopted might have been because Linda was odd and maybe 'slow'. Fortunately, she was able to remain with her foster family throughout her childhood and into adulthood.

When I met Linda, she was 14 years old, although she appeared much younger. Her foster mother brought her because she had been raped by two neighbor boys, whom she had known most of her life. I will not go into the descriptions I received about this from her mother. Linda was in special education at school and not doing well. She was easy to be with, quiet, and obedient. She did what she was told. She was told to come to therapy. She did so without protest. I saw her once a week until she turned 18 and no longer qualified for social services.

Linda was a petite child-like teenager. Her face was almost elf-like and free of any expressions of concern. I interpreted this silently as innocence. She seemingly had not been affected by her circumstances. This was incomprehensible. We could also say, it was a lie. The truth of the impact of her history lay in the reality that I could not reach her. Her story, told by others, deeply impacted me.

The first year was very painful for me, but seemingly not for Linda. She would enter the room, not look at me, and sit in my chair. She faced away from me looking out the window. I could see only the side of her. Her face was blank and still. My supervisor said she was aggressive. I did not think so. Many words were used to describe her: dissociative, catatonic, autistic, psychotic, angry, hostile, traumatized. She did not speak for many months. She did not make eye contact. It was not that she looked down or away from me. That would have been to acknowledge I was there. She moved past me as if I were a chair. Her foster mother told me she spoke at home and occasionally at school. I trusted that she heard and understood me. I do not know if she did. It appeared no one was 'home' inside of her. She didn't seem to be having unshared thoughts nor withheld feelings. She appeared blank.

At first, I remember being very uncomfortable and not knowing what to do. I talked. I asked questions. I reported what I had been told. Nothing happened. I waited. Nothing happened. To be silent felt wrong and to speak felt wrong. Her foster mother told me it was helping. When I asked how, she merely shrugged and said, "It just is". I was not sure of that. I felt Linda wasn't there, but I didn't understand my own feeling. I worked with her long before I had any idea of what 'not being there' meant psychologically. Because she was so absent and I was so present, sitting as I did in the 'patient's' chair, I was the patient. Now looking back, I realize that I was not present from her perspective, something I didn't comprehend then. She was all there was and she was blank. I didn't recognize the lie I told myself: "I was there for her". How could I be if she didn't recognize my presence? I stopped talking and just sat with her, looking out the window.

After many weeks of silence, I began to describe what I was sensing. I was very careful not to describe her because I felt that would be cruel. It also seemed that anything I said would be about me and potentially a lie about her. Instead, I sat unconsciously mirroring her posture. Eventually I noticed this and spoke about it. But first, when I began to speak, I described the natural world out the window as it shifted and changed before us: the sky, the clouds, the sun, the rain or snow, the trees swaying in the wind, the changing light. Sometimes I described birds as they flew by. Notice that these observations were of visual images. However, they were not internally generated. They were concrete descriptions.

After several months, I began to notice something else. Again, I did not describe her, nor did I 'disclose' my sensations. I intuitively began to describe sounds and sensations in the room, in the space between us. I described birdsong, the sounds of rain on the window, or wind through the trees. I described the atmosphere. I did not use pronouns such as you or I or we. I did not interpret her breathing or blinking or movement. I would say something like, "The air is heavy today". "The birds are quiet". My comments placed my observations in the space between us and not in her or me. I did not mean my descriptions symbolically, but concretely. I was not consciously speaking in metaphor. I was being as concrete as language allowed me. I also was not implementing a strategy. I was being there and making sounds. I was also describing, without attribution, my sensations, my observations. I assumed some of these were also hers. In other words, I assumed we were having a simultaneous physical experience. I was also embodied, staying aware of the rhythm of my breathing, the pounding of my heart that came and went in intensity. I had many conflicting emotions every time I was with her.

I must say, that I was most uncomfortable doing this. I felt like an intruder. I had no theories to help me. My supervisor said all the aggression was now in me. I wasn't sure. I was present to myself and trying to be present to Linda. I could not face how isolated she was, deeply inside a self she seemingly did not recognize as her own. Her passivity was unlike anything I had ever known. I was quite horrified to be so invisible to her and she to me. She certainly did not seem to be projecting into me so the analytic function of receptivity took on a whole new meaning for me.

At the same time, I felt very calm, as she seemed to be. Looking back, I imagine I was trying to feel her. I was still so as to make room for her, but I was not silent nor absent. I do not think I was dissociated, but I might have been. I was strangely lacking in imagination or daydreams or thoughts. I was concretely being a body in the room with her. I gave up having any agenda. Only after the session, did images and thoughts come to me. I imagine, again looking back, that what I was doing was inductive, not interpretive nor receptive (Blum, Goldberg, and Levin, 2023). The question is, was this process, if we name it induction, mutual?

It was several years before Linda began to talk to me. Occasionally, she would fleetingly look at me. It was such an accomplishment for her. I remember nothing of what she said. I do remember her pale blue eyes. If I were to guess, I imagine she described her days. She never expressed frustration with me or anyone. Had we been able to work longer, I imagine that would have been a possible progression. With her ability to talk more, she was able to make a friend in high school. They met on the bus. The two of them liked music and would sing along with popular songs. I don't really know what they did besides listen to music. I don't think they danced. She never dated, went to sports events, or even to the movies. She seemed more engaged with the world than before, although still emotionally distant from herself and me.

Through the years, I have thought of her, hoping her life is 'good enough' for her.

Discussion

Nothing is as simple as words make them seem. How does one lose something one has never had? How is one satisfied if one has not known satisfaction? How does one find truth when emotions are stripped from sensations? How can certainty derived from concrete relationship with the world be addressed? How can truth be found if emotional relationship is avoided? Trauma seems to disrupt natural human impulses for connection with both self and other. Denial of the essence of being and of *unrealized potential* by focusing on the concrete aspects of living, interferes with growth and development.

The instinctual need for truth and to be understood is thwarted by a cumulative traumatic relationship with parents who do not receive an infant's projections (Bion, 1958) and by infants who then fail to project (Meltzer, 1986a). Instead of a receiving object that is internalized, an obstructive object is internalized (Bion 1957; Eaton, 2005, Eekhoff, 2021). The innate *expectation of care* is not realized nor satisfied. Linda truly did not seem to project. I found this hard to believe but could not deny that if she were projecting, I was not receiving those projections. In that way, she appeared to be on the autistic spectrum. She seemed unaware of having an inside and barely aware of an outside.

Without containment in early childhood, the traumatized child perceives the instinct to communicate and the expectation to be understood as dangerous and turns away from the object, sometimes via a delusion that there is no object there at all. A delusion is a defense, a mental construction. It is not a deficit. Linda's difficulty learning may have been a deficit. I am more inclined to think of it as a defense. Perhaps it was both. In some way, a defense is preferable since it can more easily be addressed analytically. Some of the defenses Linda presented were negative hallucinations: not seeing what was there. She simply did not originally recognize others as people. We were things.

When the analyst is perceived as being a thing, the patient is alone without an object to project into. Without the registration of an object to be used as receptor, the projective identification, especially the identification aspect, is very weak, more adhesive that projective. When people are things not objects, relationship is imitative and concrete and not emotional. Relationship is transactional. Adhesive equation or *being-the-object* replaces dependency and intimacy. However, if reaching for the other is a drive (Bergstein, 2019), that instinctual need will benefit the analysis, making most people amenable to treatment. The music of the instincts (Ferenczi, 1909) will be heard. Initially, I could not sense that Linda knew I existed and so she did not psychically reach for me. She projected minimally.

The Tango Dancer

A brief story of another patient might illustrate the profound somatic symbiosis that can occur when working with severely traumatized patients who are very concrete. Lorraine was 63 years old and never married when she came to me, hoping that analysis would help her find a husband. She had had therapy previously, but "without success". Her neighbor was an analyst and had given her my name. In spite of my telling her that analysis could not promise her a husband, she agreed to come. She asserted that since I had a husband, she was sure I could help her. Her certainty was disconcerting for me. At the time we began our treatment, I was single.

Lorraine did whatever I recommended. She used the couch and came faithfully four times a week. She was on time and paid promptly. Her history of physical and sexual abuse, as she reported it, was extensive, coming from both her father and uncles. This was described as a fact, without emotional significance to her. Her only problem was not being a wife. She professed to be happy and content with her life. That was not what it felt like to me. She seemed anxious and depressed, as evidenced by pressured speech and physical gestures. She constantly shook her foot. She rubbed her fingers and thumb together as she spoke. With her other hand, she brushed the fabric of the couch, back and forth, back and forth. Clearly, she had a very sensual relationship to the setting of my office. She denied feeling either anxious or depressed, insisting her only problem was that she had never married. This was also hard for me to believe in that often she spoke disparagingly of her friends, her neighbors, and her family, which seemed like a problem to me.

This was a long and painful treatment. Lorraine's gestures and sensory preoccupations were disturbing to me, but it took me many months to attempt to interpret them in the transference. Even then, nothing changed. Her concreteness made my interpretations seemingly ineffective. I could not penetrate the wall of sensation the concreteness provided. In my counter-transference, I felt sleepy, bored, impatient, and frustrated. Nothing worked. We seemingly had no relationship at all. Except that my counter-transference responses told me otherwise. Clearly, Lorraine projected and massively. Projective identification requires a receiving object and implies relationship.

I came to understand how wrong I was about the lack of relationship. We were fused. The extent of her unconscious fusion with me became apparent when my own life changed. For years I had been dancing tango two or three nights a week. When I began a romantic relationship with my future husband, I stopped dancing to be with him. I want to be clear here, at no time did I disclose to Lorraine that I was single or married or that I danced tango in my spare time.

Within weeks of my new significant relationship, Lorraine reported that analysis was not working for her, and so she had taken the problem into own hands. She would find her husband herself. She was taking tango lessons. She was buying sexy tango clothes. Her sessions became descriptions of the tango scene I knew so well. Her teachers had been mine. Her dance partners were men I knew. Her dancing put me back into the life I had had. I was confused and disorganized in many sessions. It also seemed that I had gotten the husband she wanted.

This emotional experience of registering and recognizing the profound fusional relationship I had unknowingly been a part of for over four years shocked me. Although the work had been difficult, I had felt we were making progress. Perhaps. However, it is also possible that we had been engaged in a sensual adhesive relationship of mimicry. She was preforming and giving me what I unconsciously wanted. When I stopped dancing and she began dancing, I was able to understand the depth of her symbiotic need of me and her lack of psychic differentiation. She was more in me than I realized and perhaps, I too was in her. This woman who had no friends and had never married fused with all of her objects, myself included. Once fused, she could not think. Out of a fear of losing herself, she pushed her objects away with her concreteness and self-absorption. I thought she was pushing me away when all along she was unconsciously psychically burrowing in deeply and looking out at the world through my eyes. When she began dancing tango, I realized it was my whole body she inhabited.

Lorraine highlighted for me the psychic reality of porous boundaries in patients who have been traumatized as infants and young children. She psychically became me, entering in and possessing me against my will and outside of my awareness.

Discussion

The primordial symphony of life is common to all humans. It is a background object, a primordial Mother Nature that holds us. Our senses take this symphony in, even before we are born. Nature and nurture work together when we are embodied. Being embodied enables us to find meaning in our experiences and to relate to each other as partners in our search for what is true to us. Without each other, finding truth is not possible. Relationship with each other, just as relationship between the senses, provides binocular vision (Bion, 1950; 1962b; Molinari, 2024). Binocular vision brings dimensionality. Time and space in relationship make truth discernable.

Both Linda and Lorraine seemed to have had no relationship with me, even at a physical level. They additionally did not display any emotional connection to their other objects. People were things. They also seemed to lack an ability for *imaginative elaboration* (Winnicott, 1949) of their somatic experiences. Neither seemed to have a relationship to their own bodies. Whereas Linda seemed equally distant from herself as from me, appearing autistic, Lorraine had a seemingly highly narcissistic relationship with only herself. No one else existed. Both patients were not self-reflective nor interested in being understood. They just didn't think about it. Instead, they were extremely concrete and focused on the practical day-to-day experiences of living. The experience of coming to see me, to be with me, to talk or not talk to me, was purely part of their routine. It was not emotional. It was sensual and procedural, creating a rhythmic relationship of coming and going, much like breathing. As I look at what I just wrote, they were not coming 'to me' since I was psychically not there. Coming to therapy was not relational; it was practical.

Over the years I have come to think of an autistic state as one of somatic defenses. The somatic defenses, the taking in of the analyst's smell, the sounds and rhythm of her voice, are woven together to create a sense, in phantasy, of having a unity that ultimately results in a shape. Since this need to have a shape, to be a solid being, is essential for the *mental solids* (Friston, 2013; Solms, 2013) of the mind, any person whom the patient contacts regularly will become interwoven with the patient. When and if that interwoven nature, that unity or fusion, begins to break down, it is evidence of progress, but will initiate a difficult time in the treatment. This is the origin of being, the "ontological vibration" of Merleau-Ponty (1968) as discussed by Blum, Goldberg, and Levin (2023).

Psychic fusion needs to break up so as to enable differentiation. A relational representative process needs differentiation. However, when this breakup occurs and should an object appear, in this instance a therapist, the object is perceived as an aggressor (Ferenczi, 1932). Also, when the previous coping strategies break up, initially there is little to replace them. This is a very dangerous time because the analyst is dangerous and the patient is extremely raw, open, and vulnerable, seemingly with few defensive structures. Somatic defenses initially become stronger and somatic symptoms may appear.

I am speaking of somatic defenses, but in another way, as I said earlier, the somatic is the origin of our organizing processes. The origin of our Being occurs with our senses being in sync with each other and our bodies being in sync with other bodies. When an infant brings mouth to nipple, the sensations focus attention, enabling an integration of subjective experience. The process is one of figurability. The same is true when a patient hears the analyst's voice, for example. The sound serves as an attractor of attention, focusing and integrating soma and psyche, even if only momentarily. These sounds, smells, and sensations become defenses, rather than a means of figurability, when the object or the subject in phantasy does not exist. In health, the *somatic surround* is container of Being.

Back to Linda

I wonder whether Linda was taking her shape from me or I from her. Again, this language is in retrospect. I did not have the concept of psychic shape available to me then. I did want to reach her. I did try to find her. I found her strangely beautiful and innocent, not understanding that my perception of her innocence represented a deep body/mind dissociation in her. However, I also wondered if what I was sensing was her essence of being. Was I feeling the infant behind the autistic defenses?

I felt curious about what was happening inside of her, but could not initially even make up a believable story about her. Yet, I trusted something was happening. Looking back, I might theorize about shape changing. Linda seemed to 'become' in phantasy whomever she was with. She did not do this in the sophisticated way a hysteric might imitate or a schizoid might mimic. Rather, she blended. I have faith that someone has to be 'in' there for blending or shape changing to occur. Again, I did not have such thoughts then. And even now, I struggle with words because the fusion and lack of differentiation I experienced with Linda was outside of language.

In every session we were entangled, but more accurately, intermingled and melded. The transference took on new meaning for me. It was silent and I feared it did not exist. The silent transference (Eekhoff, 2015) is a *transference of figurability*, where the analyst is interwoven with the patient creating a second psychic skin for both. This defense is not embodiment but can be transformed. The defense against liquefying or evaporating or disappearing into nothingness can be silence – an absence of anything. It can also include pressured speech where the patient's own words are important, not for their meaning, but for their sensual qualities.

Words as sounds, as things, alleviate this primal anxiety of not existing. Words used this way are sensual things, not representations, not symbols. They are music when the sounds are related, but in this most retreated place, the notes are separated and not related to each other. When a patient has no words, when sounds may not even have rhythm, much less order, as birdsong or music does, the senses exist outside of time. I believe that was true for Linda. Each moment was unique unto itself. When this happens, moments cannot be remembered nor accumulate except in a very primal way. They seemingly do not register. In those moments, the patient appears unreachable. These moments are not *moment* (Bollas, 1978, 1987) nor are they aesthetic. These moments are not experienced as Being, either. They are neither cognitive nor affectively experienced because the Self is not present.

Back to Lorraine

This also seemed to be true for Lorraine. There was, however, a major difference: Lorraine projected and her projections enabled me to think I knew how to reach her. I made interpretations at a higher level than her most primitive anxiety as presented in the hour. I struggled with my counter-transference. I did not find Lorraine attractive, either physically or emotionally. Sometimes I was very put off by what I thought of as her selfishness and her almost sociopathic use of people at work. I did not like her. This too was disturbing for me. I tried to understand it as her projecting into me, but I didn't really believe my own theorizing outside of the hour. I sought consultation and struggled with my own interest in her. I had very physical reactions to her that disturbed me deeply. Today, I believe these were in response to the unconscious fusion I was having difficulty tolerating. I was trying to get away from the entanglement which nauseated me.

It took many years of working with Lorraine before I could sense her innocence and lost infancy. She seemingly had no lost mother of infancy because she herself had been lost so early. As I found her, she could feel her own differentiation from me. Only then could she begin to feel a relationship with me which included her need of me and her vulnerability. Initially she felt how dangerous I was, which of course, was a correct assumption on her part. This was the beginning of the breakup of a symbiotic undifferentiated relationship with each other. It initiated a very difficult and productive time.

Body Relations and the Analyst

The analyst who feels a tremendous pressure to do something: to speak, to shift uncomfortably in the chair, or to direct the patient to action, is having physical as well as emotional reactions to the patient. Perhaps merely speaking serves a function of organizing the timeless, spaceless experience of undifferentiation and fusion. Speaking is action. Speaking attracts attention, which may serve an organizing function for the patient as well as the analyst. I have said that the music of the analyst's voice, its tone, rhythm, and cadence, becomes an aspect of the setting. However, *speaking-as-action* is an acting-in on the part of the analyst, even though it might simultaneously be containing on a different level.

These moments of *speaking-as-action* mimic analysis. They make the analyst unreachable emotionally for the patient. They indicate an inability on the part of the analyst to tolerate the emotional experience of the here-and-now. When the analyst can tolerate and become aware of something happening and then can allow herself or himself to be interwoven with the patient, where self and other is confused, where inside and outside is confused, the patient can experience herself as taking shape. In this process of figurability, fusion becomes merger and the two move in and out of each other searching for the truth of self and other.

As I said earlier, I believe this occurs by becoming an attractor of attention. Once attracted, differentiation for the patient, and consequentially the analyst, can resume, but differentiation brings confusion and disorientation and often fear and anger. Becoming a confusional object for the patient that can be internalized is evidence of differentiation. It is also extremely disturbing (Eekhoff, 2022) because the primordial defensive structure is breaking down. This is the reason I wished my work with Linda had progressed to a point where she could be upset with me. A confusional object appears when a psyche is emerging from fusion. Lorraine did accomplish being upset with me. I became her bad-object after having been a no-object for so long.

Working at such primal levels can be extremely upsetting for the analyst. I believe with others (Bion, 1970; Winnicott, 1949; Bergstein, 2019) that this is partly so because our traditional methods of the 'talking cure' are only effective once contact has been made. Primal mental states are revealed in the here-and-now of the setting. The experience is not verbal and so cannot be communicated verbally. Traditional interpretations of transference, of attacks on linking, of negative therapeutic reactions, of history, are ineffective. Primal mental states must be lived and "sometimes for the first time, in the here-and-now of the analysis" (Bergstein, 2019, p. 137). In this way, the no-object becomes a bad-object before it can be internalized as a good-object. Yet primal mental states are in all of us, they are not pathological. They just are. Primal mental states can be communicated via the body relations between patient and analyst.

Conclusion

This chapter has explored the relationship between the senses and emotional links as they reveal truth. It posits that symbolization itself is dependent upon a sensory embodied emotional relationship with self and other. Emotions as represented by love, hate, and knowledge enable integration. They are also intersubjective links between two subjects and between subject and object that facilitate meaning-making and the development of a subjective sense of self. The birth of the mind and the realization of potential arises out of the harmony of intrapsychic and intersubjective relationship. Being in harmony brings psychic balance and enables the figurability of symbolization processes to function.

The chapter has explored how the analysts' body is an aspect of the setting and the frame, equally important as the analyst's mind. Sounds, for example the analyst's voice, sensations, for example, the texture of the fabric of couch or chair, smells such as flowers from the garden, are all an aspect of the primordial symphony. As the setting, they become a background environmental mother. The constancy of the analytic setting is essential for a process to be discovered. Process itself is intimately related to figurability and the development of a capacity for relationship.

This chapter has explored the symphony of life and how it expresses the beauty and truth of the world. It has described the emotional atmosphere engendered in relationship. The emotional capacity for passion – to truly love, hate, and know another person – is to register their individuality with our hearts and bodies. The imaginative leap into intimacy reverberates and resonates within and between souls. Intimacy promotes aliveness.

Finally, the chapter is about the ontology of being and becoming as it creatively evolves in the analytic relationship. Aesthetic reciprocity between analyst and analysand involves being with, not thinking with. Aesthetic reciprocity as the inaccessible yet extant presence of both analyst and analysand enables truth to be found.

References

Alvarez, A. (2006). Some questions concerning states of fragmentation: unintegration, under–integration, disintegration, and the nature of early integrations. *Journal of Child Psychotherapy*, 32(2): 158–180.

Alvarez, A. (2010). Levels of analytic work and levels of pathology: The work of calibration. *International Journal of Psycho-Analysis*, 91: 859–878.

Alvarez, A. (2012). *The Thinking Heart*. London: Routledge.

Anzieu, D. (1985). *The Skin Ego*. New Haven, CT: Yale University Press, 1989. [Reprinted London: Karnac, 2016.]

Anzieu, D. (1990a). *Psychic Envelopes*. London: Karnac.

Anzieu, D. (1990b). *A Skin for Thought*. London: Karnac.

Aulagnier, P. (1975). *The Violence of Interpretation: From Pictogram to Statement*. Sheridan, A. (Trans.). Hove and New York: Brunner-Routledge, 2001.

Bergstein, A. (2015). Attacks on Linking or a Drive to Communicate? Tolerating the Paradox. *The Psychoanalytic Quarterly*, 84: 921–942.

Bergstein, A. (2019). *Bion and Meltzer's Expeditions into Unmapped Mental Life*. The Psychoanalytic Field Theory Book Series. London and New York: Routledge.

Bergstein, A. (2020). Violent Emotions and the violence of life. *The International Journal of Psychoanalysis*, 100(5): 863–868.

Bick, E. (1968). The experience of skin in early object relations. *International Journal of Psycho-Analysis*, 49: 484–486.

Bick, E. (1986). Further considerations on the function of the skin in early object relations. *British Journal of Psychotherapy*, 2(4): 292–299.

Bion, W. R. (1950). The imaginary twin. In *Second Thoughts: Selected Papers on Psychoanalysis* (pp. 3–22). London: Heinemann.

Bion, W. R. (1957). The differentiation of the psychotic from the non-psychotic personalities. *International Journal of Psycho-Analysis*, 38: 266–275. [Reprinted London: Heinemann, 1967; London: Karnac, 1984, pp. 43–64.]

Bion, W. R. (1958). On Arrogance. *International Journal of Psycho-Analysis*, 39: 144–146.

Bion, W. R. (1962a). A psycho-analytic theory of thinking. *International Journal of Psycho-Analysis*, 43: 306–310. [Reprinted as "A theory of thinking", in Bion, W. R., *Second Thoughts* (pp. 110–119). London: Karnac, 1984.]

Bion, W. R. (1962b). *Learning from Experience*. London: Heinemann. [Reprinted London: Karnac, 1984.]

Bion, W. R. (1965). *Transformations*. London: Heinemann. [Reprinted London: Karnac, 1984.]

Bion, W. R. (1970). *Attention and Interpretation*. London: Tavistock. [Reprinted London: Karnac, 1984.]

Bion, W. R. (1973). *Bion's Brazilian Lectures 1*. Rio de Janeiro: Imago Editora.

Blum, A., Goldberg, P., and Levin, M. (2023). *Here I am Alive* (pp. 1–304). New York: Columbia University Press.

Botella, C., and Botella, S. (2005). *The Work of Psychic Figurability: Mental States without Representation*. Weller, A. with Zerbib, M. (Trans.). Hove, East Sussex, UK: Brunner–Routledge.

Botella, C. (2014). On remembering: The notion of memory without recollection. *International Journal of Psycho-Analysis*, 95(5): 911–936.

Bleger, J. (1967). *Symbiosis and Ambiguity: A Psychoanalytic Study*. Churcher, J. and Bleger, L. (Eds.); Rogers, S., Bleger, L., and Churcher, J. (Trans.). London and New York: Routledge, 2013.

Bleger, J. (2013). Psychoanalysis of the psychoanalytic setting. In *Symbiosis and Ambiguity: A Psychoanalytic Study* (pp. 228–241). Churcher, J. and Bleger, L. (Eds.); Rogers, S., Bleger, L., and Churcher, J.London and New York: Routledge, 1967.

Bollas, C. (1978). The Aesthetic Moment and the Search for Transformation. *Annual of Psychoanalysis*, 6: 385–394.

Bollas, C. (1987). *The Shadow of the Object: Psychoanalysis of the Unthought Known*. New York: Columbia University Press.

Civitarese, G. (2013). *The Violence of Emotion*. London and New York: Routledge.

Civitarese, G. (2016). *Truth and the Unconscious in Psychoanalysis*. London and New York: Routledge.

Eaton, J. L. (2005). The obstructive object. *Psychoanalytic Review*, 92(3): 355–372.

Eekhoff, J. K. (2015). The silent transference: Clinical reflections on Ferenczi, Klein, and Bion. *Canadian Journal of Psychoanalysis*, 23(1): 57–73.

Eekhoff, J. K. (2016). Introjective Identification: The Analytic Work of Evocation. *American Journal of Psychoanalysis*, 76: 354–361.

Eekhoff, J. K. (2017). Finding a center of gravity via proximity with the analyst. In Levine, H. and Power, D. (Eds.), *Engaging Primitive Anxieties of the Emerging Self:*

Papers from the Seventh International Conference of the work of Frances Tustin. London: Karnac.

Eekhoff, J. K. (2019a). Affective bridges between body and mind. In *Trauma and Primitive Mental States, An Object Relations Perspective* (pp. 15–28). London and New York: Routledge.

Eekhoff, J. K. (2019b). The body as a mode of representation. In *Trauma and Primitive Mental States, An Object Relations Perspective* (pp. 94–111). London and New York: Routledge.

Eekhoff, J. K. (2019c). Finding a center of gravity via proximity with the analyst. In *Trauma and Primitive Mental States, An Object Relations Perspective* (pp. 50–62). London and New York: Routledge.

Eekhoff, J. K. (Jan 21, 2020). "The Cruelty of Emotion" paper presented at Seattle Psychoanalytic Society & Institute in response to O. Romero's paper: "The 'Cruelty' of the Psychoanalytic Method and Antonin Artaud's Theater".

Eekhoff, J. K. (2021). Body as Dream Space. In Harrang, C., Tillotson, D., and Winters, N. (Eds.), *Body as Psychoanalytic Object: Clinical Applications from Winnicott, Bion and Beyond*. London and New York: Routledge.

Eekhoff, J. K. (2021b). *Bion and Primitive Mental States: Trauma and the Symbiotic Link*. London and New York: Routledge.

Eekhoff, J. K. (2022). Psychic Equivalency as an Aspect of Symbiosis. In Levine, H. and Moguillansky, C. (Eds.), *Psychoanalysis of the Psychoanalytic Frame Revisited" A New Look at Bleger's Classical Work*. London and New York: Routledge/IPA.

Eekhoff, J. K. (Dec, 2023). Between the Real and the Imaginary: Truth and Lies in the psychoanalytic Encounter. *American Journal of Psychoanalysis*, 83(4).

Ferenczi, S. (1909). Introjection and transference. In: *First Contributions to Psychoanalysis* (pp. 35–93). New York: Brunner/Mazel, 1980.

Ferenczi, S. (1932). *The Clinical Diary of Sándor Ferenczi*. In Dupont, J. (Ed.); Balint, M. and Jackson, N. Z. (Trans.). Cambridge, MA: Harvard University Press, 1988.

Ferenczi, S. (1933). Confusion of the tongues between the adults and the child (The language of tenderness and of passion). In *Final Contributions to the Problems and Methods of Psycho-Analysis* (pp. 156–167). London: Karnac, 1994.

Friston, K. (2013). Consciousness and Hierarchical Inference. *Neuropsychoanalysis*, 15: 38–42.

Ferro, A. (2005). *Seeds of Illness, Seeds of Recovery: The Genesis of Suffering and the Role of Psychoanalysis*. Slotkin, Philip (Trans.). New York: Brunner-Routledge.

Joseph, B. (1975). The patient who is difficult to reach. In: Feldman, M. and Spillius, E. B. (Eds.), *Psychic Equilibrium and Psychic Change: Selected Papers of Betty Joseph* (pp. 75–87). London: Tavistock/Routledge, 1989.

Klein, M. (1961). Narrative of a Child Analysis. *International Psycho-analytic Library*, 104. London: Hogarth Press and Institute of Psychoanalysis.

Klein, M. (1975). Envy and Gratitude and Other Works. *International Psycho-analytic Library*, 104. London: Hogarth Press and Institute of Psychoanalysis.

Korbivcher, C. F. (2017). Bion's theory and unintegrated phenomena: Falling and dissolving. In Levine, H. and Power, D. (Eds.), *Engaging Primitive Anxieties of the Emerging Self: Papers from the Seventh International Conference of the work of Frances Tustin* (pp. 151–170). London: Karnac.

Loewald, H. W. (1980). Ego & Reality. In *Papers on Psychoanalysis*. New Haven and London: Yale University Press (1951, pp. 3–20).

Levine, H. B. (2012). The colourless canvas: Representation, therapeutic action and the creation of mind. *International Journal of Psycho-Analysis*, 93: 607–629.

Levine, H. B. and Powers, D. G. (Eds.). (2017). *Engaging Primitive Anxieties of the Emerging Self: The Legacy of Francis Tustin*. London: Karnac.

Maiello, S. (1995). The Sound-Object: A Hypothesis about Prenatal Auditory Experience and Memory. *Journal of Child Psychotherapy*, 21: 23–41.

Meltzer, D. (1983). *Dream-Life: A Re-examination of the Psycho-analytical Theory and Technique*. Strathclyde, Perthshire, UK: Clunie Press.

Meltzer, D. (1986a). *Studies in Extended Metapsychology*. London: Karnac Books.

Meltzer, D. (1986b). Facts and fictions. In *Studies in Extended Metapsychology: Clinical Applications of Bion's Ideas* (pp. 83–92). Pitlochry, Scotland: Clunie Press, for the Roland Harris Educational Trust. [Reprinted London: Karnac, 2009.]

Merleau-Ponty, M. (1968). *The Visible and the Invisible Studies in Phenomenology and Existential Philosophy*. Leforte, Claude (Ed.); Lingis, Alphonso (Trans.). Evanston: Northwestern University Press.

Molinari, E. (2024). *Binocular Vision: An Inquiry into Psychoanalytic Techniques and Field Theory*. London and New York: Routledge.

Ogden, T. H. (1991). Some theoretical comments on personal isolation. *Psychoanalytic Dialogues*, 1(3): 377–390.

Piontelli, A. (1987). Infant Observation from Before Birth. *Int. J. Psycho-Anal.*, 68: 453–463.

Sandler, J. (1960). The background of safety. *International Journal of Psycho-Analysis*, 41: 352–356.

Solms, M. (2013). The Conscious Id. *Neuropsychoanalysis*, 15: 5–19.

Winnicott, D. (1945). Primitive emotional development. In *Through Paediatrics to Psychoanalysis: Collected Papers*. New York: Basic Books, 1958.

Winnicott, D. W. (1949). Mind and its relations to the psyche-soma. *British Journal of Medical Psychology*, 27: 201–209. [Reprinted in *Through Paediatrics to Psychoanalysis: Collected Papers*. New York: Basic Books, 1958.]

Winnicott, D. W. (1969). The use of an object. *International Journal of Psycho-Analysis*, 50: 711–716. [Reprinted in *Playing and Reality*. London: Tavistock, 1971.]

Chapter 8

Perceptual Identification as Analytic Receptivity of Dissociative States

Analytic reverie is severely challenged when working with patients who have suffered early accumulated trauma – that is childhood trauma that was an aspect of their everyday lives from birth to emancipation from their families. Often these are the patients who come to us with life-long pain and frustration, but seemingly without feeling much of their childhood trauma. They can tell us many stories. They *know* they had a difficult childhood, but seemingly they have not *suffered* their pain (Bion, 1970). They have used primary dissociation, that is, separating their bodies from their minds (Bion, 1967; Lombardi, 2017; Goldberg, 2021; Eekhoff, 2021) to escape the pain and frustrations of their abuse. Primary dissociation involves precocious mental development that forecloses mind body cohesion and integration. Their emotions are also much reduced in that they seem unable to express or feel them. Sometimes they know this. Sometimes they do not. Often, they tell us something is missing in them. Sometimes they tell us they cannot love. More often still, they tell us they feel isolated, but are most comfortable being alone.

Goldberg (2021) describes what he calls *beta function*, the ongoing not-ever-to-be-represented body as background object. Although I would not use the words beta functioning, I believe he is describing a very important element of what it is to be embodied and the pleasure the body brings. In this chapter, I am focusing on the opposite of that: diffusion of the self and a defensive foregrounding of sensation that occurs in response to trauma. In using the body and the senses as defense, pleasure is lost as is a capacity for intimacy. Lack of representation is also both defensive and the result of an external attack that overrode the apparatus for thinking and interfered with its development. Without the capacities to represent relationship, complexity and depth of that which was experienced are lost (Bion, 1965). Lost also are the capacities to love and to grieve the loss of a love. As one patient asked me, "How I do I grieve something I have never had?" For these patients, primal dissociation of severing the body mind union is more prevalent than is dissociation via splitting and projective identification or repression. Each of these require an object. Primary dissociation forecloses the possibility of an

DOI: 10.4324/9781003544470-8

internal containing object and in doing so forecloses further development of a subjective sense of self.

For me, this dissociation occurring in infancy involves dispersal of the self via excessive splitting and projection into infinity instead of projection into an object (Eekhoff, 2021, pp. 5–6). States of primary undifferentiation result. These states appear to be primary narcissism, something neither Klein nor I believe in. Rather these undifferentiated states are defensive and the result of an overwhelming traumatic experience. Undifferentiation is accomplished by dissociation of body and mind, during which the mind becomes more important than the body, hence initiating precocious mental development that includes a premature cruel superego. Auto-sensuous defenses separate the person from his or her objects, reinforcing an unconscious phantasy of no objects available. Since trauma survivors use primal dissociation and primary undifferentiation as extra-ordinary protections (Mitrani, 2001), they also suffer from unmentalized states and unrepresented states. These are present, not as holding and containing background objects, but as an *unthought known* (Bollas, 1987) that persecutes.

When an adult patient seems to have primitive states wherein there is little differentiation between the internal world and the external world, chaos and violence reigns. As infants this lack of differentiation is more comfortable, especially if there is a good enough background of safety provided by the caregivers. In dissociating in order to survive their childhoods, these adults limit their possibility for growth and development. For as Bion (1970) says, "The patient who will not suffer pain fails to 'suffer' pleasure and this denies the patient the encouragement he might otherwise receive from accidental or intrinsic relief" (p. 9). Since projective identification can be a means of communicating and receiving help in dealing with unprocessed pain, it is an important part of coping with difficult circumstances. We know he also says that projective identification is the foundation for thinking and that it can be disrupted, thus disturbing the development of thinking itself. He (Bion, 1958) says,

> In some patients the denial to the patient of a normal employment of projective identification precipitates a disaster through the destruction of an important link. Inherent in this disaster is the establishment of a primitive superego which denies the use of projective identification.
>
> (p. 146)

When parents are the cause of accumulated childhood trauma, they are denying their children the use of themselves as receptors of projective identifications. Their children cannot communicate their pain, even unconsciously via projective identification. This ultimately disrupts these projective and introjective processes. Children subsequently develop premature superegos and internalize obstructive objects (Bion, 1958; Eaton, 2005; Skogstad, 2013). Bion (1967) says they prematurely become aware of their own personalities.

I use prenatal and postnatal infantile experience as a model for the work we do with these patients. I do not equate the adult with the infant or even attempt to have the patient regress to infancy. That infancy is always present in the hour. Again, quoting Bion (1994),

> Winnicott says patients need to regress: Melanie Klein says they must not: I say they are regressed, and the regression should be observed and interpreted by the analyst without any need to compel the patient to become totally regressed before he can make the analyst observe and interpret the regression.
>
> (p. 166)

For me, this implies that an analyst will be able to use reverie as a means of anticipating a patient's response to an interpretation. This is not necessarily via the reception of projective identifications, rather it may come through adhesive identifications. This requires the analyst's unconscious use of perceptual identification.

Sometimes the unconscious-to-unconscious reception occurs via reverberations or resonances that are discovered in the body of the analyst. These impressions present as somatic counter-transference. These are derivatives of impressions or traces of experience that have not been mentalized. However, I also believe that not every analysand/analyst dyad is a good fit for each member.

In health, the mother's love for her unborn and newly-born infant is communicated via her reverie. Her joy, passion, and awe at the mystery of life invoke representation and a rich mental life in her infant. It impacts the infant's growing ability to dream meaning into experience (Monteiro, 2023, p. 128). I believe infants are born object related even though their primary mode of relating is body relations. During nursing the infant is taking in the body relations and the object relations of its mother. Along with milk comes the mother's love or hate, and it is this emotional link that enables the infant's mind to be called forth in a healthy relational manner.

Trauma disrupts this process and object relations. Traumatized infants and children retreat to their bodies as defense. Their body relations are proximate and sensual, without bringing pleasure; sensations and sensory perceptions dominate as defense. At the same time, they may also persecute, resulting in hypersensitivity that feels like too much for them. This results in a loss of the object and inhibition of introjection. Without awareness of the other, the budding subjective sense of self is also delayed. The *primal dissociation* of soma and psyche protects these trauma survivors from awareness of being projected into and not received.

With accumulated childhood trauma, both the mental apparatus for processing relationships and the emotional complexity of being human is compromised. This means that projective and introjective processes that are the foundation for future thinking become inadequate. As Bion (1965) says, "The growth of insight depends, at its inception, on undisturbed functioning of projective identification" (p. 36). Patients who were abused as young children and who use primal dissociation and undifferentiation as defenses have retreated from parents who seemingly were *obstructive objects* (Bion, 1958; Eaton, 2005) – that is, they did not often enough receive their infant's projective identifications through their reverie. Bion (1970) says the way a mother shows her love for her infant is by reverie: "...when a mother loves the infant what does she do it with? Leaving aside the physical channels of communication my impression is that her love is expressed by reverie" (pp. 35–36).

An analyst working with a person who does not always split and project and then re-introject with proficiency faces challenges to his or her imaginative conjecture, receptive openness, and even the unconscious communication such processes promote. Reverie in the face of a psychically absent other, such as the primally dissociative patient I am describing, is difficult. Without receiving the expected emotional contact from the patient in the form of projective identifications, interpreting the transference can become a mental activity, not one of intuitive understanding. This is a repetition of the primal dissociation of the patient and evidence of an obstructive internal object in the analyst who does not notice the lack of connection and/or in the patient who bounces the analyst's projective-identification-as-communication back. The obstructive object can be in either the patient or the analyst or both.

In instances where projective processes are damaged, I believe we do the best we can, using our reverie and our openness to 'find' the person with us. Bergstein (2019, p. 39), quoting Meltzer "...in these unmentalized states, the analyst must be capable of imaginative thought, or dream-thought, that embraces the intra-uterine experience as a 'world' quite different from the 'world' of projective identification" (Meltzer, 1986, p. 36). The world these patients bring us is a world we must enter if we are to be of service. This is a world of body relations, of synchrony and rhythmicity, of sound and sensation. It is a world of music and dance. It is a mysterious world outside of the symbolic order.

When our receptivity and openness, important analytic values, are met with indifference and seemingly little response, we can fall back upon Bion's belief that "Receptiveness achieved by denudation of memory and desire (which is essential to the operation of 'acts of faith') is essential to the operation of psychoanalysis and other scientific proceedings. It is essential for experiencing hallucination or the state of hallucinosis" (Bion, 1970, pp. 35–36). Hallucinosis is an aspect of everyday analytic work (Civitarese, 2012; 2015). However, analysts often find such a state uncomfortable and threatening, since it can evoke a feeling of not existing psychically for themselves or for the patient. Included in this may be the analyst's own defensive blockage of psychic aliveness.

When it seems that we do not psychically exist for our patients, our own narcissistic needs to exist interfere with disciplined stances of no memory and desire. Mind takes over and analysts can be drawn into thinking too much.

Such thinking interferes with reverie. For example, when this happens to me, I find myself thinking about theory or watch myself observing and mentally describing what is happening. I talk to myself, "Remember this. What is happening here?" These side trips away from my patient are important means of holding myself, but that is the point. They are not the result of my receptivity of unconscious communication, or of projective identification, or even of psychic deadness coming from my patient – not that all those things do not also happen. Such 'side trips' are not a reverie to be used for understanding my patient. However, they are an hallucinosis – a state where I become my dissociated patient and am no longer embodied. I then become an obstructive object.

There can be words coming from both patient and analyst. Sometimes there are too many words. Words can be used as shields, sounds not to be interpreted for their content but for their auto-sensuous function of protection. Some of these words are more than mimicry or self-soothing, but finding the symbols of truth beneath the mimicry and self-soothing can be difficult. Sifting through the debris and sounds of words might put the analyst into an experience of being the patient.

Again, for me such an experience is terrifying because at once, I am witness to my patient's self- annihilation even as I myself am being obliterated. Further, this symbiosis seems to happen in the presence of the other without effort, passively. At the most primal level, symbiosis does not include violence or attacks on the psyche. It occurs via bodily proximity, even on screen. It is in the sensual link, the symbiotic link between patient and analyst. Hence it is the arena of perceptual identity and primary process. Symbiosis is a foundational experience, found in all of us (Bleger, 1967), however it can be and is also used defensively.

One could say analytic symbiosis is akin to maternal preoccupation, but not quite. It is outside of awareness until it can be gathered and slowly, over time, named and described. This is the bodily gathering of the transference (Meltzer, 1986). Goldberg (2021) believes that some of these bodily sensations are never to be named – but serve as beta functions – like a backdrop to the self. My language for this is slightly different, but if I understand him correctly, this arena of the self – undifferentiated and undrawn, but none-the-less present, is backdrop for us all. I believe Bleger (1967) is also exploring this primal position of the self, which is a body relation filled with sensuous pleasure in the physical sound and sensation of another. That is the healthy aspect.

Rather now, I am writing about, trying to find words for, a primal dissociative state of nonexistence that includes few represented and few projected states. It is the arena of experience of the *unrepressed unconscious*. If the unconscious is conscious (Bion, 1970; Bergstein, 2019), without a repression barrier or a contact barrier as protection, there is no need for projection. There is also little opportunity to use projective identification as a means of communication because undifferentiation between self and other wipes out an object to project into. Without an object, the projection into the universe that occurs can only be used to rid the psyche of debris. The primal dissociative state becomes a background of the self and what is presented is behavior without true relationship. If I am correct, this helps us understand the force that keeps trauma alive year after year, seemingly without diminishment.

When patients have withdrawn so far into themselves or exploded into infinite space, it is very hard to be with them. It is difficult to be open and receptive to the nothingness of mindless states. This is true especially when the patient is able to present a false self or an as-if self of mimicry. I believe that whereas patience and non-intrusiveness are extremely important, so too is calling a patient forth, saying "Come, come" (Eekhoff 2019; 2021) or "Hey, there" (Alvarez, 1992). This is done by remaining in the here and now with the mystery and awe of getting to know this other person and being actively engaged.

Clinical Example: Dennis

Let me tell you of a patient and my attempts to find him. I have written of him before (see Chapter 4) as an example of primal hope. Of course, this story that I tell of him does not begin to convey the truth of our meetings. There was so much more than anything I might say. The mystery and depth of our work cannot be described.

Dennis is now in his 80s. He came to me when he was 74. Initially, I was not sure why he came. His attempts to describe his need for a second analysis were vague. I registered his ambivalence: he told me he had called me several times in the past ten years, listening to my voice but not leaving a message. He said my voice was "too deep". After our first visit, he asked for a referral, telling me "You are too far away". A month later, he returned, saying he wanted to work with me. He was a pleasant, well-groomed man who seemingly engaged easily. Since he was retired from a good job, he felt he had time to get to know himself better.

Dennis was college educated but reported, "It took me a few extra years because I had difficulty remembering things and I couldn't think". As with everything else he told me in these beginning years, his voice was calm and matter-of-fact. He reported without feeling. He told me he decided to come now, "because my cat died". He had had a previous ten-year experience in college with analytic group therapy. This ended when the analyst died. Later he had a nine-year analysis as well as a ten-year live-in relationship with a man who died of AIDS. He reported without feeling, although he described both of these later relationships as bad for him. I noticed that he seemed to almost equate his former analyst with his live-in partner. We began at once a week, soon moved to twice a week, and then to three times a week. He did not use the couch, "because I don't like women".

I began to fear the work we were doing, since I imagined he would suffer greatly if we connected deeply and emotionally, as is usual in analysis. This fear of mine, I believe, was the first evidence that he was beginning to project into me and to make use of me. But I worried. Would analysis only make him suffer? Would he die before our work was finished? He was so determined to be 'better', but I did not think he knew what that would require.

I learned that Dennis was an unwelcome child (Ferenczi, 1929; Eekhoff, 2022). He was the fourth child and the third boy. Purportedly, according to family myth, his mother wanted another girl and thrust the infant back at the nurses with disgust, telling them to keep him. Three other children followed – all girls. The home he was born into was not a happy one. His parents fought continually, and the children were frequent victims of physical and emotional abuse, from their parents and from each other. Much later, he told me several of his sisters had accused their father of sexual abuse. He didn't know if it was true or not, but concluded anything was possible in that house. Dennis described his childhood home as a "house of horrors". He did not bring friends there.

School was escape for him, but he did not do particularly well. He said he always had trouble concentrating and lived in a dream world. He focused on having friends, many of them girls. He also took refuge at his grandmother's house who claimed him as her favorite. In spite of seemingly being a 'good boy', he described getting beaten by both parents. I did not ask for these stories. They were part of the script Dennis believed every analyst wanted.

When I remarked on our process, he would sometimes look confused. He told me I talked more than his first analyst did, which made him doubt our work was anything but social. He regretted that he had used the couch or stayed so long with his former analyst. He did not want to make the same mistake with me. He described being paranoid and obsessive, because his first analyst had told him he was. Apparently, he had also been told that there was no treatment for either paranoia or obsessiveness.

When I attempted to interpret the transference, he would continue talking as if I had said nothing. If I commented, he would say, "This isn't about you". When I said he seemed to want me to know all of his history, he said his first analyst did. So did his second. If I attempted to add to what he was saying, he would say, "I didn't say that". There was no rancor in his voice. He was merely stating the fact. He seemed to have no idea that two analysts were not the same or that a conversation could build on itself, with each participant contributing and elaborating an idea or a feeling. I began to think that he was not in relationship with me because there was really only room for one of us. Should he become aware of me, I could only become identified as an aggressor (Ferenczi, 1933. This would interfere with his purpose.

I am not sure how long it took me to recognize that when I spoke, he would dissociate. The difficulty was that if I didn't, he would dissociate too. Silences were difficult for him because he told me he fell into "mindless places". Previously (see Chapter 4), I described him as blinking on and off like Christmas tree lights, but this coming and going was not splitting. Rather it was what Ferenczi (1932) has called *atomization*. He was dissolving or evaporating in front of me and seemingly without form. In those moments, he was experiencing *"objectless sensation"* (Ferenczi, 1920–1932) as well as an *inhibited attempt at splitting* (Ferenczi, 1920–1932). He con-formed with me, taking shape via the setting of my office (Bleger, 1967). He began to speak about my office, describing it and missing it when he was not there. He said, "When I am in your room, I feel I am in my lower garden where I have room to feel these things". When I said he equated my office with me, he just looked at me, blinking. After a while he said, "Maybe". Today, I might say he equated my office with his garden, alive. He did not seem to equate my office with me. I was not yet a person to him.

He displayed little agency and seemed extremely passive. His primary activity other than his analysis was working out three or four hours a day at a local gym. He also continued to read his many books on psychoanalysis and to talk to me about Karen Horney. Once he said, "You know you look like her, don't you?" Another time he described listening to her on YouTube and told me "You sound like her". Here again we have evidence of equating two people in an almost hallucinatory manner.

As I began to experience his dissociation, I felt increasingly upset by it. I could never be sure if he heard me or even registered my presence, although he watched me intensely. On the one hand, he appeared alert, almost hyper-vigilant and hyper-sensitive to changes in the frame. On the other, he appeared indifferent and very young, almost newborn or even unborn. Sometimes, his rapid blinking would turn into a stare. I began intuitively to describe what was happening in the room, in the atmosphere, so to speak. Whenever I told him it was time to end our session, he would abruptly rise and exit, without looking back.

Once, when Seattle suffered a major snow-storm, he came anyway in spite of his fear of driving. Later, I went outside to get the mail, and discovered someone had shoveled my sidewalk and driveway. It was he.

There are many things I could say about Dennis, but I want to focus on an important aspect of our work together. Our relationship was seemingly devoid of feeling. I found working with him pleasant, but not initially sti-mulating. I also did not feel as if I 'received' any projections from him. Nor was I bored or sleepy or even confused. I was mildly curious as to why he was with me. In the initial stage, it seemed he was repeating what he had told his previous analysts.

Slowly, our relationship came into being. Once he told me he had read about dissociation and realized that he had been "gone my whole life". He wanted to be real and spontaneous, but he could not imagine how that was possible if he were gone. He said I talked to him as if he were present and he was grateful for that.

In the second phase, he began to have many somatic symptoms. I will let you get a sense of his voice:

P: I have been psychically dead all my life. You told me dissociation was a type of death and I did not want to hear you, but now I agree.

A: You are having good insights, using your stress to come alive, and breaking your routines opens the possibility for more spontaneity.

P: It makes sense, but uh...first I thought the headaches were physical. I thought it was a tumor or cancer of some kind.

   And I ache all over.

A: You are afraid of dying now that you are coming alive.

P: Yes, I have a red mark on my skin. I also fear I am going blind.

   You know I am taking very seriously things I didn't take seriously before. The other day walking around my yard loving the flowers, I asked myself what kind of person am I? But I am being more spontaneous.

   (Silent) Lots of bad stuff is coming up too. I used to say, it's just my unconscious.

   (Silent)...but I can do a lot. It is me, and I can do something with what comes up...it is me.

   I think about my psychic death, how I died and changed, not for the better.

Gradually over time, our relationship deepened. He began to bring me dreams and he began to grieve his past. He rarely cried, but he described crying at home. Always I was impressed how he would take these horrible feelings of pain and dread and say, "It must be good that I can feel this now".

He remembered a day when his father had demanded that he and the girls dig a basement under the house. This had been going on for months and his parents fought about it. The chimney actually began to tilt, so he said, due to their digging. The girls said they weren't going to dig anymore and their father went after them with a shovel. Dennis stepped in and got knocked to the ground while the girls ran away. Afterwards, he ran away too. He was given a ride to another part of town by his older brother. He said he was frightened. Then he accidentally saw his mother in front of the grocery store. He told me, "And I felt my soul leave my body". When he returned home, he went to the edge of his garden, looking down on the neighboring houses and shouted, "Can't anyone see what is happening here? Help us! Help us!" No one came.

Another time when he told this story, he added:

She saw me and had a goofy look on her face, was no help to me at all and that is when I had that experience; missing something. Thinking about my life... and authenticity chipped away year after year and hardly anything left...the effect they had on me emotionally, ...and how I could not cover it up...my friends must have seen it, but I do not think their souls left their bodies and they weren't being beaten and stuff.

In fact, previously Dennis had told me something was missing in him. He didn't know what was missing, but he thought it had something to do with not being real. I commented on how each time he told me his stories, they were different. He was moved, saying his former analyst thought he was obsessive, going over and over things again and again. He laughed, "Sounds obsessive to me". I said it was sometimes difficult to notice little changes, that sometimes he has a hint of a feeling in his words. He laughed and said, "Not me".

Dennis came alive, and was able to describe mood changes within a single day, something that surprised him. He always brought me dreams, having learned they told him about himself. Then he told me of a day following one of our sessions: he suddenly noticed that he no longer felt something was missing in him: "I felt solid, like I have an inside. I walked around the house saying, I am alive. I am alive". He began to play Elvis music on his recorder and to dance.

Accompanied by himself now, he began to notice his dissociations. With analysis, he began to observe what had happened just prior to them. More and more he felt himself and in doing so, felt his need for contact with others. He said, "It is hard to explain. I always knew what happened to me but now when I think of it, I feel it. I feel lots of things now, not like before". He deepened relationships and made new friends. He stayed in touch with his siblings. He told me how much he valued his first analysts and that he loved his partner. Much more could be said, but I am writing specifically about his primal dissociations.

Discussion

Dissociation is a valuable ability. We all use it to help us focus and to facilitate our creativity. I believe differing forms of dissociation can be found in each of the psychic positions – primal, paranoid-schizoid, and depressive (Eekhoff, 2021). In excess, primal dissociation takes the life out of the psyche due to the extreme separation of soma and psyche. It interferes with the development of projective identification and an apparatus for thinking.

Receptivity seems an insufficient word to use in describing how I found Dennis. If he was not transmitting truth via projective identification, but rather maintaining stasis as a means of ridding himself of excess stimulation, how could I find him? If I mistakenly believed he was projectively identifying with me as a possible container for him, I might have been confused for a very long time. I would be mistaking my imaginings as coming from him. My illusion of at-one-ment with him would be my hallucination and delusion. Symbiotic at-one-ment in the hour must be of my experience of the two of us in whatever primal place we are. It enables growth in both participants.

Dennis was good at self-observation which he reported to me. He was not so good at self-reflection. His observations allowed me to reflect on our process and slowly over time to report it. This could be risky, since as I had to constantly guard against providing more material for mimicry. Analysts since Freud have known this: Bergstein (2019) quoting Freud, "When the patient runs out of associations…we intervene on our own; we fill in the hints, draw undeniable conclusions, and give explicit utterances to what the patient only touched on in his associations" (Freud, 1933, p. 12). When Dennis ran out of associations, which was frequent, he often simultaneously lost contact with me as a separate other. I became a symbolic equation at best. Our contact was proximal, only at a physical concrete level. At first, I thought this was his distancing from me, but I came to understand in that moment that he was lost to himself. He was dissociating body from mind, and lost contact with himself, having no sensorial awareness. Differentiation of himself from me too was lost.

Since often these patients are so concrete as to be unable to associate, the filling in happens unconsciously first at the level of bodily relations (Bleger, 1967). Even when the patient and the analyst are speaking to each other, it is the sound and rhythm of the speech that is of primary importance. There is not aggression or defense since the union forecloses an awareness of twoness. The interaction merely is concrete, material, true in a physical manner. Any elaboration by the analyst is not possible under those circumstances, because as I reported earlier, the patient will say, "I didn't say that". Such a concrete comment is evidence of a difficulty in thinking and learning from experience (Bion, 1962a; 1962b). As Goldberg (2021) says "where there is dissociation, the function of association is disabled. This means that the therapeutic function of receptivity and introjective identification are much reduced in the treatment of dissociation" (p. 125).

Conclusion

Using a clinical case, I have described somato-psychic dissociative states that foreclose meaning-making rather than use the sensual to find meaning. Such states, when shared in the analytic hour, can be transformed so that experience is not only observable but can be reflected upon and used for the coherence and development of the self. Learning from experience is then possible.

I have described a kind of analytic reverie that includes physical proximity, sensation and sound, and rhythm and synchronicity. I have used Bleger's (1967) description of this as symbiotic. Being receptive of primal states of mind requires the perception of bodily experience. These states are always nonverbal, and in fact may never be fully symbolized in language. Receptivity via a body relation also requires the analyst be present and attuned not to the symbolic order but to the perceptual order of immediate experience. Perceptual identity of both patient and analyst enables growth. Analytic receptivity enables previously unrepresented and poorly represented states to move from presentations of experience to representations of experience.

References

Alvarez, A. (1992). *Live Company.* London: Routledge.

Bergstein, A. (2019). *Bion and Meltzer's Expeditions into Unmapped Mental Life, Beyond the Spectrum in Psychoanalysis.* London and New York: Routledge.

Bion, W. R. (1958). On Arrogance. *International Journal of Psycho-Analysis*, 39: 144–146.

Bion, W. R. (1962a). A psycho-analytic theory of thinking. *International Journal of Psycho-Analysis*, 43: 306–310. [Reprinted as "A theory of thinking", in Bion, W. R., *Second Thoughts* (pp. 110–119). London: Karnac, 1984.]

Bion, W. R. (1962b). *Learning from Experience.* London: Heinemann. [Reprinted London: Karnac, 1984.]

Bion, W. R. (1965). *Transformations.* London: Heinemann. [Reprinted London: Karnac, 1984.]

Bion, W. R. (1967). *Wilford Bion: Los Angeles Seminars and Supervision.* Aguayo, J. and Malin, B. (Eds.). London and New York: Routledge, 2013.

Bion, W. R. (1970). *Attention and Interpretation.* London: Tavistock. [Reprinted London: Karnac, 1984.]

Bion, W. R. (1992). *Cogitations.* New extended edition. London: Karnac.

Bleger, J. (1967). *Symbiosis and Ambiguity: A psychoanalytic study.* Churcher, J. and Bleger, L. (Eds.); Rogers, S., Bleger, L., and Churcher, J. (Trans.). London and New York: Routledge, 2013.

Bollas, C. (1987). *The Shadow of the Object: Psychoanalysis of the Unthought Known.* London: Free Association Books.

Civitarese, G. (2012). *The Violence of Emotions: Bion and Post-Bionian Psychoanalysis.* London and New York: Routledge.

Civitarese, G. (2015). Transformations in hallucinosis and the receptivity of the analyst. *International Journal of Psycho-Analysis*, 96: 1091–1116.

Eaton, J. L. (2005). The obstructive object. *Psychoanalytic Review*, 92(3): 355–372.

Eekhoff, J. K. (2019). *Trauma and Primitive Mental States: An Object Relations Perspective.* London and New York: Routledge.

Eekhoff, J. K. (2021). *Bion and Primitive Mental States: Trauma and the Symbiotic Link.* London and New York: Routledge.

Eekhoff, J. K. (2022). The Unwelcome Child and the Acceptance of New Ideas. *American Journal of Psychoanalysis*, 82(4).

Ferenczi, S. (1920–1932). Notes and fragments. In *Final Contributions to the Problems and Methods of Psycho-Analysis* (pp. 216–279). London: Karnac, 1955. [Reprinted London: Karnac, 1994.]

Ferenczi, S. (1929). The unwelcome child and his death-instinct. *International Journal of Psycho-Analysis*, 10: 125–129. [Reprinted in *Final Contributions to the Problems and Methods of Psycho-Analysis* (pp. 102–107). London: Karnac, 1994.]

Ferenczi, S. (1932). 14 June 1932. Permanent disturbance of object-libido. In *The Clinical Diary of Sándor Ferenczi* (pp. 122–124). Dupont, J. (Ed.); Balint, M. and Jackson, N. Z. (Trans.). Cambridge, MA: Harvard University Press, 1985.

Ferenczi, S. (1933). Confusion of the tongues between the adults and the child—(The language of tenderness and of passion). In *Final Contributions to the Problems and Methods of Psycho-Analysis* (pp. 156–167). London: Karnac, 1994.

Goldberg, P. (2021). Embodiment, dissociation, and the rhythm of life. In Harrang, C., Tillotson, D., and Winters, N. C. (Eds.), *Body as Psychoanalytic Object: Clinical*

Applications from Winnicott to Bion and Beyond (pp. 118–133). Oxford and New York: Routledge.

Lombardi, R. (2017). *Body-Mind Dissociation in Psychoanalysis: Development after Bion.* Oxford and New York: Routledge.

Meltzer, D. (1986). *Studies in Extended Metapsychology.* London: Karnac Books.

Mitrani, J. L. (2001). *Ordinary People and Extra-ordinary Protections.* New Library of Psychoanalysis. Philadelphia: Brunner-Routledge.

Monteiro, J. Sousa (2023). *Bion's Theory of Dreams: A Visionary Model of the Mind.* Oxford and New York: Routledge.

Skogstad, W. (2013). Impervious and intrusive: the Impenetrable Object in Transference and Countertransference. *International Journal of Psychoanalysis*, 94: 221–238.

Chapter 9

Between the Real and the Imaginary

Truth and Lies in the Psychoanalytic Encounter

Actual reality is unknowable. The reality we do know, and often vehemently declare *is* real, is filtered through imagination. Our imagination links conscious and unconscious somatopsychic processes. Our sensations, which we claim to know, are filtered through the process of perceiving. All perceptions are mediated by our imaginative mind. Awareness of internal and external reality as facilitated by our consciousness differs radically from one person to another. No two people experience the same event in the same way due to this somatopsychic sifting of experience.

Our consciousness effects where we place our attention and how we interpret what we notice. At the same time, in our deep unconscious – that is, in our somatic processes which are the essence of our being – we are symbiotically attached to our intimate others (Bleger, 1967). Bion (1971) says the real and imaginary occur when two parallel lives meet in the sensual domain. To me, this means we are always in relationship to our internal and external objects, even when it may appear otherwise. These internal and external body relations and object relations impact our experience of reality via imagination.

Although the real and the imaginary are inseparable in practice (Eekhoff, 2022a), keeping them differentiated or apart psychologically is necessary for our sanity. What I'm suggesting is that sanity itself is dependent upon the relationship between the two. The real and the imaginary must be psychologically separate enough for a relationship between them to be possible. At the same time, they must be related for psychic dimensionality to develop. Similarly, maintaining a sense of sanity is dependent upon our experience of reality and unconscious processing of experience. The real and the imaginary are equal aspects of being human.

If one is terrified of the real, without access to imagination, life becomes concrete and practical with a concomitant reduced capacity for emotional interpretation of experience. Often patients who have been physically or sexually abused in early childhood cannot accept the emotional reality of their experiences. They dissociate what they know to have been a reality from emotional or bodily responses to those experiences. This bodymind dissociation enables them to function operationally in the world. Their lives, while

DOI: 10.4324/9781003544470-9

efficient, may be experienced as dull or flat. Others may describe these persons as two dimensional and uninteresting.

On the other hand, if one is persecuted by reality, this may drive one toward living excessively in the imaginative realm. Life might then become difficult to manage because of imaginative eccentricities. The stereotype of the absent-minded professor or the artist who needs a partner to manage the practical aspects of life comes to mind. Too much imagination, with one's head in the clouds, means a common-sense view of reality is lost.

Since actual reality is purportedly the foundation for emotional truth, truth itself is unknowable. Unknowable truth is a reality beyond personal differences and outside of universal agreement. Bion (1965; 1970) designated actual reality and unknowable truth as 'O'. 'O' or Origin exists outside of our capacity to comprehend it. 'O' is the emotional reality of the unknown and the unknowable, of the unspoken and the unspeakable. We may at moments glimpse it. Actual reality is infinite and the comprehension of 'O' impossible. Bion (1965) says, "The thing in itself is not mediated by the senses which means that it is the unknown…the essence is not known because all of our perceptions come into it" (p. 4). The moment our perceptions come into the sensorium, sensual experience becomes a construction of the mind. At that moment, we become uniquely ourselves.

Even though psychic reality is a somatopsychic construction, reality is not exclusively subjective. Material reality is knowable though our senses. Psychic reality is not. Furthermore, there is an illusion that we can control what we experience with our senses. For example, we can turn away, change directions, shut off the radio. We cannot control our imaginations, which are the end result of a dream process we cannot alter (Monteiro, 2023). Psychic existential reality is a mix of the real and the imaginary. It is a dynamic somatopsychic process of the relationship between the two. Our psychic existential realities are simultaneous and multiple, not a once and forever static thing. They are mysterious and unknowable except as derivatives of our own somatopsychic construction.

Truth in Transit

Generally, we have a consensus or common-sense agreement that allows individuals, couples, families, cultures, and nations to come together. Common sense, in the ordinary meaning of the term, refers to an agreed-upon reality amongst humans who live together. Our humanity unites us as we explore our emotional experiences of living. With consensus between individuals in relationship, the real and the imaginary come together in agreed-upon terms.

The most obvious way consensus is acknowledged is through language. Words typically have shared meanings. When we communicate with each other via language we share an illusion of understanding. Even though each of us uses words laden with our own perceptions, we presume that we are using words in the same way our listener is using them. Of course, language is limiting; and mutual understanding of the words we use is limited. This is equally true in the field of psychoanalysis. As Bion (1994) says, "for different people the same words have in addition to their common meaning, a different penumbra of associations" (p. 63). Whereas, this is true of concrete descriptive words, such as dog or horse, blue or green, the 'penumbra of associations' about emotional words that link, such as love, hate, and curiosity, is more difficult to ascertain. Associations to words enrich emotional experience, while propelling differentiation and individuation. Idiosyncratic associations to emotional words create confusion or agreement based on misunderstanding. Common-sense associations enable us to understand each other.

When using common sense and finding ourselves in an agreed-upon order, psychic reality and the ability to stay psychically alive, healthy, and related to one another becomes satisfying. Our psychic emotional vibrancy enhances how we function in the world. It facilitates love, laughter, and life itself. When these characteristics are integrated into our sense of being, we feel passionately alive. Then, we are able to dream ourselves into being. Meltzer (1984) succinctly describes this process when he says "it is the poetry of the dream that catches and gives formal representation to the passions which *are* the meaning of our experience so that they may be operated upon by reason" (p. 47). Monteiro (2023) summarizes this beautifully, noting how dreaming ourselves into being is an ongoing bodymind process that involves inner relatedness.

We experience the dynamic emotional truth of personal inner relatedness. Inner relatedness involves simultaneous multiple states of being and states of mind. Inner relatedness creates cohesion and includes communication of self-with-self that is outside of language (Bion, 1958b). This is our dreaming process, present from birth and most likely beforehand as well (Monteiro, 2023). The dreaming process and the meaning it brings is continually changing. Bergstein (2015; 2019) names this "truth in transit". This personal emotional truth is verified via intersubjective relationships with others. These relationships of being are embedded in very personal histories of each member of the couple or dyad. Included in this history is the primary relationship of the infant at the breast or the child-in-the-adult for each person of the dyad. This dynamic of continually changing personal 'truth in transit' is the focus of this chapter.

Truth and Lies

Common sense requires a relationship between emotional truth and the somatopsychic acceptance of both material reality and emotional reality. Lies interfere with the spaces between reality and imagination, between inside and outside the psychesoma. Lies collapse the common order. The word 'lies' may be thought of as a conscious manipulation of truth. I am not using the word in this way. I am speaking of the unconscious disguises, deceits, and distortions we use in order to escape an unbearable pain of facing an overwhelming personal emotional truth.

The lies we unconsciously tell ourselves are dangerous because they affect the ways in which we organize experience in order to make meaning of it. There can be no experience of reality without an organizing perspective. All perspective is subjective. Perspective requires a gap, a space, a distance between the observer and the observed, between the "thing-in-itself" (Bion, 1962b) and the awareness of emotional experience. Imagination also requires a distance from reality. When the real and the imaginary are not distinguished, psychic space is diminished. Perspective is lost and truth becomes a lie. When the psychic distance between the real and the imaginary collapses, ordinary material reality and common sense is lost. Depending upon the severity of emotional illness, common sense may be momentarily lost, or in cases of autistic retreat or psychotic processing, it may be seemingly gone. In such circumstances, the patient believes it is also gone in the analyst; that is, that the analyst's mind operates in the same manner as the patient's (Bion, 1958b).

With the loss of common sense, confidence that we know what is real is diminished or lost. Corrosive doubt emerges. Blurring the boundary between truth and lies creates confusion and despair, while covering unbearable psychic pain. It is a protection that has a terrible cost in emotional relationships and personal satisfaction. The emotional links of love, hate, and curiosity become perverted.

Bion's New Idea

Bion (1965; 1970) helps us to understand the mental processes involved in using imagination to make sense of reality. Further, he helps us to grasp our experiences of these processes. Patients who present primitive material in analytic sessions require much of their analysts. Bion (1971) says,

> The analysand operating on a primitive level comes close to acting on the principle of "act first, think later". Usually, the analysand in such an episode is acting in relationship with the analyst as if, to put it in a mixture of real and imaginary terms, an extremely active, flexible and speedy unconscious were being pursued by a slow, rigid, lumbering conscious.
>
> (pp. 25–26)

Further, he links the processing of emotional experience with mental health. If emotions are not processed, they can only be evacuated or take the form of hallucinations, delusions, and somatic symptoms (Bion, 1958b). When this happens, unprocessed raw emotions interfere with the development of a thinking mind.

Bion (1962b) describes the emotion-to-thinking process saying,

> Alpha-function transforms sense impressions into alpha-elements which resemble, and may in fact be identical with, the visual images with which

we are familiar in dreams, namely, the elements that Freud regards as yielding their latent content when the analyst has interpreted them.

(p. 7)

The visual image becomes a mediating symbol between the emotional experience and the *unknowable truth we cannot bear*. The image – a product of emotional imagination – leads us to the use of language and speech for the purpose of communicating. I am referring here to both inner and outer speech. This process is foundational and inherent in the drive to communicate (Bergstein, 2015; 2019).

Bion's (1965; 1970) idea that *minds require truth in order to develop* is, in my view, unsettling and disturbing. Disturbing because he is telling us we need to grow a mind in order to cope with emotional reality. Our minds are too vast to hold themselves; they do not function in isolation. Without another mind, we leak, spill, evaporate, split, fragment, and explode. Or, if we are less traumatized by experience, we may distort, deny, and minimize. In order to grow a mind, we need the mediating mind of another. Without such emotional contact, our primitive agonies force us to dissociate, distort, and deceive ourselves.

In order to keep dreaming ourselves into existence, we need the order and organization another bodymind provides. We also require another to enable meaning-making. Without reverie – that is, the alpha function of another bodymind (originally the mother) – we cannot contain the infinite experience of being (Bion, 1965). Actual reality comes in too soon and is too much. Without mediation, outside reality impinges upon our psychic perceptions of reality and we become disoriented. We become lost in the chaos of infinite experience. Associations become idiosyncratic and we begin to doubt what is real. Even a sane person hallucinates when reality is too much.

I think of a patient, 'Dennis', who was severely emotionally and physically abused as a child. I have written of him previously in Chapters 4 and 8, Dennis had told me the following story many times. He was grateful each time that I wanted to hear his experience again. Each time, I noticed something slightly different in his story. The words were almost always the same, but their expression varied. In this particular instance, he shared his experience in a new way, with new words. His father had required him and his sisters to dig an additional basement under their home. His sisters who were younger than he, got tired and threw down their shovels and walked away. His father grabbed a shovel and went after them. Dennis stepped in, telling his father to stop. His father punched him hard in the face, knocking him to the ground. The pain, he told me, was indescribable. Such is the story Dennis had recounted many times.

This time, Dennis said that he too ran away but not to get away from his father. He ran to the house and into the bathroom in order to see himself. Upon being hit, Dennis experienced his face as becoming distorted. His jaw and mouth went sideways, separating from his eyes and forehead. His face stayed that way. He was horrified, feeling he was permanently deformed. When he looked in the mirror, he saw the truth that his face though battered, was *not* deformed. He could barely believe what he saw, still feeling he was deformed for life. Then he ran away from home.

Dennis' experience illustrates how difficult it can be to differentiate emotional truth from concrete reality and a lie we tell ourselves. When our inside world does not match the outside world, we cannot believe our own experience; we psychically scramble in order to make the two relate to each other. Sometimes, we have to dissociate and create an alternate reality as Dennis did in order to cope.

If we can tolerate the frustration of dissonance between our inner and outer associations, our personal relationships with ourselves and others will be creative and passionate. Mystery and wonder can be tolerated. We will learn from our experiences (Bion, 1962b), embedding them in who we are and what we feel. This is how we become multidimensional humans with depth and scope, firmly embedded in our emotional relationships with others. If we can tolerate frustration, we can grow.

When our internal and external worlds do not match, we become disturbed. If we are unable to tolerate the frustration of that disturbance, we may lie to ourselves and ultimately to others, thus impeding communication and understanding (Bion, 1970, p. 60). When communication is disrupted, emotional upset disturbs psychic balance. If we cannot tolerate the frustration of not knowing, we cannot use the process of thinking to problem solve. Our psychic equilibrium becomes further compromised.

Tolerating frustration does something else: it creates an opportunity for *authentic pleasure* (Rezze and Braga, 2019). Authentic pleasure is a moment of intense satisfaction when the inside and the outside, the real and the imaginary, unite. I agree with these authors when they note that intense satisfaction can indicate moments of at-one-ness and internal coherence. This is a moment of transformation in 'O' and of becoming 'O'. There is momentary contact with truth and beauty. Furthermore, authentic pleasure, like passion, is a moment of integration of the emotional links of love, hate, and knowledge (Chapter 2). Passion integrates because "passion is evidence that two minds are linked" (Bion, 1963, p. 13). Authentic pleasure is linked with passion.

The Patient Who Did Not Exist

It might be useful to think of the following excerpts from sessions with a patient who originally came to treatment suffering from post-partum depression after the birth of her third child and haunted by the ghost of her second child. Her live baby grieved her; her dead baby from 18 months previously was still *alive* in her mind. It took many years before I could comprehend that her dead baby, although of course a terrible tragedy, also represented her own internal dead and dying baby. This was true because of the lies she told herself, and by extension the lies she told me. We were, in this way, both deceived. It was also true because the person she brought to each session covered an empty core and hid the lack of a subjective sense of herself. Psychically, my patient believed she did not exist, so the 'person' she brought to me was a conglomerate composed of bits and pieces of others whom she admired.

When I first met my patient, whom I call Natalie, I was impressed. Natalie was attractive, vivacious, and immensely successful professionally. In addition, she was funny, insightful, and seemingly open to learning. A former teacher, who left teaching after a few years to pursue a career in project management, she now earned six figures. Yet she seemed unaware of her accomplishments and her beauty. At the beginning of treatment, she was a young mother of a three-month-old and a three-year-old.

At the end of the first session, I said something that surprised me. After hearing the matter-of-fact outline of Natalie's story, I told her that analysis would be "extremely painful" for her. I realize now that I must have been subliminally aware of just how many lies this bright, engaging, successful woman told herself. I was afraid for her and dreaded being the bearer of bad news – the emotional truth – of her life. After the session, I questioned myself, fearing what was to come. In retrospect, I think of my responses as premonitions (Eekhoff, 2024), which were aspects of my receptivity to her worry and fear of contact communicated via projective identification. Natalie mostly dissociated her life-long pain, denying that the events from her childhood had any impact on her current life. My intuitive grasp of her life-long pain allowed me to feel what she did not. I believe I was also unconsciously in touch with a profound bodymind dissociation process that disrupted our intimacy.

The first session I describe occurred during the COVID-19 pandemic, when Natalie's baby was a toddler and we were working via Zoom. When she met me on screen, she was leaning forward, so close to the camera that I could not see her whole face. Her mouth filled my monitor. Instantly, I had an image of a hungry baby at my breast. She was laughing and seemed happy to see me. After some time, Natalie moved back, looking at me intensely. She was silent for a minute and then began to describe how she had been flirting with her husband, trying to get him to engage with her. She felt sad that they had not been sexual since their daughter was conceived. She described her husband as unavailable and lost in his devices. When Natalie touched him, he would move away. I did not interpret the transference, although I might have.

I felt sad, recognizing that we too were lost in our devices, separated physically from one another. The loss seemed overwhelming and I felt close to tears. Natalie was working so hard to reach me, flirting and laughing. Suddenly she sat back and said, "Oh, I just had an image of myself, at maybe my baby's age – one year or so – on the ground with my hands held up to my mother. She is walking away".

We were silent for a time. Natalie's picture of herself as a baby – first an image of herself that morphs into a moving picture of herself in relation to a mother walking away – helped her begin a process of discovering a lost aspect of herself as helpless, vulnerable, and abandoned. She went on to wonder if some part of her had died as an infant. She began to tell me of her alcoholic and drug-addicted parents and their abject poverty. Natalie described being hungry and scrounging for food. She told me she felt confused and terrified most of the time. Pretending and taking her cues from others helped her to know what to do, yet she felt unable to know her own wishes and desires. Before this moment in our work together, her history of abandonment and neglect and their devastating impact upon her had been denied. She not only hadn't told me about this aspect of her life, she hadn't told herself either. She knew it, but she didn't feel it.

After these images emerged, Natalie's system of dissociation and denial began to further break down. She described what she saw in her mind's eye. The images came unbidden, a product of imagination apparently evoked by her telling me about her husband. She had an unconscious emotional association via the image to an infantile experience of holding up her hands to a mother who was walking away. Whether these images were memories of actual reality or symbolic of early experiences is not as important as her here-and-now experience with her analyst-mother.

What had I done in the moments before Natalie's image of herself emerged, seemingly evoked by the story of her husband? I too had had an image of an infant at my breast. Both images were laden with emotion. Why had she leaned her body toward the screen, showing me her mouth and tongue while see-mingly searching my face with her eyes? Why did her image of her baby-self come to her mind just then? Was it before, during, or after my own image of her as an infant at my breast?

Undeniably, I had a profound emotional experience. I was deeply moved by Natalie's image of herself as a reaching-for-mother baby. I could imagine, see, and feel her reach. I was experiencing her deeply, in spite of our working remotely. As previously mentioned, my patient had leaned toward the screen, seemingly trying to get closer to me. Then when the image of her baby-self popped into her mind, she abruptly sat back. My experience of her coming closer and retreating from me psychically was mirrored in her physical rela-tionship to the computer monitor.

Natalie and I were no doubt experiencing a degree of frustration in work-ing remotely. It would be easy to attribute frustration to the pandemic neces-sity of working at a distance. Perhaps too Natalie may have felt me as emotionally distant. I was silent, waiting for her, present but not speaking. My silence may have felt too difficult. When I did speak, my words may not have demonstrated understanding. We cannot know. I do, however, believe that something in our connection stimulated visual imagery for both of us, including the particular moving picture image for Natalie of her mother walking away. It seems there was a moment of emotional truth between us, a moment of at-one-ment. Although we can never directly know what Bion (1965) calls "the thing in itself", we can know what we as analysts or as patients feel has happened.

In a session several weeks later, Natalie said,

> As a child, I was always looking for something outside myself in order to orient. Maybe I still am. I don't think I can *feel* my own desires. I remember being in my bedroom when I was four or five, sitting on the floor and spinning and spinning, around and around, looking at the objects in my room: the closet door, my bookshelf, the toys, my bed, the carpet, the grey walls. The turning comforted me, but now thinking back I wonder, where was I? Where was my mother? What was I doing: spinning, spinning, spinning?
>
> I still do that. [Natalie said continuing.] I think it is partly why I am so successful at work. I look at everything and somehow get comfort putting the pieces together. I figure out what people want and give it to them. I always seem to sense what is missing in a procedure or a process. Except now, I am so overwhelmed with the virus, trying to do everything while sheltering at home – work, clean, mother, cook, be a wife. Home was never a comforting place for me. It certainly isn't now.

In this second example, I find Natalie's images emotionally moving. She is describing a memory, and her description evokes feelings and images in me. On both occasions, the images and emotions that form in my mind are vivid, although Natalie's presentation is matter-of-fact and unfeeling. Bion (1973; says, "The dominance of the ocular senses, both real and imagined, is such that it affects our capacity for thought" (p. 8). Shortly thereafter he adds, "The verbal formulation of a visual image is more comprehensible and probably more false" (p. 9). If I follow his meaning, Bion is describing one means of lying to oneself by failing to use emotion for the purpose of communicating. He is telling us that images are transformations that presumably make the truth we cannot bear more bearable. In other words, as much as we need language it fails to represent *the full emotional truth*. Thus, emotion that is not transformed into thought is, in a sense, a form of lying to ourselves (Meltzer, 1998).

Bion (1962b) asserts that visual images, such as those we find in nighttime dreams or in waking reveries, bring information to those who would seek emotional truth. These visual images come as flashes that provide intuitive access to the here-and-now emotional relationship between analyst and patient. As alpha-elements, they emerge into consciousness as associations to emotional experience. When this occurs, the analyst is able to use her imagination to find meaning. What we imagine is not reality per se. Rather, imagination is a transformation of experience into a bearable, knowable image. Images, what we imagine, hold an emotional truth.

The aforementioned vignettes were, as it turns out, covering a more disturbing psychic reality for Natalie. She unconsciously firmly held to a defensive negative hallucination of *not existing*.

A few months later, Natalie is silent for several minutes as our online session begins, looking deeply into my eyes, then looking away. I feel sad, although I do not see sadness on her face. She says, "I am in a weird place. I feel like there is something wrong with the boundary of myself". She gestures to her skin and continues saying, "Like I don't know if I am going out, like evaporating, or coming in, like absorbing something…it's weird".

After a while, Natalie wonders if her habit of buying candy with her allowance as a kid and then putting it in a sack and not eating it is related to similar behaviors she has now. For instance, she buys alcohol which she barely drinks, putting the bottles back in her cupboard. Or she buys Girl Scout cookies; several boxes of each kind and puts them in the cupboard "just in case" she needs them. I wonder aloud if she is doing something similar with me; gathering images during our sessions and secretly tucking them away inside of herself, "just in case" she needs to 'see' me later, so she knows that through me she exists. I wonder if she is always looking for missing pieces of herself and of me. She looks at me, nods, and says, "Maybe".

Natalie's "maybe" is important as it marks the beginning of a real and truthful relationship with me as her analyst. *Maybe* I was wrong. *Maybe* I was right. She was unable to discriminate which felt true. Previously she was 'inside' of me, so to speak, and it took a while for me to grasp the symbiotic nature of our connection. We were barely differentiated as separate subjectivities since she did not yet experience herself as existing.

In both online and in person settings, Natalie's relationship to me was sensual, not emotional. Like the other physical objects she saved (candy, cookies, alcohol) she needed me as both a hard and soft object (Tustin, 1981; 1986) in order to experience herself as existing. She was not yet at a stage in the analysis where she could make use of me as a transitional object (Winnicott, 1951). Rather, she related to me as a confusional object (Tustin, 1981; 1986; 1990; Eekhoff, 2022a). Initially, I chose not to interpret this confusional dynamic, which included lack of clarity about who was who in our dyad. I felt that attending to our body-to-body 'conversation' was essential to locating or finding the 'dying baby' inside of Natalie's bodymind and nursing it back to life. From her psychical position inside of me, she had no need to project. We reverberated and were in sync.

The symbiotic link was a body relation (Bleger, 1967; Eekhoff, 2022a; 2022b; 2025); one that was severely disturbed when we had to suspend in-person sessions and work remotely due to the COVID-19 pandemic. However, the symbiotic relationship between us was still present, via imagination. The shift to a virtual setting reenacted the abandonment Natalie experienced in childhood that took us several years to elaborate and come to understand. The shift from working in my office to online forced us prematurely into a different kind of communication.

In our virtual sessions, Natalie no longer used the couch, explaining that she needed to be able to see my face. She was curious that she really didn't miss me over the weekend or during planned holidays. She said she didn't even think of me during these times. I was not surprised by this, given Natalie's powerful capacity to dissociate. Still, it saddened me to imagine how isolated she was from herself and from me. Telling me she didn't miss me reminded her of going to live with her aunt when she was eight or nine years old. Her parents dropped Natalie and her younger brother off, leaving them for no apparent reason. Natalie said she dealt with it and didn't feel much nor miss them. Although she saw her parents occasionally, she *never again lived with them*.

Natalie's "Maybe" marked a shift in the transference as well as an internal shift in her ability to have her own thoughts as well as to hold me in mind. She was slowly coming to realize that her life had been a sham. Before becoming a mother, Natalie wasn't sure she had ever loved anyone. Indeed, she described herself as living a lie, appearing as if she existed, when she felt she did not exist, except as a clone of whomever she was with. Now, she needed to feel me and see me in order to know that *I was real*. By extension, she needed to see me and sense me feeling her in order to know that *she was real*. With "Maybe", came a host of nighttime dreams, which she recognized as communications from inside of herself to herself first and then to me. Natalie was beginning to find her emotional truth. However, she still felt very little emotionally and found that "interesting". She also felt confused, wondering who was who? Were these her thoughts or mine? Natalie wasn't sure.

More feeling began to emerge following Natalie's decision to separate from her husband. After three years of analytic work together, she was beginning to show evidence of accepting her vulnerability and dependence upon me. She no longer needed to lie to herself that she didn't need anyone. After a two-week hiatus due to work obligations, she came to an online session looking startled and wide-eyed. She burst into tears, sobbing for several minutes, all the while keeping her eyes open and looking at my face. I returned her gaze and waited. When she was able to speak, Natalie said, "I missed you". She then sobbed for several minutes. I met her eyes with mine and nodded.

Discussion

Both neurotic and psychotic aspects of the personality are simultaneously present in all of us and can interfere with the perception of internal and external reality. Misperception leads to faulty assumptions and false assertions about what is emotionally true. Emotion, as the link between mind and body, is a communication that facilitates reality testing. When emotion is discharged through the body via acting out and not processed by the mind symbolically in dreaming and thinking, lies are the result. These unconscious processes of deceit are an attempt to make psychic reality bearable.

The ability to tolerate emotion is important because emotion accumulates into an awareness of self. Such awareness is essential since a relationship with oneself fosters congruence between self and the expression of wishes and desires. Only then can behavior be dependent upon thought and can action be derived from thinking. Natalie did not initially have much of a sense of herself, of her own subjectivity. When we met, she did not know what she liked or disliked, what she wanted or didn't want. She took her cues from the external world. She became what others wanted, mimicking their behavior in an effort to belong. Once a boyfriend left her, she told me, because she automatically did whatever he wanted without contributing anything of herself to their relationship. He told her she was boring. Natalie told me that what he said was correct, even though at the time his statement confused her.

When one does not have a relationship with oneself, one's focus is on the concrete external world and behavior tends to be reactive to circumstances. If the reactivity is to the internal processes one is experiencing without acknowledgment or to the external perception as a mirror of the unknown internal, then one may appear impulsive or explosive or its opposite, passive and indifferent. One then clings to one's internal and external objects via adhesive identification (Meltzer, 1974) and unconscious mimicry (Eekhoff, 2019; 2022a).

Patients who have been traumatized as infants and children by not being welcomed into the family (Ferenczi, 1929) nor emotionally received have no words to say what they experience (Eekhoff, 2022a). What appears as an alive, functioning adult is deceiving. As unwelcome children, these individuals become mute and passive, dissociated from their bodies and trapped in an unembodied material world. As adults, poor personal decision-making, especially in relationships, derives from this dissociation. The resultant immobilized psyche is hidden by fusing with its objects while seemingly not needing or ignoring them. Such is the nature of one of their biggest lies. Their unconscious fusion with internal and external objects leaves them passive and emotionally disconnected. Their conscious ability to give their employers and partners what they want leaves them successful, but unsatisfied and confused.

It is the analyst's task to find the mute and dying infant within the seemingly functional adult. Only after such an individual becomes mute and feels as if she or he is dying, can awareness of their psychic reality and the lies engendered emerge. Emotional truth enables a subjective sense of self to evolve within the analytic relationship. Only then, can the analyst begin to interpret the transference relationship. Paradoxically, a certain degree of understanding can only come after a symbiotic relationship with the analyst has begun to break up.

Bleger (1967) says, "giving names to things is only possible when they (fused patients) acquire a certain identity as a consequence of discrimination" (p. 93). For this to occur, the analyst must be willing to give up his or her own autonomy and separateness in order to experience fusion with the patient. According to Meltzer (1967), this means that the analyst must be "lost" in the inner experience of his patient's material, trusting to his analytic virtuosity in the session to carry on both the technical management and interpretive work. But he must "surface" in repose to understand what he has in fact been doing and what area the analytic process has traversed.

(p. xvi)

As analysts, working in the here-and-now of the session is the only means of realizing the depth of the patient's dissociation from themselves and the pervasiveness of their internal battle against emotional truth. As psychoanalysts we use all that we experience – thoughts, sensations, images, and emotions – to connect with the deepest aspects of the patient's experience. When we make an interpretation, it is only our opinion as to what is happening in the session. With patients like Natalie, we are challenged to pay careful attention to the impact we have because such individuals often take their cues from us, not from their own experience. They struggle with silence because they tell us and feel that there is nothing inside of themselves to discover. There is no one and nothing there. They do not exist. We do not want to believe this, but we must, because having nothing inside is the truth of their experience. Sometimes they tell us they do not exist, like Natalie came to believe, or they are invisible. Silence with a patient who feels they do not exist is dead, unlike the silences occurring when the patient experiences themself as existing. The later silences can reflect thinking or resistance and are communicatively alive.

Whereas developmental psychologists have traditionally asserted that symbolization occurs when a child begins to speak, I believe a primitive capacity to represent and to symbolize is biologically present at birth awaiting the response from another person. Symbolization originates in relationship via the emotional experience of the baby and the mother. The capacity to use the senses, transforming affect into emotion, precedes putting experience into images and words. Such emotional capacity enables the baby to put two or more things together and to tolerate and remember experience that can be used as motivation for thinking. Emotional experience provides the structure for finding language to represent these links. Emotion links the complexities of multiple affective states called into being via experience with an alive, caring, receptive other. Emotion also serves a linking function with internal others and the complexities of our experiences of them.

Patients who have not experienced parents or caretakers capable of 'reading' or intuiting their infantile emotional states often cannot tolerate the anxiety inherent in experiencing "memories in feelings" (Klein, 1975) or "memories in sensorium" (Eekhoff, 2019). Another way of saying this is that internal experience overwhelms such patients, inhibiting their capacity to use memory to unite self with accumulated history. Memory's origin in emotional development serves to aid integration and differentiation, something that counters fusion with internal or external objects.

Back to Natalie

Pleasurable emotional experiences can be difficult to bear (Meltzer and Williams, 1988). Dennis, whose vignette I shared earlier, said, "How can I miss what I have never known?" For him, good experiences evoked discomfort and a sense of loss. The same was true for Natalie. She lied to herself in feeling that she needed no one. When someone was genuinely interested in her, she ran away. Love was frightening, even though she said she wanted it. However, there was also a wish to know the truth about herself, as frightening as that was, and so she stayed in her analysis.

Natalie's overwhelming emotions began to surface, first in images, then in dreams, and finally in session with me. Bion (1958a) says,

> Briefly, it appears that overwhelming emotions are associated with the assumption by the patient or analyst of the qualities required to pursue the truth, and in particular a capacity to tolerate the stresses associated with the introjection of another person's projective identifications. Put into other terms, the implicit aim of psycho-analysis to pursue the truth at no matter what cost is felt to be synonymous with a claim to a capacity for containing the discarded, split-off aspects of other personalities while retaining a balanced outlook.
>
> (p. 145)

Such is the unspoken promise I brought to my work with Natalie. Such is the unspoken promise analysis brings to every patient.

Natalie did not consciously know she was lying to herself. She told me that her mother used to play a Simon and Garfunkle song that she loved, called "I am a rock" (Simon & Garfunkel, 1966). She said her analysis had helped her realize why. One day she brought me the lyrics and said the song would never again be a favorite of hers. She cried as she said she no longer felt isolated and alone, a rock without feeling or life. She wasn't sure if she had built walls around herself leading her to feel that she did not exist or whether in reality she had built walls so early as to not have developed a self. Natalie told me whereas she had felt at the beginning of her analysis that she *was incapable of love*, she now felt that she loved her children, herself, and me. She was a rock no more.

Conclusion

In this chapter, I have described how truth and lies relate to the real and the imaginary. A clinical case was given to illustrate the use of extra-ordinary protections against emotional truth. Further, I have applied these ideas to the role emotion and imagination play in the development of a subjective sense of self. When early childhood trauma creates unbearable emotional experience that is unmediated by caregivers, perceptual and cognitive distortions arise as a means of protecting the psyche from overwhelm.

I have described how in extreme cases, body and mind become dissociated from one another, thereby interfering with an ability to know what is real. Bodymind dissociation includes a focus on the sensual at the expense of the relational. Such a focus results in 'as if' relationships and mimicry as a defense. When this occurs, I have demonstrated how analytic work involves *being the patient* until imagining the patient and *being with* her or him is possible. Being the patient, at an unconscious level, involves a somatopsychic link that enables processes that have been suspended to be mobilized. This mobilization happens quite viscerally as visual images and other sensory experiences evoked in the session are employed by the analyst to make meaning of the here-and-now relationship with the patient. To engage with patients who feel as if they do not exist, is to participate fully in the horror of *not* being as well as the ongoing birth of being and becoming.

References

Bergstein, A. (2015). Attacks on Linking or a Drive to Communicate? Tolerating the Paradox. *The Psychoanalytic Quarterly*, 84: 921–942.
Bergstein, A. (2019). *Bion and Meltzer's Expeditions into Unmapped Mental Life*. The Psychoanalytic Field Theory Book Series. London and New York: Routledge.
Bion, W. R. (1958a). On Arrogance. *International Journal of Psycho-Analysis*, 39: 144–146.
Bion, W. R. (1958b). On hallucination. *International Journal of Psycho-Analysis*, 39: 341–349.
Bion, W. R. (1962a). A Psycho-Analytic Theory of Thinking. *International Journal of Psycho-Analysis*, 43: 306–310.
Bion, W. R. (1962b). *Learning from Experience*. London: Karnac.
Bion, W. R. (1963). *Elements of Psycho-Analysis*. London: Heinemann. [Reprinted London: Karnac, 1984.]
Bion, W. R. (1965). *Transformations*. London: Karnac.
Bion, W. R. (1970). *Attention and Interpretation*. London: Karnac.
Bion, W. R. (1971). *The Complete Works of W. R. Bion: The Grid*, Volume X, pp. 1–32. Mawson, C. and Bion, F. (Eds.). London: Karnac, 2014.
Bion, W. R. (1973). *Bion's Brazilian Lectures 1*. Rio de Janeiro: Imago Editora.
Bion W. R. (1994). *Cogitations*. New extended edition. London: Karnac.
Bleger, J. (1967). *Symbiosis and Ambiguity: A psychoanalytic study*. Churcher, J. and Bleger, L. (Eds.); Rogers, S., Bleger, L., and Churcher, J. (Trans.). London and New York: Routledge, 2013.
Eekhoff, J. K. (2019). *Trauma and Primitive Mental States: An Object Relations Perspective*. London and New York: Routledge.
Eekhoff, J. K. (2022a). *Bion and Primitive Mental States: Trauma and the Symbiotic Link*. The Routledge Wilfred Bion Studies Book Series. London and New York: Routledge.
Eekhoff, J. K. (2022b). Psychic Equivalency as an Aspect of Symbiosis. In Moguillansky, Carlos and Levine, Howard B. (Eds.), *Psychoanalysis of the Psychoanalytic Frame Revisited*. London and New York: Routledge.

Eekhoff, J. K. (2024). Premonition: Hope and Dread in the Analytic Hour. *Jahrbuch der Psychoanalyse*, 87: 41–67. Nissan, B. (Ed.). Berlin, Germany.

Eekhoff, J. K. (2025). Truth and Lies: The Perversion of Truth and the Disruption of Passion. In *Bion and the Truth/Lies Enquiry*. Fortuna, T. (Ed.). Manila: Phoenix Publishing House.

Ferenczi, S. (1929). The unwelcome child and his death-instinct. In Balint, M. (Ed.), *Final Contributions to the Problems and Methods of Psycho-analysis* (pp. 102–107). New York: Basic Books, 1955.

Klein, M. (1975). Envy and Gratitude and Other Works 1946–1963. Masud, M. and Khan, R. (Eds.). *International Psycho-Analytical Library*, 104: 1–346. Richmond: Holgarth Press and the Institute of Psycho-Analysis.

Meltzer, D. (1967). *The Psycho-analytical Process*. London: Heinemann. [Reprinted London: Karnac, 2008.]

Meltzer, D. (1974). Adhesive identification. In Hahn, A. (Ed.), *Sincerity and Other Works: The Collected Papers of Donald Meltzer* (pp. 335–350). London: Karnac, 1994.

Meltzer, D. (1984). *Dream-Life: A Re-examination of the Psychoanalytical Theory and Technique*. Pitlochry, Scotland: Clunie Press for The Roland Harris Trust Library No. 12. [Reprinted 1994.]

Meltzer, D. and Williams, M. H. (1988). *The Apprehension of Beauty: The Role of Aesthetic Conflict in Development, Art, and Violence* (pp. 1–258). London: Karnac Books.

Meltzer, D. (1998). *The Kleinian Development*. London: Karnac, published for the Harris Meltzer Trust. [Reprinted London: Karnac, 2008.]

Monteiro, J. S. (2023). *Bion's Theory of Dreams: A Visionary Model of the Mind*. London and New York: Routledge.

Rezze, C. J. and Braga, J. C. (2019). Authentic pleasure: capture of moments of unison with reality. In Alisobhani, A. K. and Corstorphine, G. J. (Eds.), *Explorations in Bion's "O"* (pp. 63–70). The Routledge Wilfred Bion Studies Book Series. London and New York: Routledge.

Simon & Garfunkel (1966). "I Am a Rock"; Single by Simon & Garfunkel; from the album *Sounds of Silence*; B-side, "Flowers Never Bend with The Rainfall"; Released, May 1966 (1966–1905).

Tustin, F. (1981). *Autistic States in Children*. London and New York: Routledge & Kegan Paul.

Tustin, F. (1986). *Autistic Barriers in Neurotic Patients*. New Haven: Yale University Press, 1987.

Tustin, F. (1990). *The Protective Shell in Children and Adults*. London: Karnac.

Winnicott, D. W. (1951). Transitional Objects and Transitional Phenomena. In *Collected Papers: Through Paediatrics to Psycho-Analysis*. London: Tavistock Publications, 1958.

Chapter 10

The Perversion of Truth and the Disruption of Passion

Churchhill (2000) says "In wartime, truth is so precious that she should always be attended by a bodyguard of lies" (p. 308). In psychic reality, lies are the bodyguards of psychic truth. They are used to protect against the terror and horror of an internal world that is devastatingly threatened by absolute reality. The internal combat between facing reality and hating reality distorts truth. The battle of truth and lies is waged on the battlefield of internal object relations where what it is to be human is expressed passionately in relationship.

Psychoanalysis has always been interested in this battle and the psychic means used to fight it. The exploration of the psychic struggle between truth and lies has sparked many theories. These in turn have provoked analytic controversies as to whether the search for truth is of internal or external importance. Many have asserted that liars cannot be analyzed. And yet, given how terrifying actual reality is, we all lie to protect ourselves from truths we cannot bear. Psychoanalyses analyzes these by labeling them defenses. Freud focuses on the intra-psychic processes of repression, where truth is relegated to the unconscious. Klein highlights the processes of splitting and projection, where truth is dissected and relegated outside in phantasy to the other. Neither speak of lies, except privately.

Bion and Meltzer do. Bion (1970) links the ability to tolerate frustration as integral to the search for truth and describes lies as means of evading frustration. He sees truth as food for the mind. Meltzer elaborates on Bion. In Freudian, Kleinian, and Bionian terms, knowing the truth is central to analytic work, even when it is recognized that absolute reality can never be known. Absolute reality can never be known for it is always transformed by our minds into something we can bear. Some aspect of those transformations may be lies used to protect ourselves from the unbearable truth; psychic truth can then be far from absolute truth. We use each other in order to test reality and discover what is true. We also use each other when our own protections are not strong enough to guard truth. Yet, we aspire to knowing.

DOI: 10.4324/9781003544470-10

Blass (2016) says,

> desires to know and to not know are fundamental expressions of love and
> hate, of life and death instincts. Thus, the analytic process of becoming
> open to truth is one of being able to give greater expression to the ana-
> lysand's capacity to love.
>
> (p. 307)

To love requires a capacity for separation and difference. Lies distort this
reality of separateness. Lies deny difference and otherness. Sometimes, lies
destroy a subjective sense of being and existing.

The most dangerous lies are the lies we tell ourselves, not via inner speech
and thoughts, although those too are significant, but via a misunderstanding
of our perceptions and our emotions. Perceptions are already a mentalization
of our bodily experiences. These unconscious misunderstandings interfere
with our embodiment and therefore impact our object relations. Further, I
believe with Bion (1962a; 1965; 1970), Bleger (1967), and Monteiro (2023)
that the birth of the mind is dependent upon both body relations and object
relations. The psyche in relationship is always in construction or, we might
say with Bion, in the process of becoming.

Unlike Freud and Klein, who believe the development of the psyche is
primarily a biological imperative, Bion does not take the continual construction of the somato-psyche for granted. He does not believe the self naturally
unfolds as from bud to flower. Rather change happens throughout life as the
mind struggles to find meaning in relational emotional experience. He says,
"An emotional experience cannot be conceived of in isolation from a relationship" (Bion, 1962b, p. 42). Subsequently, he adds: "Everything that 'later
becomes known...derive (s) from realizations of two-ness as in breast and
infant'" (Bion, 1967, p. 113, in Levy (2020), p. 102). Twoness involves a passionate intimacy with another.

The 'O' of Truth

Truth is. Without transformation, truth is also impossible to bear. Bion
named truth 'O' in order to be able to talk about its mysterious unknowable
nature. In order to bear truth, we resort to representation. Illusion, imagination, and symbolic representation make truth uniquely personal to each of us.
That is not to say truth is only subjective and constructed for the sole use of
the individual. Although we can only ever see or know the world around us
except through the lens of our own organizational processes, we are dependent upon others for reality testing. Individual subjective experience is reflected in the group. These organizational processes are structured, and
depending upon the vertex that we use, our experience of 'O' alters. An
everyday way of saying that is that our moods, as well as our unconscious

phantasies, effect what we perceive as psychic truth. The degree to which our emotional experience and 'O' align measures our mental health. Bion's 'O' is all that we cannot know.

Truth and the lies that distort our experience are essential elements that we deal with in ourselves and in our patients. Subjective truth is a transformation of 'O'. Any such modification is always a distortion in that it cannot contain the whole reality. Without relationships to actual live others, the distortions are greater. Without cohesive relationships with our internal objects, distortions also occur. Passion is lost, intimacy is shallow, and external relationships become procedural.

The 'O' of Truth exists outside of us in its purity. It belongs to all of us and to none of us. The awesome nature of the 'O' of Truth keeps us humble. If experienced, Truth is transformed to something we can bear. The degree to which we are able to transform absolute reality with minimal distortion is related to our ability to tolerate frustration, recognize our inter-dependence with others, and appreciate the awe and mystery of Life. I link it with the ability to love and to hate and to move in and out of the depressive position. From the vertex of the depressive position, our relationships to and with others is valued and our hate is modified by love. At the same time, absolute reality remains unknowable and needs no one to create it or protect it (Bion, 1970).

Lies and the Liar

Lies, on the other hand, require a person to manufacture them (Bion, 1970). Blatant denial of truth requires someone to replace truth with a substitute that Bion calls minus K or alpha function in reverse. There are lies of omission and lies of commission. Both create a delusion of certainty with a moral assertion of truth that confuses others and perverts object relations. Both rely on material facts used in a twisting of emotional truth. Lies, both conscious and unconscious, damage and distort object relations.

Lies also create a perverted relationship with self. Love then becomes a lie, a means to manipulate and control others rather than a means of knowing the truth about ourselves. We need each other to discover the lies we tell ourselves. We need to love and hate each other in order to clarify what is true. We need to love in order to become more of our potential. Unfortunately, the lies inside of us fight to destroy love and hate and curiosity, even as they protect us from the unbearable battles raging within us.

Bion (1970) suggests persons who come to analysis risk becoming aware of the lies they tell themselves. Those persons include analyst and analysand alike. Further, he goes on to suggest that discovering our lies is experienced by us as a catastrophe (Bion, 1966), because lies are used to protect us from realities we cannot bear. So, lies are our protections against unbearable truth and pain. They are the bodyguards of psychic truth.

Further when we discover our lies, it is catastrophic because the consequences to our internal organizational structures are devastating. These
structures come into question and have to change if the emotional truth is
recognized and experienced in relationship. Only through this personal catastrophe where lies are challenged can growth and change occur. The modification of our internal organizational structures is inevitable when we
passionately love or hate someone. Love and hate improve reality testing and
activate growth. Relationship, with an alive, emotional, and thinking other
facilitates evolution.

No wonder the liar resorts to certainty and rigid thinking. No wonder the
liar has difficulty with whole object relationships. A reversal – where truth
feels disturbing and lies feel calming – maintains a perverse structure that
avoids the awareness of catastrophe. The turmoil of change is diminished. In
addition, the clever liar uses truth to tell the lie. No wonder also that our
institutes require us analysts to have an analysis in order to become analysts.
Without our own analysis, we are vulnerable to the power of the lie and the
confusion that follows when even a little bit of truth within the lie exists.

The lie, using truth to confuse, gains power through the protection from
struggle that it brings. The lie created to hide the truth changes the nature of
the internal battlefield. What happens when our hatred of reality is greater than
our curiosity? What happens when our minds select an aspect of truth that
forecloses the whole picture? Then the very means of meaning-making, what
Bion (1962a; 1962b; 1963) calls the apparatus for thinking, does not adequately
develop. Then the apparatus for thinking – for making meaning itself – is
damaged. We become unable to dependably recognize the significance of our
emotions. Then we lie to ourselves and do not know that we are lying. Again,
quoting Blass (2016): "Hatred informed by love is lived differently than hatred
in isolation" (p. 311). The lie perverts intimacy and unleashes violence.

The Perversion of Truth

I am suggesting that the perversion of truth is a symptom of a hatred of reality where love and hate do not mingle. An element of that perversion is a
hatred of the reality that we are both separate from and connected to those
we love. We are both dependent on them and cannot control them. We are
both together with them and isolated from them. These paradoxical tensions,
when we can tolerate them, aid us in discovering personal truth and accepting
reality. They serve to elaborate our knowledge and understanding and
increase our capacities in every human dimension.

Perversion is an infantile distortion of desire. In speaking of perversion, I
am limiting our discussion to our earliest and most primitive emotional lin-
kages. These are unconscious. I am not speaking of a higher level of using lies
to control and intimidate such as can be found in domestic violence or political strategizing. Rather, I use the word perversion to describe an internal

object relationship that denies differences and separateness. In doing so, external relationships also become twisted and distorted.

The perverted object relationship uses mimicry to create a false intimacy. True intimacy, which occurs only with wholeness and three dimensionality, is evaded instead of sought. Parts are incongruously linked with other parts. Internal structure collapses leaving a hollowness and a flatness. Mimicry is a surface-to-surface relationship, an adhesive bodily relationship that uses sensations as links instead of emotion as links. It denies both subject and object. This mimicry is a desperate act that covers an unconscious phantasy of having died before being born (Amir, 2013; Eekhoff, 2017; 2019; 2022). Such a phantasy of psychic death destroys subjectivity and a subjective sense of self. Without an ongoing sense of self, internal and external relationships become distorted. The mimic is left alone, but does not feel lonely.

Becoming the Lie

It is not that mimicry is the only means of lying. Certainly, all primitive defenses are used to avoid the frustration of reality. In this chapter, I have specifically chosen a very primitive kind of protection where a person becomes the lie (Bion, 1970). Becoming the lie means that language is no longer trustworthy as the bearer of symbolic truth. Both Paul (1997), in writing about the imitation of human speech, and Amir (2013), in writing about chameleon language, address the use of language, not in its symbolic function, but in its function of perverting truth by creating the delusion of intimacy where none exists. The delusion of intimacy is created via psychic fusion and mimicry.

In mimicry, adhesive identification (Meltzer, 1974) is with the surface of the other. Dimensionality – having a psychic inside – is reduced. Mimicry is accomplished via acute observation of gestures, movements, rhythms, tones, and timing. The mimic unconsciously co-opts others' characteristics as a means of survival that includes a seduction and a manipulation of relationship. In becoming the other via mimicry, difference is denied. The relationship itself is perverted due to the erroneous impression of a subject object two-person emotional connection, when in reality the relationship is a one-person relationship with one or the other member foregrounding (Eekhoff, 1994).

Amir (2013) says "Perversion is simultaneously an attempt to deny separateness, by means of creating a pseudo-twinship, and an attack on intimacy through the perverse subject's refusal to allow any expression of his or her deep core. It is the attempt to penetrate the other without being penetrated (Parsons, 2000). It is, at one and the same time, a lie that seems truthlike and a truth that appears as a lie". She goes on to say that "...if psychosis is an attack on meaning, perversion is an attack on meaningfulness" (p. 395). I agree with Amir, although I might not use the word 'refusal', which implies more agency than I have experienced with perverse patients.

I have previously written about a differentiation between fusion and merger involved in this process. Fusion denies difference and hence forecloses intimacy and learning from the object, while merger enables a movement in and out of the object in phantasy that is creative and productive (Eekhoff, 1994; 2016; 2022). Hence in a perversion of the truth, the perverse relationship is not a true relationship between equals. It is a lie. According to Parsons (2000), quoted in Amir (2013), the analyst is penetrated, the analysand is not. Identification is not with the internal essence of the object, but uses astute hyper-sensitivity to ensnare and possess the object via mimicry. She says: "Adopting the other person's syntax, the perverse subject actually employs it to trap and subjugate him or her. This entire production has the aim of ensuring that the 'chosen' other will not only fail to find out that she or he is under attack, but in fact will not register that she or he actually is in the presence of a stranger" (p. 397).

The fusion, where it takes two people to make one person, creates a delusion of a relationship and is destructive rather than creative. It is parasitical link rather than a mutually beneficial link as is found in the healthy symbiotic link (Bleger, 1967) or in love (Bion, 1966, p. 38.) The relationship is a lie because the person is a lie. Congruence between truth and self, between self and self, and between self and other enables life to have meaning. Without congruence, there is struggle and heartbreak. There is no hope.

It is even possible according to Bion for someone to be a lie. He says: "It is possible to be a lie and being so precludes at-one-ment in 'O'" (Bion, 1970, p. 104). Being a lie forecloses at-one-ment with Truth and inhibits using the other as an aid in finding Truth. Instead, a person is so out of touch with themselves that what they present to themselves and others is imitative, not authentic. They become the other and so the relationship is psychically a one-person relationship. In a two-person relationship where truth is valued, otherness and difference are valued. Spontaneity and freedom create new growth-producing experiences that are in touch with the reality of not just two people but of the space between – of a third.

After so many years of believing lies we tell ourselves, it is painful to uncover them. The reality that people believe the lies they tell is incomprehensible to us. Yet we know they do. For example, Trump and his followers believe they won the 2020 election. Putin claims to believe that invading Ukraine was in the interest of peace and was humanitarian. Beliefs treated as knowledge, as truth, cause harm (Britton, 1998).

The Disruption of Passion

Many of our patients come to us doubting they can love. At some level, they seem to know that they are lying to themselves about their relationships. They tell us their emotional relationships are flat, dull, and lacking passion. Bion (1963) suggests that passion itself is only possible between two whole people. He says,

By "passion" or the lack of it I mean the component derived from L, H, or K. I mean the term to represent an emotion experienced with intensity and warmth though without any suggestion of violence (and) is not to be conveyed by the term 'passion' unless it is associated with greed.

(CWB, Vol V, p. 19, Elements)

By implication, passion involves the union of two bodyminds to create a third and includes a hunger or greed for contact with the other. We might say, a passionate link is required to have a greater sense of what is true. Implicit also is the idea that humans have an ontological instinct of being and becoming as an aspect of the epistemological instinct, an innate drive to know and understand.

Freud (1909), as quoted by Blass (2016, p. 316), says "A man who doubts his own love may, or rather *must*, doubt every lesser thing" (p. 241, italics in original). Lies are symptoms of corrosive doubt and are dangerous because they disrupt passion. They unconsciously create a perverse parasitical relationship with self, that inevitably affects the ability to love others and includes an inability to love one's self. A parasitical relationship with self inevitably creates dangerous parasitical relationships with others.

We could say lies are self-destructive doubts pronounced as certainties. They interfere with our perceptions and even distort our relationship between our bodies and our minds. Again, quoting Bion (1970), "The link between one mind and another that leads to destruction of both is the lie" (p. 104). Bion adds another element when he suggests that lies also interfere with our passionate external intimate relationships, so much so that a lying link destroys both liar and the believer of the lie.

The link is parasitical and perverse and destroys rather than creates. Nothing new comes of such a link. In fact, a link based on lies is designed to prevent change. The building of a relationship dependent upon lies cannot promote growth and further development in either self or other. Reality and passion, so essential to vitality, are thwarted.

Clinical Case

David was a man of God. He came for analysis when his third marriage was failing. His wife had given him an ultimatum: analysis or she was leaving. He truly did not feel he needed any help. He described himself as a loving and good man. He had had three perfect families with three beautiful wives and two children by each. Everyone was happy and good. He explained his former wives leaving him as their inability to live with such perfection. Each wife had complained that he loved God more than he loved them. They doubted that he loved his children. This confused him since he had "done all the right things". One wife had even told him he acted as if he were God. He thought that was a compliment since from childhood he had been taught to "be like Jesus".

David was imposing. Initially. I found him bright, witty, and charming. He dressed immaculately. He spoke in trite phrases and frequently included quotes from Scripture. He told me the Bible was the only book he needed. As a successful professional who earned six figures, he was able to support three families somewhat easily. He could also afford analysis. He looked deep into my eyes and said he found me "perfect for him". He told me he loved my voice. And yet, after the initial six months of four times a week, I began to feel the analysis wasn't progressing. In spite of his seeming compliance and acceptance, transference interpretations went nowhere. In fact, they confused him. He agreed with other interpretations, but nothing changed. He rarely disagreed with me, saying, "You're the analyst". Our relationship seemed superficial and to be one of habit, with him dutifully reporting his good deeds and his wife's irrational complaints. The sessions had become flat, boring, and repetitive.

David purportedly had had a difficult infancy and childhood, but I am not sure those details are relevant to the analysis that was not developing. Rather, the details would become part of an entertaining story of his triumphs over adversity. His voice, reminiscent of an old-time radio announcer, was deeply resonant. It soothed away any doubts about his sincerity. He had a slight accent, which was perhaps English, maybe Australian.

Yet, other than as audience to his stories, I was superfluous – a means to an end. Realizing this and attempting to speak to it was painful for me. I simply could not get through to him. Often, he would smile and nod his head as if thinking. Sometimes he would turn around on the couch to look at me. Sometimes he said I sounded like his wife, but nothing got in. This took a while for me to understand, because frequently he would repeat something I said to him weeks afterwards. I thought this meant he had understood and introjected his understanding. I came to realize this was not so. The words held little or no meaning for him. He was using them and repeating them almost obsessively, and in doing so, he stripped them of their significance.

Interpreting his imperviousness and impenetrability also seemed to go nowhere, except to make him feel misunderstood. This marked the beginning of a change. Soon he complained that I was negative, jealous of his successful life, and trying to make him feel bad about himself. He said I was gaslighting him. Once he said to me, exasperated, "How can you say that? Are you crazy?" He felt his confidence must be intimidating me. When I commented on his perfect appearance and perfect life as being an 'as if' life, he replied that everyone's life was 'as if'. He was just better at it than most.

David's wives and children felt he could not love. This baffled him, because he told me he always told them that he loved them. It was so frustrating for him not to be believed. As his analyst, I too doubted that he loved. I doubted that he noticed others as existing at all. He certainly did not notice me. Rather, others seemed to be an extension of him, myself included. David insisted he loved everyone including "his neighbor as himself". He seemed to be a chimera of a person, built of bits and pieces of persons and ideals he admired or thought he should be. He saw himself "as Christ". Finding the true person, the ordinary human being, within the rhetoric seemed impossible. David seemed to personify Bion's idea that a person could be a lie.

I began to fear the work with him, agonizing after sessions about what I was doing, and imagining that if the truth were to dawn on him, it would be devastating. I remembered Meltzer's admonition about the analyst needing to worry as an acceptance of the patient's unconscious worry (Monteiro, 2018). David became more and more upset and instead of learning from his experience, he began to rage. At the same time, he reported that his wife was less upset with him; his estranged children from his former marriages were maintaining regular contact. I alone doubted him. Once he said to me, "You do not believe anything I say". Another time he said, "Who do you think I am?" He reminded me that to think a negative thing was to "have sin in one's heart". Somehow, I was tempting him to have negative thoughts, sinful thoughts.

Each night at dinner, David read a portion of the Bible to his family. I feel a turning point in his analysis came when he brought me this quote from the Bible: Isaiah 45, verses 5–7:

> I am the Lord, and there is none else, there is no God beside me: I girded thee, though thou hast not known me:
> That they may know from the rising of the sun, and from the west, that there is none beside me. I am the Lord, and there is none else.
> I form the light and create darkness: I make peace and create evil: I the Lord do all these things.

He told me he believed there was no other god but God. I did not know his Lord, and in not knowing Him, I was a danger. He did not understand how I could see anything but good in him unless I was from the Devil. He, David, was a good man, striving to be like God. I was tempting him to sin.

I told him that having an analyst from the Devil enabled him to keep his own dark side and evilness out of mind. He seemed to see himself as God. I said that in bringing these particular verses to me, he revealed his knowledge of these places in himself, as well as in his God. He was silent.

However, this content, although interesting, was not the most important aspect of the turning point. When he was reading the Bible verses to me, I had a flash image of my favorite uncle Wiert. The image emerged from the sound of David's voice which reminded me of the rhythm and resonances of my uncle's voice. He was a radio minister and pastor of a large church. I loved him dearly. Often, he would read the Bible aloud to me.

As I pondered this memory after the session, I realized that David's voice had changed since I met him. It was sounding more like my own, which reflected my identification with my father and my uncle. By recognizing his mimicry of me, I realized something of the impasse we were in. I began first just to observe and soon found other instances of myself in him – his gestures, glances at me, and even in the way he said hello and goodbye. David was reflecting me back to myself, but David seemed not to be present. Gradually, I found ways to just name what I was observing in the here-and-now of the session.

Slowly overtime, we were able to explore his mindless states, although not easily. He feared that anything he did not know was from the Devil. A mindless state provided a gap for the Devil to get in. He feared the Devil was taking his relationships from him. He wished to stay married and maintain his ideal of having the perfect family. This wish kept him in analysis when his doubts about me and about himself surfaced.

I want to emphasize that my understanding of David as a lie has nothing to do with his faith in God. Rather, it was his belief that he was God that needed to be addressed. He was everyone and everyone was him. His spiritual beliefs had been co-opted by his powerful feelings of helplessness, vulnerability, and mindlessness. In spite of his financial and social success, David was an innocent newborn. Slightly above his innocent child, was a bad boy who felt unworthy of love. As David became able to look inside himself, he became more human. Only then could he grieve. David's analysis was long and became less tumultuous. His pain was great and his grieving came and went, depending upon how much truth he could bear.

Discussion

A profound organization of the universe and of life integrates truth within and outside of us. This innate order is the source of beauty and creativity. Awareness of it is what makes us human. It is not a once and forever awareness, but an order that develops over time and in relationship. A hidden and mysterious connection between life and death, and between self and other, celebrates change. Lies function to confuse and destroy this hidden order and to keep everything the same. Lies destroy relationship and pervert truth. They are a perversion of passion and intimacy. Lies attack the loving and hating links between and within persons. Connection that denies difference is not connection, nor is it intimacy. It is a lie that serves to keep everything the same so as to make our fear of infinity and change manageable. Passionate intimacy requires two separate and connected individuals.

If we consider the lie a symptom (Civitarese, 2016, p. 169), then liars can be analyzed. It is not easy to do so, because we are as vulnerable to the lie as are our patients. The pain of not knowing, of being dependent upon the unconscious internal forces within us, leaves us helpless without each other and humbles us. The mind develops in relationship to truth and in relationship.

A free mind remains connected to reality and to others. The mind of the thinker evolves in order to cope with personal emotional experiences. More poetically, Bion says that instead of a thinker finding thoughts, it is the thoughts that force the development of a thinker (Bion, 1966; 1965; 1970).

Thoughts without a thinker are in and around us, waiting for us to be able, via our organizational structures, to recognize them and make use of them. Further, becoming a thinker occurs in relationship to real external objects as well as in relationship to self and the infinite internal world.

Yet, the development of a thinker cannot be taken for granted. Meltzer (1981) says,

> Parts of the personality that are bound in dependence, and potentially in a love relationship to the good object, are constantly being pulled away by lies to abandon that relationship to the truth. This is, then, the "Primal" source of mental illness. If, as he (Bion) says, truth is the nourishment of the mind and lies are the poison, then the mind, given the truth, is able to grow and develop itself while, conversely, if poisoned by lies, then it withers into mental illness—which can be seen as a kind of death of the mind.
>
> (p. 182)

During all of our lives we need each other in order to learn the truth about ourselves. Otherwise, our distortions and delusions will take us further and further away from the truth and further and further away from intimate relationships.

In health, our bodily sensations are background objects and represent the body of the containing mother and father. In health, these contribute to the passion of our love for our internal and external objects. Without truth, without recognition of our love and our hate, our life and our death, forces will be caught in a battle that results in the death of the world as we know it. Catastrophic change cannot be stopped.

Bion (1970) places this in a context that helps us understand our daily work as well as the cultural clashes and wars around us. He says:

> In psycho-analysis the liar is a significant fact and gains significance from the lying nature of what he says. The parasitic relationship between liar and environment, corresponding to the parasitic relationship between the thinker and the lie, denudes the environment of significance. The analyst who accepts such lies is acting as host; if he does not, he contributes to the feelings of persecution by "being" an unthought thought, a thought without a thinker. The thought to which a thinker is not necessary is also a thought that the thinker would not regard as likely to contribute to *his* significance. On the contrary, once he has expressed a truth the thinker is redundant.
>
> The lie is peculiar to a relationship between the host mind and the parasitic mind and destroys both. The thinker can harbour thoughts if he does not need thoughts to contribute to his significance and can tolerate thoughts that do not do so. If essential to the thought, the thinker conflicts with other thinkers who feel themselves to be essential to the thought. The envy,

jealousy, and possessiveness aroused are the mental counterparts of toxic elements in physical parasitism. They contribute to the destructive nature of the culture that develops from the development of the lie.

(pp. 104–105)

Churchill's (2000) comment: "In wartime, truth is so precious that she should always be attended by a bodyguard of lies" (p. 308) reminds us that the battleground within us is populated by both truth and lies. In war, Churchill implies, lies are necessary in order to win the fight against evil. In analysis, knowing the difference between Truth and Lies is not easy. As in war, each side asserts a righteous connection with truth. Without truth, the destruction that follows is catastrophic. No one wins. With truth, a catastrophe enables growth and creativity.

Truth unites us. Lies destroy the natural order and distort the power of the universe. If we as analysts hope to be able to work productively with the lies we find in our consulting rooms, it may help us to remember Meltzer (1981) who says: "After all, we can, in our consulting rooms, be Counsel for the Defence of the loving and creative aspects of the patient's personality rather than the Prosecuter of his criminal side" (p. 101).

References

Amir, D. (2013). The Chameleon Language of Perversion. *Psychoanalytic Dialogues*, 23: 393–407.

Bion, W. R. (1962a). A psycho-analytic theory of thinking. *International Journal of Psycho-Analysis*, 43: 306–310. [Reprinted as "A theory of thinking", in Bion, W. R., *Second Thoughts* (pp. 110–119). London: Karnac, 1984.]

Bion, W. R. (1962b). *Learning from Experience*. London: Heinemann. [Reprinted London: Karnac, 1984.]

Bion, W. R. (1963). *Elements of Psycho-Analysis*. London: Heinemann. [Reprinted London: Karnac, 1984.]

Bion, W. R. (1963/2014). *The Complete Works of W. R. Bion: Elements of Psychoanalysis, Vol. V* (pp 1–86). Mawson, C. and Bion, F. (Eds.). London: Karnac.

Bion, W. R. (1965). *Transformations*. London: Heinemann. [Reprinted London: Karnac, 1984.]

Bion, W. R. (1966/2014). Catastrophic Change. In Mawson, C. and Bion, F. (Eds.), *The Complete Works of W. R. Bion: Elements of Psychoanalysis, Vol. VI*, (pp. 27–43). London: Karnac.

Bion, W. R. (1967). *Second Thoughts: Selected Papers on Psychoanalysis*. London: Heinemann. [Reprinted London: Karnac, 1984.]

Bion, W. R. (1970). *Attention and Interpretation*. London: Tavistock. [Reprinted London: Karnac, 1984.]

Blass, R. B. (2016). The Quest for Truth as the Foundation of Psychoanalytic Practice: A Traditional Freudian-Kleinian Perspective. *Psychoanalytic Quarterly*, 85: 305–337.

Bleger, J. (1967). *Symbiosis and Ambiguity: A psychoanalytic study.* Churcher, J. and Bleger, L. (Eds.); Rogers, S., Bleger, L., and Churcher, J. (Trans.). London and New York: Routledge, 2013.

Britton, R. (1998) *Belief and Imagination: Explorations in Psychoanalysis.* London and New York: Routledge.

Churchill, W. S. (2000). *The Second World War, Vol V: Closing the Ring.* London: The Folio Society.

Civitarese, G. (2016). *Truth and the Unconscious in Psychoanalysis.* In association with the Institute of Psychoanalysis. London: Routledge.

Eekhoff, J. K. (1994, unpublished manuscript). *Paper presented at the Black Butte Psychoanalytic Conference – "Fusion and Merger in Intimate Relationships".*

Eekhoff, J. K. (2016). Introjective Identification: The Analytic Work of Evocation. *American Journal of Psychoanalysis,* 76: 354–361.

Eekhoff, J. K. (2017). Finding a center of gravity via proximity with the analyst. In Levine, H. B. and Powers, D. G. (Eds.), *Engaging Primitive Anxieties of the Emerging Self: The Legacy of Francis Tustin* (pp. 1–19). London: Karnac, 2017.

Eekhoff, J. K. (2019). *Trauma and Primitive Mental States; An Object Relations Perspective.* London and New York: Routledge.

Eekhoff, J. K. (2021). *Bion and Primitive Mental States: Trauma and the Symbiotic Link.* London and New York: Routledge.

Freud, S. (1909). Notes upon a Case of Obsessional Neurosis. *The Standard Edition of the Complete Psychological Works of Sigmund Freud,* 10: 151–318.

Levy, F. (2020). *Psychoanalysis with Wilfred R. Bion: Contemporary Approaches, Actuality and the Future of Psychoanalytic Practice.* London and New York: Routledge.

Meltzer, D. (1974). Adhesive identification. In Hahn, A. (Ed.), *Sincerity and Other Works: The Collected Papers of Donald Meltzer* (pp. 335–350). London: Karnac, 1994.

Meltzer, D. (1981). The Kleinian Expansion of Freud's Metapsychology. *International Journal of Psychoanalysis,* 62: 177–185.

Monteiro, J. S. (2018). *Long-Term Psychoanalytic Supervision with Donald Meltzer: The Tragedy of Triumph.* London and New York: Routledge.

Monteiro, J. S. (2023). *Bion's Theory of Dreams: A Visionary Model of the Mind.* London and New York: Routledge.

Parsons, R. D. (2000). *Ethics of Professional Practice.* Boston: Alyn & Bacon.

Paul, M. (1997). On the imitation of human speech. In *Before We Were Young* (pp. 165–192). Binghamton, NY: ESF Publishers. [Reprinted London: Free Association Books, 1999.]

Chapter 11

Body Relations and the Black Hole

The body is the background of every analysis. Yet, as an aspect of the setting (Bleger, 1967), the body may go unnoticed since the mind is infinitely interesting for those of us committed to analysis. Bodies are also psychoanalytic objects (Harrang, Tillotson, and Winter, 2021) when they become represented. Our bodies represent our most infantile and perhaps even our prenatal experiences of our own and our mother's bodies. As such, our bodies both hold and trap us. In health, our bodies are symbols of our mothers' bodies and represent a background of safety. In pain, our bodies betray us, reminding us of our difficult existence and our inability to escape that pain.

Primitive unformed and forming body states are closely linked with perceptual identities – the deeply unconscious mechanisms that organize the chaos of our emotional and sensate experience into meaningful order. They are an aspect of primary process. Meltzer, in summarizing Bion, asserts that "...at this primitive level the ego does not make mental representations 'of emotional experiences but both construes them *as* bodily states and reacts to them *with* bodily states and actions" (Meltzer, 1986, p. 35). Body states are intimately connected to emotional life and form the foundation of meaning-making. Simultaneously, without the organizing function of the mind, these states can persecute. Body states also form body relations with actual live objects that defend against the awareness of psychic separateness.

In health we are embodied and fluid, shifting with ease from state to state. Our bodies and our minds are not separable. We have free minds and responsive bodies. Our defenses serve to protect us from too much stimulation – either physical or psychological. Our bodies are background objects (Eekhoff, 2021a; 2021b; 2022) to our Selves. Our senses, our perceptions, and our consciousness work together. Our attention floats from inside to outside, from outside to inside, from concrete to abstract, from abstract to concrete, from sensation and sensuality to thought and action. We are within ourselves and between others who are also within themselves and between us. When we are embodied, our bodies become dream spaces (Eekhoff, 2021a) and enable us to organize and use the information we perceive.

DOI: 10.4324/9781003544470-11

The accumulated effect of linking our sensations, our perceptions, our emotions, and our identifications on our *somatopsyche* is coherence. All our experiences are integrated and unified. We become at-one-with ourselves. We are embodied. Everything coheres giving us a sense of who we are. Not that we are ever only one thing. Our identities themselves are fluid and multiple. All are affected by both our body relations (Bleger, 1967; Eekhoff, 2021b) and our object relations (Klein, 1975). These relations are not only internal objects and representations; they are actual concrete external relationships that are somatic and proximate.

In this way our identities are intimately affected by our actual external physical and emotional relationships with others. When these relations are disrupted for any reason, trauma occurs. When the disruptions occur in infancy or early childhood and the disruptions are of premature bodily separation from the primary caretaker, they result in catastrophic mis-perceptions of bodily experience, which create a secondary trauma. *Secondary trauma* (Eekhoff, 2021b; 2022) results in a lack of coherence – in fragmentation. Fragmentation that repeats over time accumulates and itself becomes a source of trauma. Primary and secondary traumas interfere with the representational processes innate in humans. The development of an apparatus for thinking (Bion, 1962a; 1962b; 1970; 1992) is disrupted.

These disruptions can be overwhelming, causing psychic collapse. When infants and young children experience repeated collapses, auto-sensuous behaviors create an encapsulation. Tustin (1981) describes this as *primary encapsulation*. She says, "In this type of encapsulation, the child seems to us to be in a shell in which, in a global state of unintegration and undifferentiation, he lies dormant, waiting for more propitious conditions for development." (p. 47). When premature separation from the mother occurs in infancy or early childhood, encapsulated pockets are formed as extreme protection against the reality of separation. The infant's arousal functions *as if* an aspect of his or her own body has been lost. Hence the separation creates an experience of loss of both the physical other and the psychical self. Psychic death threatens.

Primal and primitive mental states of being remain present throughout life as memories in feelings (Klein, 1961; 1975) or memories in sensorium (Eekhoff, 2019) but cannot be thought about and processed. These states, especially in the case of patients who have suffered early childhood traumas, become linked to hopelessness and despair. Time becomes frozen around these encapsulated states. Space collapses. Further, in some cases, these states seem to be linked to a delusion of not existing and to a psychic collapse into a hallucinatory Black Hole. The Black Hole are the words my patients use to describe their implosions.

The Black Hole and Nonexistence

The Black Hole is a dense sucking experience of annihilation and undifferentiation. It is primarily a somatic experience (Eekhoff, 2021b; 2022). It is not that patients are only in a black hole. The Black Hole is all there is. They are a Black Hole. Nothing else exists. Their words 'black hole' are used to mark a memory of a psychic collapse. The word 'hole' is used to describe a perception of a gap caused when a part of the body has gone missing. The nipple has left, taking the mouth with it. Skin has left, taking skin with it. The result is a hole in the body. The vagina has left, taking the penis with it. The penis has left, taking the vagina with it. Holes in bodies interfere with keeping things in. Things spill out. All body cavities can come to represent a loss of the self, not via projective identification, but via spilling, evaporating, or atomizing. Psychic dimensionality itself collapses.

The psychic collapse called a Black Hole first occurs early in life. Through clinical experience, I have come to believe these collapses occur in the first months of life. Early collapse creates a vulnerability to collapse. It is both a breakdown and a fear of breakdown (Winnicott, 1974). Instead of projecting out, exploding into the world in search of a container, the person psychically implodes. The implosion wipes out everything and everyone. In such a catastrophe, the object is lost, as is the subject. The person cannot even experience themselves as an object. Everything is nothing because the apparatus for processing experience is damaged or does not adequately develop.

Persons who talk about the Black Hole will frequently tell us they do not exist, exemplifying Bion's ideas regarding a negative hallucination. In spite of concrete somatic evidence of existing, they experience themselves as nonexistent. Bion (1970) says of nonexistence, "Non-existence, immediately becomes an object that is immensely hostile, and filled with murderous envy towards the quality of function of 'existence,' wherever it is to be found" (p. 20). Bion is, in part, describing self-envy (Lopez-Corvo, 1995) that attacks the live part of the person or in the case of the transference, the live analyst. The experience is fleeting. However, it can be felt by the analyst via imaginative conjecture and analytic intuition as a dense impenetrable otherness, that like an astral black hole sucks in and destroys life. The *psychic event horizon* of the Black Hole is a ring of chaos that cannot be symbolized. It is somatic experience. Patients will describe sensations of heat, burning, vertigo, and nausea just before the collapse.

Language and the Black Hole

This psychic experience of not existing defies language because language operates at a different psychological level of functioning. In the realm of perceptual identity, it is the body that organizes experience. Language intrudes even as it supplies order by bringing an awareness of time and space.

The *perpetual now* of the perceptual realm makes the rhythm and sound more important than the words themselves. The result is that language used may be vague and lacking in emotion. Again, I turn to Bion (1965), who says,

> The analyst's transformations employ the vehicle of speech just as the musician's transformations are musical and the painter's pictorial. Though the analyst attempts to transform O, in accordance with the rules and discipline of verbal communication, this is not necessarily the case with the patient. He may, for example, transform O into what may *seem* to be a verbal communication but is to the analyst something akin to hallucination. Such transformation (Tp ⊠) belongs to the domain not of verbal communication but of hallucination, be it auditory, visual or tactile. It should therefore be helpful if, by analogy with painting, music or verbal communication, it were possible to understand the discipline and rules, so to speak, of hallucination.
>
> (p. 71)

The rules of hallucination are not so easily discovered. Hallucination is intimately connected to the body, using the senses in reverse (Bion, 1958); but each person has his or her own process.

Since these hallucinations are outside of consciousness, they are particularly difficult for analysts to observe. Bion gives us an idea of how to do this when he says that one can interpret what a patient describes as being an actual perceived external object or as an object that has come from inside the patient and is "ejected through his eyes" (p. 342). Bion is describing a process of double meaning where the use of verbs of sense indicates an hallucinatory process.

Bion also describes this as an attempt to heal. He says,

> Hallucinations and the fantasy of the senses as ejecting as well as receiving, point to the severity of the disorder from which the patient is suffering, but I must indicate a benign quality in the symptom which was certainly not present earlier. Splitting, evacuatory use of the senses, and hallucinations were all being employed in the service of an ambition to be cured, and may therefore be supposed to be creative activities.
>
> (Bion, 1958)

The negative hallucination of not existing originates as a defense against catastrophic loss. It is a means of encapsulation making it possible for normal development to occur around the Black Hole. Body relations and object relations are affected, but premature mental development often compensates for the losses.

Precocious mental development often includes early speech development and, in adults, an articulate use of language. Paradoxically, patients who suffer from the Black Hole are often highly verbal. Using the senses in reverse may be covered over with other than sensory words. This is particularly true of the abstract and philosophical patients. Since words are the medium of psycho-analysis, there is an immediate difficulty for the analyst. The analyst may become lost in the words and not understand the unconscious process occurring, where the words are being used as things and for their sensory qualities. The content, even though it is not symbolic, may be treated by the analyst symbolically.

Our words automatically constitute and limit our experience. Some of the chaotic trauma of preverbal experience is that it cannot be limited or contained with words. If the original trauma of premature awareness of separateness occurred in the preverbal stage of development, it has never been symbolized in language. Preverbal trauma is only remembered in feelings and sensations. How then, are we as analysts to reach these patients? Meltzer (1986) asks, "Are these experiences only historically pre-verbal or are they essentially unverbalisable?" (p. 81). I agree that these somatic experiences may be unverbalizable, but they do exist as traces that repeat in the patient's and the analyst's body relations.

Since the words of the patient suffering from a collapse into the Black Hole are often vague and seemingly difficult to understand symbolically, the analyst must rely on his or her somatic responses in the here and now of the session in order to discover meaning. Somatic counter-transference, what Bergstein (2019) equates with analytic intuition, becomes the only accurate indications of the unconscious communication coming from the patient. Further, the traumatic disruptions of representations have interfered with the normal back-and-forth of projective and introjective identifications, leaving the com-munications somatic and adhesive in nature. Since projective identification is essential for thinking, emotional growth is stunted.

The process of repetition of the collapse may appear to have emotional meaning, but in cases of early childhood trauma, preverbal and preconceptual (Lopez-Corvo, 2014) experience is somatic. It cannot be recalled; its repeti-tion can only be concretely acted. Initially it also cannot be recognized by the patient. However, it can be recognized by the analyst. Emotional transfor-mation and psychic change occur slowly and first in the analyst. Then, the analyst brings it to the patient, as often as is possible. Even as I write this, I mislead because I make it seem so simple. The symbiosis involved in working with body relations and un-nameable states is anything but simple.

I have not named it symbiosis until now, but the relationship between patient and analyst on the somatic level is a body relation that is symbiotic. Bleger (1967) says,

> Symbiosis is a close interdependency between two or more persons who complement each other in order to keep the needs of the more immature part of the personality controlled, immobilized and in some measure satisfied. These parts demand conditions dissociated from reality and from the more mature or integrated parts of the personality.
>
> (p. 79)

Undifferentiation is an aspect of symbiosis. It is an aspect of the primal position. Undifferentiation is also an element of autistic encapsulation.

I believe the *primal position* (Eekhoff, 2021a; 2021b), named glischro-caric by Bleger (1967/2013) and autistic contiguous by Ogden (1989a; 1989b), is evoked when working with patients who were traumatized in early childhood. It becomes a primary focus of the analytic work. The symbiosis, so essential for establishing a relationship, needs to be broken up. Analytic work with traumatized patients is work that enables differentiation and then categorization and subordination of emotional experience. It strengthens the apparatus used for processing information. Since the apparatus itself (Bion, 1965; 1970) has not adequately developed or, more accurately, has developed leaving pockets unformed or undrawn (Alvarez, 2010; 2012), only somatic body relations provide a sense of safety. No wonder these patients fuse with their analysts, adhesively clinging to them. Proximity comforts. Symbiosis creates a delusion of safety for them. These somatic body relations also provide hope for transformation in that they communicate themselves via the body to the other. Somatic experience is communicated via resonance to the analyst who may find meaning in it.

Since their projective and introjective processes have not sufficiently developed, patients caught in a black hole of sensation are not able to make good use of their objects. They unconsciously cling to them as surfaces. They do not experience them as dimensional. Their communication falters, and they symbiotically fuse in order to survive. Often, they have no emotional awareness that a containing object is available for them. Relationships are thus superficial and functional. Body relations, which are symbiotic (Bleger, 1967), are primarily a means of self-regulation and delusional coherence. Over time, the analyst transforms the symbiotic body relations and its primal communication into language. Object relations deepen.

I am generalizing here about our loyal and reliable patients who come to us with a life-long history of pain. They work hard, faithfully attend and promptly pay for their analysis even though they continue to suffer without relief. The more we analyze them and they analyze themselves, the more the analysis seems to flounder – caught in a rhythmic wave of words. The analyst may be fooled into believing these words have meaning, as I initially was with Ronald, whom you will meet shortly. Of course, at a higher level, a symbolic level, words do have meaning. However, analyzing their content threatens the analysis with meaninglessness, nothingness, and the Black Hole (Grotstein, 1990a; 1990b; 1990c). Perhaps it is more accurate to say that words cover over the meaninglessness and nothingness of the Black Hole, even while evoking it. The content may have different meaning from its manifest one to each member of the dyad. Each member interprets the content of the language differently.

What I am describing about adults who suffered collapse as infants, Meltzer (1975) has articulated regarding post-autistic states in children. He explains a failure to represent as originating in the post-autistic child's need for sensual contact which includes an intense relationship with the mother's body. He describes these children as sensuous, highly oral, and tender. They are neither sadistic nor aggressive, but can be very possessive. They fuse with their objects by physically engaging them and behaving as if they were one body. He attributes this to a failure in achieving a capacity for projective identification (p. 18). Post-autistic patients communicate via the senses using adhesive identification. Their representations are primitive and at a body level.

The Black Hole is a sensory representation. It is an alarm, signaling a catastrophe (Eekhoff, 2021b). The sensory representation is both defense and communication. The repetition of collapse adds to its traumatic nature. Learning from collapse does not happen since the experience is a sensory one that comes and goes. There can be words about feeling bad, but understanding what the process has been or even what happened does not develop. It is as if collapse happens *for the very first time* each time. Another characteristic is that recovery from the collapse can sometimes be rapid, which also surprises the analyst.

Clinical Case: Ronald

Ronald is a patient who accessed his hallucinated black hole. Of course, my story of Ronald is just that – a story. I hope that I am able to convey an emotional truth of my work with him that my words alone cannot do. I am excerpting a long and painful analysis for the purpose of demonstrating his sensate hallucinatory experience of the Black Hole. Also, I want to emphasize that Ronald was neither borderline, autistic, nor psychotic. His psychological structure was primarily neurotic. He was at once overly concrete and overly abstract.

Ronald first came to see me following a divorce from his second wife. He felt suicidal and despairing. He told me there was something missing in him. He did not feel fully human in that he was not sure he was able to love. He said he was forever searching for "my missing piece" in the women he met. He described himself as always lonely, but rarely alone. Although he was physically faithful to his wives, he always had "a woman or two in the wings". During his analysis, he married and divorced again.

He taught me much about body relations and disrupted object relations. He challenged all my Kleinian ideas regarding projective and introjective identifications. It was not that he did not project, he did; however, there was a deeply primitive aspect of him that could not project into or identify with anyone. This part of him was prone to collapse and he would despair, unable to mobilize. Almost as quickly, he would re-group himself, usually by manically connecting with a woman. Just to be proximate to a woman helped him, but it was even better if he could be held. Every touch was eroticized and often he was sexual. At first this ability to re-group so quickly was confusing to me. He would enter my consultation room extremely suicidal and despairing and leave happy, eager for new adventures.

Trying to understand him helped me rediscover Ferenczi, Klein, Bion, and Meltzer. I reread Bleger and Ogden. However, ultimately, it was my experience of him that helped me understand the theories. My understanding that his use of his own body and mine was more important than trying to make interpretations about his dreams and phantasies. Understanding that his growth of an apparatus for projection and introjection had been stunted in infancy came later. From the depths of him came only blankness and despair, while at higher levels of organization he was extremely proficient.

When first I met Ronald, I was impressed. He was a self-made millionaire working in high finance. He was charming and funny. Although not physically extraordinary, he exuded accomplishment. He was of medium height and build, beautifully dressed in a casual Northwest style. His eye contact was intense, and frequently I felt him coming into me through my eyes. I found his intrusion deeply unsettling, but did not feel angry or even irritated by it. I wondered why it did not feel hostile. His impressive voice was deep and resonant. In spite of his accomplishments, he seemed a very gentle man. We began twice a week, facing each other.

Ronald spoke articulately and almost poetically about his life, telling me he had been anxious and depressed for as long as he remembered. He said he was always mildly suicidal, sometimes intensely so. He described times in his childhood, when he stood outside himself and noticed how sad he was. As his story unfolded, I noticed myself being drawn in and charmed by what seemed to be self-reflection. I say drawn in because in those first few months, I did not yet feel the flatness that would emerge. Later, I came to recognize that much of what I had thought was self-reflection was mimicry in the form of regurgitated self-help books or imitated movie scenes. The verbal processing itself was an *auto-sensuous action* not self-reflection.

Ronald was a very busy man. He sought to always be a better person. He joined toastmasters and learned to speak "like a Greek orator", writing inspirational speeches. After joining a political party, he ran for office on a liberal, taking-care-of-others ticket. Volunteering in homeless shelters and prisons became a way of life. People looked up to him as a good man fighting for just causes. He stayed physically fit by careful diet and daily exercise. High-risk sports such as white-water rafting, helicopter skiing, and mountain climbing thrilled him. He ran marathons and did triathlons. The challenge excited him, although after a particularly strenuous or dangerous activity, he often felt depressed and suicidal for days.

He studied philosophy, psychology, literature, and religion. He travelled all over the world seeking adventure in foreign cultures and what he called "primitive peoples". He idealized Buddhism, Hinduism, and ancient Aztec and Mayan culture, being particularly curious about human baby sacrifice. He had many friends and social activities. In spite of being very successful professionally, he was as unhappy with himself as he was with his relationships.

Although successful in business, Ronald was unlucky in love. He told me he fell hard and fast for a woman and soon tired of her. For most of his life, he had had two or more women who loved him. This originated in childhood, always having an intense relationship with his female teachers as well as with his mother. He described a high school teacher who took him on outings, hired him for small jobs, and whom he adored, much to the chagrin and confusion of his mother. He smiled as he said this, claiming he could always find someone, but thought he was forever seeking his "lost mother of infancy". This statement rang true to me, but I wasn't sure why. Everything he told me about his childhood seemed "good-enough" (Winnicott, 1953). However, knowing that he was seeking someone – his lost mother of infancy – who was obviously already gone, changed nothing. I wondered if this apparent insight wasn't also something he had read, but did not feel. Later I would learn that the wish was based in a concrete reality.

Ronald's difficulties with intimacy signaled a non-symbolic arena of his personality that relied on somatic and adhesive involvement rather than the emotional meaning-making inherent in projective and introjective identification. His process of symbolization was selectively inhibited. In this psychic arena, his body relations were primary and his internal object relations were perverted. He needed women desperately and had an almost compulsive sexual drive. He longed to "be devoured by a woman who can't get enough of me". His aloofness and constant disappointment in women kept them pursuing him, which met some of that wish. His work in analysis, where he attempted to crawl inside me and stay curled up there, appeared to be superficial, but unconsciously was a deep and profound fusion. As the analysis deepened, I experienced his aloofness and inaccessibility in the transference.

The superficiality of our relationship began to show when after seven months, he agreed to come four times a week and use the couch. It was also about this time that he told me, in passing, that he had been adopted. According to him, his adopted family was "devoted and distant". I began to think of him as both an unwelcome baby (Ferenczi, 1929) and a wise child (Ferenczi, 1923). His quiet gentle ways began to seem something else. There was a notable lack of curiosity about me in the transference. He seemed to take me as an actual concrete thing in the room rather than as someone with an internal emotional life. A profound lethargy threatened. Furthermore, his passivity seemed untouchable. When I first met him, he appeared ambitious, gregarious, as well as highly competitive and successful. His docility and inability to act surprised me.

Over time, his passivity and indifference to me began to change. Whereas previously I had considered him difficult to reach, he began to experience me as unreachable and "above or beside it all". In the silences, his anger and disappointment in me became palatable, although he never complained. If I attempted to name it, he always denied feeling anything but gratitude for me. At other times as he lay on the couch, it seemed he was dissolving into the fabric, disappearing into some unreachable place away from me. Sometimes, the idealization that he had for me, as well as for the women he met, seemed difficult to comprehend. He did not seem to be splitting and projecting into me as one would expect. Instead, the idealization seemed based on actual physical proximity, as if he were gaining something essential via osmosis and proximity.

After more than two years on the couch, his silences became something other than despair. He reported dreams that were without images or sounds; "just sensations and a feeling of doom and dread". Then he began to sense something in the silences. Sensations seemed meaningless, but were accompanied by indescribable pain. His pain was very different from despair. He described physical sensations in his chest, "as if my heart were breaking". Over time, these sensations were accompanied by images that began to appear in his mind and in mine.

At first, he named his sensations of loneliness: "my Black Hole". He equated them with a "lack of anyone". He admitted that all of his relationships were superficial and shallow. He told me he liked his Black Hole. He said, "Judy, in some strange and perverse way, there's been such comfort in this Black Hole". He said it was like a good mother – always there. Furthermore, his Black Hole was more comforting than people, it wanted him. Again, his words: "It explains why I've been attached to it. The Black Hole is who I've been. It has been far more real than my attachment to wives, children, lovers, friends. It is a reality more real than they are". About this time, he told me, "I've just gone to the 'beyond words place'. You are with me but on the edge of it all. I'm not looking forward to the next four days without you".

The *"beyond words place"* became an expression for a somatopsychic experience that paradoxically used my physical presence and the setting of my office as protection against an unbearable reality of my emotional presence and his separateness from me. He told me,

> There is something about being in your room, the essence of it, that comforts me. You don't even have to speak, but when you do, it is not so much what you say, but how you say it, the sound of you does something to me I cannot explain.

This comfort however did not last and a threatened separation over night or over the weekend could bring us to a beyond words place and the Black Hole. In this state, Ronald could not function nor speak. He collapsed. He could not feel my presence. The silence that ensued was not a creative one. It was dense and dark. It sucked us both in. It was a Black Hole of sensation without meaning. It was *objectless sensation* (Ferenczi, 1949). He also over time began to describe a feeling that I did not exist.

Soon, each time there seemed to be a difference between us, the collapse threatened. Difference was equated with a loss of me. To leave Ronald in this impenetrable silence felt immeasurably cruel. Yet, to speak too soon was to defend against my own primitive states and abandon him. To speak too soon was also to deny our separateness and perpetuate a delusion that we were one. I had to be there with him without abandoning him. When I failed this, I learned to speak to the consequences: the collapse and the separation between us. The dangerous and seductive gap became a Black Hole. At first, my words were incomprehensible to him, even though I tried to use words I had heard first from him. They only made him feel worse since they were evidence of our separateness and my lack of understanding.

Eventually he was able to articulate his loss and his anger. He said,

> This is the deepest, most tormented I've felt since seeing you. I am angry with you. It feels like you caused it. Abandonment is too nice a word. I'm isolated, unconnected to anyone. Yesterday felt like I was going crazy, absolutely disconnected - somewhere out in a black hole of space, floating, not grounded to anything. Being sucked deeper and deeper in. I didn't know what to do. Call you? I felt so desperate, I was talking to my dogs: "Don't leave me." "Don't leave me".

He began to tell me that it was no wonder he could not feel me in the room even though he saw me physically. He said he wasn't sure that either one of us existed except as actual concrete bodies. This might be demonstrable with a short vignette from a later session:

RONALD: I am an empty shell. On the outside, I do what I am supposed to do. But inside there is a vacuum. I cannot experience you. You act like you are present and understand. I do not experience that. You behave as if you have faith and trust that I will change from the inside out. But there is nothing inside of me that makes it possible to experience you. You do not exist for me. Worse still, no matter how I try to tell you that, your faith suggests you do exist. You just don't get it.

ANALYST: Perhaps if I truly understood your despair, you believe I too would be despairing and not have faith.

RONALD: Maybe.

ANALYST: Then we would be the same. Two of us helpless and despairing.

RONALD: And I wouldn't be alone. Both of us would at least exist.

This brief excerpt shows the terrible dilemma. If neither of us could think, we would be the same. In sameness, there is an illusion of unity and security. Sameness stays the same. If I think and respond to him, we are separate. The gap between us is dangerous. The gap becomes the Black Hole, sucking us in. He is lost forever. Instead of seeking his lost mother of infancy, he may be seeking his own lost infant. As this realization of difference dawns on him, he becomes angry with me for not being him.

This is progress even though he cannot yet express his anger. He can talk about it, which is the beginning of differentiation. It is also evidence of psychic existence.

However, differentiation is hard to bear. Existing is threatening, yet non-existence, as Bion has said, is unbearable and hostile, evoking envy. The fleeting awareness of the reality of life and death requires another kind of defense. The negative hallucination that I am not there is as difficult to alter as is the parallel delusion/negative hallucination that he does not exist. Not existing is safe. Giving up negative hallucinations is to give up safety. Also, since hallucinations are bodily in nature, they are convincing and hard to alter. These hallucinations include the body of the analyst in a two equals one experience. In those moments, there is no room for two of us in one space. It is dangerous. We must be one.

Ronald demonstrated a profound dependency that left him vulnerable to psychic disorganization – a return to an unindividuated state where he is fused symbiotically with whomever he is with. The sensory of sexual inter-course gave him a second skin, to aid in his coherence, while at the same time created an illusion of oneness with the other. The delusion/hallucination of being in union and secure via the skin of the other was broken the moment any form of differentiation aroze. Misunderstandings and disillusionment followed with intense affective storms and suicidality.

Sometimes even to say something – make an interpretation, rather than stay completely in agreement – was experienced as a violent attack, as if when I spoke, he could not stay inside his own skin but came over into mine. He became me, and in that action, annihilated himself. Sometimes my breathing distracted him from himself. He needed me to breathe with him, disappear myself into him, or he would be lost, floating away, evaporating into the air around us.

Several months later, Ronald is able to articulate his experience of me as existing as someone who was hurting him. This happened whenever I did not immediately understand him as well as when we were physically separated. He tells me it makes his head hurt and then in session, he fantasizes lying in a coffin with his head separated from his body. Only his head is alive. When I interpret it as evidence of my being separate from him, he is silent and says, "Uh huh. Uh huh. [Silent]. You know the moment you said that, I felt the band around my head. I feel you are quite removed. You are not down here with me". He then is silent and I feel his withdrawal. He tells me he has no room for me in the intensity of his experience. I again name his retreat from me. He agrees and says, "Yes, yes. [Silent for several minutes]. Boy, this is a weird memory. I am back 45 years ago, playing football, quarterback, throwing to a wide receiver, completed, but just as I released the ball, a defender hit me in the head, laid me out. A cheap shot to the head that laid me out".

I say, "So you imagine I use my words to lay you out with a cheap shot to the head". He agrees, saying, "Yes. The expression 'laid out' is key – what I felt last weekend in my depression was laid out".

I add, "It is also what they do with dead people in coffins – lay them out".

These initial forays into describing feeling hurt by me, by our separation between sessions, as well as by my interpretations that do not exactly match him, also demonstrate a change in his ability to tolerate silence. Silence was no longer equated with the Black Hole.

Soon the anger and rage were replaced by an erotic transference. Ronald's fantasies and daydreams in and out of the sessions became sexual. The sensations and images intruded into the hour, taking his breath away and stopping his words. Silences became tinged with alternating eroticism and deep shame. However, the collapses and dense silences of the Black Hole decreased. Depressive anxieties gave way to paranoid fears that I would hurt him and take pleasure in it. These in turn also became sexualized. Eventually these images became focused on my breast. I was able to interpret his infantile need of a constant nipple in his mouth or even of an umbilical connection that would require no action on his part. Such a connection would forever remain unbroken.

I will leave the elaboration of that process for a later time. I mention it here to give you some idea of the movement out of the concrete somatopsychic experience of the Black Hole into a relational world where the infantile experiences could become represented and the process of revery and containment internalized. The process involved moving from concrete somatic experience of sensation to images and finally to words. This process repeated over and over again with sensation becoming images or words evoking images and sensations which evoked other words.

Towards the end of his analysis, Ronald felt compelled to find his birth mother and learn of his origins. What he learned was that he had been born in a home for unwed mothers and kept in a nursery for three weeks while his 16-year-old mother decided whether or not to give him up for adoption. She had periodically held him and nursed him during those weeks. He was eventually adopted when he was five weeks old. This information confirmed our constructions gained in the transference of his perceiving me as being both warm and loving and horrifically rejecting, cold, and cruel. He was able to imagine himself alone and bottle fed in a dark room. Whether or not this was accurate was not as important as was his capacity to grieve the loss of his "lost mother of infancy". His suicidality and rage, first turned against himself and then at me, dissipated. His loss was grieved. He left me feeling sad but no longer in despair. He could love.

Discussion

The Black Hole is a sensory representation, via sign and signal, of an early developmental catastrophe where reality came in too soon (Eekhoff, 2022a; 2022b) and the developing psyche collapsed. The representation is both defense and communication. The experience is somatic and destroys psychic awareness of object relations and body relations. Everything shatters and collapses inside, like the death of a star. The implosion wipes out a sense of the object as well as a subjective sense of self.

The ongoing repetition of collapse adds to its traumatic nature. Learning from collapse does not happen since the experience is a sensory one that comes and goes and damages the apparatus for thinking. There is simultaneously a destruction of the self and the object. There can be words about feeling bad, but understanding what happened does not develop. Each time there is a collapse into the Black Hole, it is *as if for the very first time* because the experience does not become sufficiently mentalized. With each collapse and hallucinatory experience comes hopelessness and dread and often suicidality.

Similarly, for the patient, it is as if each time the unverbalized is experienced and verbalized by the analyst, it is a surprise. The first time is repeated again and again as seemingly nothing accumulates. Words become somatic manifestations used for auto-sensuous protections. They are not used for meaning-making which requires accumulation and change. Auto-sensuous protections prevent change. Initially, only the analyst remembers, recognizes, and transforms via naming the shared somatic experience. Over and over again, the analyst must name something that has previously been un-nameable. Naming the *perpetual now* is recognizing and drawing attention to a process, even when the process is one of denying the movement of time. The patient does not consciously remember the analyst as having noticed, much less named something. To remember would enable an experience of separateness. Rather than indicate separateness, the analyst's words become part of the chaos of the Psychic Event Horizon and go into the Black Hole never to return. They have become meaningless things.

This puts more pressure on the analyst. The unbearable experience must be borne. The unspeakable must be spoken. Words, as a wall of sound, must be broken up in order to have meaning. Further, the analyst's responsibility is to neither repel the experience and hence the patient, nor to prevent the experience resonating within the patient and the dyad by intruding via his or her own personal projections. Since the mutual experience is intense and raw, the analyst's first task is to survive as a whole emotional and thinking being in order to be present to and for the patient. Containment is silent without words long before the experience can begin to be articulated.

When psychic overwhelm floods the emotional link between the patient and the analyst, the bridges between mind and body are broken. The mind implodes or explodes in response. The body restricts, becoming tight and rigid. Relationships seemingly cease. There is in that moment a very specific and very detailed response needed from the analyst that *cannot be guessed by him or her*. The response is needed instantly so there is no time nor inquiry that can be used to find it. It must be instantaneously correct. To inquire is to prove you are not with the patient. You do not feel or empathize accurately.

To hesitate is evidence you have failed him. You do not understand. Moreover, you are helpless to do anything about it. This is so because, in that moment, the patient requires that you be them. You are not them, nor are you psychic or clairvoyant. You are separate and your failure to be the patient communicates that unbearable truth. The despair for both analyst and patient is horrific.

It is those times when doubt arises.

Without faith in the human psyche and faith in the analytic method, analysts working with patients who suffer from the Black Hole may lose faith in themselves. Without faith, our space narrows and corrosive doubt destroys our patience and our security (Bion, 1970). Without faith, we need the concreteness of actual experience. Without faith, we may fall back on reassurance which maintains the symbiotic link. With faith, our doubts are creative, serving to open up space for a new idea or thought.

Conclusion

I have described a psychosomatic hallucinatory experience of the Black Hole using my patient Ronald as a clinical example. I have used Ronald's story to describe a psychic catastrophe of imploding into the self which follows infantile experiences of trauma. I have used the designation "Black Hole", first named by a patient of Francis Tustin (1981; 1988), to differentiate the implosion into the self from repression and introjection. The resultant psychic Black Hole consists of compacted fragments of the self and others. The compaction must be broken up via relationship with an actual other person, the analyst, if change is to occur.

At the same time, I have described how the Black Hole marks a catastrophic suspension of development, which creates deficits in the capacity to symbolize. Cognitive and emotional development proceeds unevenly with patients who suffer the Black Hole. Some of these patients achieve impressive intellectual and professional accomplishments by encapsulating their relational traumas. I have also explained how the analyst using psychoanalysis may be able to reach and treat a difficult-to-reach patient whose representational processes have been frozen. In this way, our theories, models and methods facilitate the process of representation and symbolization, and enable healing from childhood trauma.

References

Alvarez, A. (2010). Levels of analytic work and levels of pathology: The work of calibration. *International Journal of Psycho-Analysis*, 91: 859–878.

Alvarez, A. (2012). *The Thinking Heart*. London: Routledge.

Bergstein, A (2019). *Bion and Meltzer's Expeditions into UnMapped Mental Life: Beyond the Spectrum in Psychoanalysis*. London and New York: Routledge.

Bion, W. R. (1958). On hallucination. *International Journal of Psycho-Analysis*, 39: 341–349.

Bion, W. R. (1962a). A Psycho-Analytic Theory of Thinking. *International Journal of Psycho-Analysis*, 43: 306–310.

Bion, W. R. (1962b). *Learning from Experience*. London: Heinemann. [Reprinted London: Karnac, 1984.]

Bion, W.R. (1965). *Transformations*. London: Karnac Books.

Bion, W. R. (1970). *Attention and Interpretation*. London: Tavistock. [Reprinted London: Karnac, 1984.]

Bion, W. R. (1992). *Cogitations*. New extended edition. London: Karnac.

Bleger, J. (1967). *Symbiosis and Ambiguity: A psychoanalytic study*. Churcher, J. and Bleger, L. (Eds.); Rogers, S., Bleger, L., and Churcher, J. (Trans.). London and New York: Routledge, 2013.

Eekhoff, J. K. (2019). *Trauma and Primitive Mental States; An Object Relations Perspective*. London and New York: Routledge.

Eekhoff, J. K. (2021a). Body as Dream Space. In Harrang, C., Tillotson, D.. and Winters, N. (Eds.), *Body as Psychoanalytic Object: Clinical Applications from Winnicott, Bion and Beyond*. London: Routledge.

Eekhoff, J. K. (2021b). *Bion and Primitive Mental States: Trauma and the Symbiotic Link*London and New York: Routledge.

Eekhoff, J. K. (2022). *Psychic Equivalency as an Aspect of Symbiosis*. In Levine, H. and Moguillansky, C. (Eds.), *"Psychoanalysis of the Psychoanalytic Frame Revisited" A New Look at Bleger's Classical Work*. London and New York: Routledge/IPA.

Ferenczi, S. (1923). The dream of the clever [wise] baby. In *Further Contributions to Psycho-Analysis* (pp. 349–350). Compiled by Rickman, J.; Suttie, J., et al. (Trans.). London: Hogarth Press, 1926 (2nd edition, 1950). Reprinted London: Karnac Books, 1980.

Ferenczi, S. (1929). The unwelcome child and his death-instinct. *International Journal of Psycho-Analysis*, 10: 125–129. [Reprinted in *Final Contributions to the Problems and Methods of Psycho-Analysis* (pp. 102–107) London: Karnac, 1994.

Ferenczi, S. (1949). Notes and Fragments [1930–32]. *International Journal of Psycho-Analysis*, 30: 231–242.

Grotstein, J. S. (1990a). The "black hole" as the basic psychotic experience: Some newer psychoanalytic and neuroscience perspectives on psychosis. *Journal of the American Academy of Psychoanalysis*, 18: 29–46.

Grotstein, J. S. (1990b). Nothingness, Meaninglessness, Chaos, and the "Black Hole" I—The Importance of Nothingness, Meaninglessness, and Chaos Psychoanalysis. *Contemporary Psychoanalysis*, 26: 257–290.

Grotstein, J. S. (1990c). Nothingness, Meaninglessness, Chaos, and the "Black Hole" II—The Black Hole. Contemporary. *Psychoanalysis*, 26: 377–407.

Harrang, C., Tillotson, D., and Winters, N. (Eds.) (2021). *Body as Psychoanalytic Object: Clinical Applications from Winnicott, Bion and Beyond*. Routledge, London.

Klein, M. (1961). Narrative of a child analysis. *International Psycho-Analytical Library*, 55.

Klein, M. (1975). Envy and Gratitude and Other Works 1946–1963. Masud, M. and Khan, R. (Eds.). *The International Psycho-Analytical Library*, 104: 1–346. London: The Hogarth Press and the Institute of Psycho-Analysis.

Lopez-Corvo, R. (1995). *Self-Envy: Therapy and the Divided Inner World*. New Jersey, London: Jason Aronson, Inc.

Lopez-Corvo, R. (2014). *Traumatised and Non-Traumatised States of the Personality: A Clinical Understanding Using Bion's Approach*. London: Karnac.

Meltzer, D. (1975). The psychology of autistic states and of post-autistic mentality. In Meltzer, D., with Bremner, J., Hoxter, S., Weddell, D., and Wittenberg, L. *Explorations in Autism* (pp. 6–29). Strath Tay, Perthshire, UK: Clunie Press. [Reprinted for the Harris Meltzer Trust, London: Karnac, 2008.]

Meltzer, D. (1986). *Studies in Extended Metapsychology*. London: Karnac Books.

Ogden, T. H. (1989a). *The Primitive Edge of Experience*. Northvale, NJ: Jason Aronson.

Ogden, T. H. (1989b). On the concept of an autistic-contiguous position. *International Journal of Psycho-Analysis*, 70: 127–140.

Tustin, F. (1981). *Autistic States in Children*. Boston: Routledge & Kegan Paul.

Tustin, F. (1988). The 'black hole'. *Free Associations*, 1(11): 35–50.

Winnicott, D. W. (1953). Transitional Objects and Transitional Phenomena—*A Study of the First Not-Me Possession*. Int. J. Psycho-Anal., 34: 89–97.

Winnicott, D. W. (1974). Fear of breakdown. *International Review of Psycho-Analysis*, 1: 103–107. [Reprinted in *Psychoanalytic Explorations* (pp. 87–95). Winnicott, C., Shepherd, R., and Davis, M. (Eds.). Cambridge, MA: Harvard University Press, 1989.]

Chapter 12

Missing Emotional Links

Analysts today are working in circumstances of collective trauma that are diffi-cult. We are also working with patients who are difficult to reach (Joseph, 1975). Reaching patients who have survived early childhood trauma and have no words to say what they are experiencing in the here-and-now (Eekhoff, 2021; 2022) communicate unconsciously with their analysts. This communication is extre-mely primitive and often leaves the analyst feeling confused or non-existent. The content of their patients' words may not have symbolic meaning, but the fact of them communicates. For analysts to understand and be with traumatized patients who use *speech-as-action* requires analysts to use their own bodies as instruments of observation and find words for patients who have none.

Further, many of these patients appear to be 'missing in action'. They tell us they do not exist or that they died before they were born. Such declarations of psychic experience are difficult for us to comprehend in light of our somatic experiences of their presence. Try as we might to empathize, our very aliveness interferes with our understanding. When we attempt to be with our patients in their pain, we experience ourselves also as missing in their minds. Not only is the patient missing in action, but from the patient's vertex, so is the analyst. These missing links are disturbing and can even be perceived by the analyst and the analysand as attacks. Sometimes they are. At other times, they are signs of negative hallucinations that mark deficits that I would call *missing links*. These missing links or lost links contribute to internal pockets of empti-ness, what Ada described as being made of Swiss cheese. These negative hal-lucinations are very disconcerting as they put us in touch with primal states of body and mind that are very difficult to impact. These missing links (Britton, 1989) also are indicative of a lack of dimensionality and three-person relating or, we might say, of working through of the oedipal situation.

Clinical Example

Lewis was 54 years old when he came requesting analysis due to lifelong experiences of anxiety and depression. His wife of 27 years had recently asked for a divorce. His children were leaving home. He feared he was enmeshed

DOI: 10.4324/9781003544470-12

with them, often unable to differentiate their feelings from his own. "I am my son", he once told me. Although a successful professional educator, he said he never really lived up to his potential.

From the first session, I found it extremely difficult to think with Lewis. Initially, I just listened. He talked on and on, not seeming to notice me as quiet. Looking back, I do not think he really registered me as present, a person in the room. My difficulty thinking seemed to derive from being overwhelmed by his smells. He reeked of new and old smoke. The stink of ingested alcohol leaked from his skin. He attempted to cover his smell by adding a strong cologne. When he left my office, his odor lingered.

His nauseating smell made it impossible to think or feel. In spite of hour after hour of stories of a terrible childhood, I was unmoved. This also bothered me. I could not understand my lack of empathy in light of his tragedies. Often, I could not distinguish the veracity of his stories, doubting him. The more blank I became, the faster his stories came.

He had been an unwanted and unwelcome baby (Ferenczi, 1929), conceived to trap his father into marriage. When this failed, his mother purportedly attempted to abort him. When he was born, and his father did not succumb to the power plays of his mother, he was given up for adoption. However, his mother failed to fill out the paperwork, so the infant was placed in foster care.

Foster care was also not reliable. Purportedly his first placement failed after six months when the state discovered the abusive conditions within the home. The second placement lasted for approximately 18 months until his foster mother died. Numerous other placements followed. When he was four years old, the state found his biological father, who was married with two younger children. His father agreed to take him, even though his step mother did not want him.

Lewis described himself as "a nobody, or at best a zombie". He thought of himself as the living dead and told me he was a chameleon, able to become anything anyone wanted him to be. He said he was aborted before he was born, psychically dead upon arrival, and missing in action. Initially, I could not fathom what that felt like for him. I found it strange that I felt so little. I too seemed dead. At times, I seemed to counter my deadness by feeling a pressure to act – to do something, anything to reach him.

Action threatened to replace thinking or feeling in both of us. He memorized my interpretations and repeated them as if they were his. Yet, he did not seem to know what they meant. Nothing seemed to accumulate. He acknowledged, "I live in the moment. There is nothing else. No before or after. I guess I am really evolved, right?" He was not really living in the moment. He was living outside of time.

Discussion

Of course, I am providing a mere snapshot of my patient and not details of the long and often painful treatment. Perhaps Lewis may stimulate associations in you of other patients like him. Clinical evidence suggests that adults who experienced early parental abuse and neglect do not perceive the world as others do. Early primitive representations of undifferentiation become a delusion of non-existence that permeates and changes the way in which they view the world.

When an infant's projections are not received and metabolized by the parents, the infant begins projecting into his or her own body. This disrupts development of a sense of self as existing separate from others. Such an early experience becomes mentalized as bad internal objects. Bion (1970) says, "Non-existence, immediately becomes an object that is immensely hostile, and filled with murderous envy towards the quality of function of 'existence,' wherever it is to be found" (p. 20). Patients who believe they do not exist become excessively concrete, even when they describe themselves as not existing or as Lewis did of "missing-in-action". His actions and his sensations and smells substituted for being. He was not able to use his concreteness so as to develop generalizations about himself or the world. Hence, he resorted to mimicry.

My patient Lewis demonstrated his existence, without feeling it, by reeking of stale cigarettes and alcohol, substances that gave him the illusion of coherence. Under this sensory second skin (Bick, 1968) were primal states of body and mind that included undifferentiation, formlessness, and extreme passivity. Initially these states could not be verbalized because he did not experience the dyad nor the triad. He was not differentiated from me, and I was overwhelmed by the concrete sensory experience of being with him.

For Lewis and patients like him, language, which requires a subject and an object, is of a different order. It is not a symbolic ordering of experience. Speech was important for its tone and rhythms, returning him to an infantile world of sounds and sensations not yet given meaning. The many words of his oft-repeated stories were sensory and non-symbolic, stripped of meaning by his obsessional repetition. Sometimes he spoke without using a pronoun. Sometimes his descriptions were vague and seemingly interchangeable. Mindless and self-less states were defenses against trauma that created deficits in his functioning. Access to these states occurred when the autistic and psychotic defenses against them began to break down via relationship with me.

Although these defenses must be broken down for therapeutic change to occur, the process is extremely disturbing somato-psychically. Awareness of somatic responses is an aspect of both body relations (Bleger, 1967; Eekhoff, 2021; 2022) and object relations. Since these states are always present, they underlie other, more developed verbal states that are the usual focus of analysis. Under usual conditions these somatopsychic states form the floor for experience (Ogden, 1991; Eaton, 2015; Eekhoff, 2019). They are outside of consciousness and include somatic sensation. A floor for experience assumes psychic cohesion, something that is achieved by trauma survivors only rarely.

Instead, cohesion comes from second-skin processes (Bick, 1968; 1986). Second-skin processes use sound and sensation to provide substance and keep awareness of the object at bay. They can also contribute to an unconscious delusion of not existing. As I have said elsewhere, "Primal processes use the sensory modalities as precursors of the visual imagery that leads to language" (Eekhoff, 2022, p. 4; see also Chapter 10). In extreme cases, the subject of the patient is also kept at bay, missing in action. When these second-skin processes fail, the fragile floor for experience collapses.

Second-skin defenses, like Lewis's smell, are protections from formlessness and mindlessness. In these primal states, the patient exists in the atmosphere of the consulting room, seemingly outside of body and mind. Seemingly is an important word here, because another unconscious patient phantasy is that of being inside the analyst's body. Eventually the analyst may experience somatic symptoms resulting in subtle agitation and irritability that are indicative of such primal psychic processes. With Lewis, I felt that I had something in my throat and needed to cough, or worse still to gag and vomit.

Bion (1967) differentiates these analysts' states from counter-transference. The responses are the analyst's own. Previously (Eekhoff, 2022), I have written of primal processes of communicative connection that do not include projection and introjection but are vibrations and reverberations. These occur especially when the processes of projective and introjective identification have broken down in early childhood due to trauma. One of the analytic tasks is to distinguish primitive mental states that are communicated via projective identification from even more primal states, proto-mental states, that are communicated via somatic resonance (Eekhoff, 2022). When the communication is via resonance, the analyst is in *symbiotic unison* (Civitarese, 2018) with the patient. This union, which Bion calls at-one-ment, enables the analyst to use his or her self-awareness of somatic states as an instrument to comprehend the patient. They are useful indications of the *analytic ambiance* and help keep the analyst psychically alive during deadening encounters with patients who are missing in action. Somatic states also aid the analyst when he or she is confused and cannot think. They are the *environmental mother*.

Emotion as the Link

Emotion as the link (Eekhoff, 2019) between perceptual and thought identity must be generated in the immediacy of the hour. Emotions are simultaneously experienced by both the patient and the analyst without being the same, enabling analytic progress. Since trauma both arouses primitive defenses and interferes with the normal development of apparatuses for perceiving, registering, and thinking about internal and external experience, simultaneous emotional experience with another person is rare for trauma survivors. Simultaneity is not the same as being in sync. Even when such simultaneity occurs, often it barely leaves an impression in the patient. Further, if there is awareness of the impression, it is one of danger because it is evidence of the presence of the object/other. Spontaneity, a necessary ingredient for simultaneous emotional connection, is absent. This is sometimes difficult for the analyst to imagine.

Since everyone utilizes perceptual identity as a floor for experiencing reality, the differences between the analyst and the patient become key unconscious elements of every encounter. The patient, whose floor for experience (Grotstein, 1990) is mindless and formless, typically has difficulty with psychic fluidity and approaches experience from a concrete and rigid vertex. In theory, the patient must be met and found by an analyst whose floor for experience enables movement between vertices. Fluidity is not a function of formlessness although it may be present at a different unconscious psychic level. Both members of the dyad have to meet each other where they are. Their difference is an element of therapeutic interaction. However, a more conscious element of the analytic task is to imagine living life without a perception of being a subject.

This requires analysts to trust their own internal worlds, which again differentiates them from their patients. These patients do not trust what is inside of them and often are not aware of the three-plus dimensional space that exists psychically. They are motivated by what they experience as external reality, not internal reality. They are expert in conforming to what they believe they perceive. In fact, the external via unconscious phantasy is made to conform with their unrecognized internal need for conformity and uniformity. For this reason, such patients are usually adept at noticing pattern variation and inconsistency. They do not trust anything that varies from their patterns. New experiences are therefore suspect and disbelieved. Other people, if psychically noticed, are perceived as dangerous. Change is therefore catastrophic.

Even when an emotional experience provides a new experience, holding onto this experience perceptually requires structural change. There need not be a negative therapeutic reaction for the change to fade. Rather, the rigidity of previous patterns returns creating once again conformity to an internal reality that is thought to be external. Rather than changing the structure or the container, that which has been experienced is changed to fit the previous pattern and structure. The structure as well as the perception of external experience, then remains the same.

Looking at the familiar gestalt picture of a figure of either a vase or a woman will remind us how this works. What I am speaking of is not a point of view, but a vertex – the organizing function of experience – that is sensual. An example of sensual distortion comes by eliminating the visual, say by use of a blindfold, and asking a person to name what they are touching. Peeled grapes are not eyeballs. Spaghetti noodles are not worms. The mind influences what is perceived and distortions are greater when the senses are kept apart – dismantled – as a defense. Nonetheless, Bion says these sensuous experiences return as *traces of reminiscence* (Bion, 1967, p. 63). As such, they include information for the analyst.

Conclusion

This chapter has explored the psychoanalytic task of working with patients who maintain an unconscious delusion/hallucination of not existing. They are missing in their actions and unable to consistently use their emotions of love, hate, and curiosity as a link with themselves and others. Without a subjective sense of self, they maintain only superficial relationships. They use their senses to defend against emotion that is too much for them. Learning from experience is compromised. Internal change does not hold because the senses themselves hold fast to previous perceptions. Patients cannot trust either what they perceive or what enables them to make sense of their perceptions, due to a delusion of not existing, of having no subjective sense of self. With such a delusion they are outside of time. Instead, they have an external scaffolding of mimicry and as-if behavior.

Even when we have an internal intellectual model for understanding these primitive states of mind, we cannot help our patients with their internal perceptions unless we experience them with them. I have described this process with the hope that it will aid other analysts in recognizing these primitive delusional states of undifferentiation in their adult patients who were traumatized as infants and small children.

References

Bick, E. (1968). The experience of skin in early object relations. *International Journal of Psycho-Analysis*, 49: 484–486.

Bick, E. (1986). Further considerations on the function of the skin in early object relations. *British Journal of Psychotherapy*, 2: 292–299.

Bion, W. R. (1967). *Wilfred Bion, Los Angeles Seminars and Supervision.* Aguayo, J. and Malin, B. (Eds.). London and New York: Routledge.

Bion, W. R. (1970). *Attention and Interpretation.* London: Karnac.

Bleger, J. (1967). *Symbiosis and Ambiguity: A Psychoanalytic Study.* Churcher, J. and Bleger, L. (Eds.); Rogers, S., Bleger, L., and Churcher, J. (Trans.). London and New York: Routledge, 2013.

Britton, R. (1998) *Belief and Imagination: Explorations in Psychoanalysis.* London and New York: Routledge.

Civitarese, G. (2018). *Sublime Subjects.* London and New York: Routledge.

Eaton, J. (2015). Building a floor for experience: a model for thinking about children's experience. In Tracey, N. (Ed.), *Transgenerational Trauma and the Aboriginal Pre-school Child: Healing Through Intervention.* New York: Rowan and Littlefield.

Eekhoff, J. K. (2019). *Trauma and Primitive Mental States: An Object Relations Perspective.* London and New York: Routledge.

Eekhoff, J. K. (2021). *Bion and Primitive Mental States: Trauma and the Symbiotic Link.* London and New York: Routledge.

Eekhoff, J. K. (2022). Psychic Equivalency as an Aspect of Symbiosis. In Levine, H. and Moguillansky, C. (Eds.), *Psychoanalysis of the psychoanalytic frame Revisited" A New Look at Bleger's Classical Work.* London and New York: Routledge/IPA.

Ferenczi, S. (1929). The unwelcome child and his death-instinct. *International Journal of Psycho-Analysis*, 10: 125–129. [Reprinted in *Final Contributions to the Problems and Methods of Psycho-Analysis* (pp. 102–107). London: Karnac, 1994.]

Grotstein, J. S. (1990). The "black hole" as the basic psychotic experience: Some newer psychoanalytic and neuroscience perspectives on psychosis. *Journal of the American Academy of Psychoanalysis*, 18: 29–46.

Joseph, B. (1975). The patient who is difficult to reach. *Psychic Equilibrium and Psychic Change*. London and New York: Routledge Books.

Ogden, T. H. (1991). Some Theoretical Comments on Personal Isolation. *Psychoanalytic Dialogues*, 1(3): 377–390.

Chapter 13

Time, Space, and Dimensionality as Somatic Representations

Psychoanalysis began as a Talking Cure. Today it is a Talking Art – an experience of the aesthetic that provokes, stimulates, and inspires. Like all great art, psychoanalysis focuses on the unknown evolution of experience and the internal forces that block its transformation. Psychoanalysis now looks to the future and the magical mysteries of Life. It has shifted from a one-person focus to a two-person focus that acknowledges the importance of emotional relationships as essential for learning. It has shifted away from being a cure, to being a discovery of the Self. Trauma disrupts emotional relationships with both self and other, with subject and object, and with body and mind unity. It also disrupts the capacity to mourn and the creative freedom to be and become one's Self. In doing this, trauma also disrupts the ability to learn from experience.

Loewald (1980) understood trauma and the importance of object relations. He was particularly interested in mourning as a necessary registration and recognition of the loss involved in differentiation. At the same time, he recognized that differentiation and de-differentiation are losses that, if mourned, can result in internalization and integration, thereby fostering the development of a mind. He explored archaic object relations, recognizing that narcissistic patients who previously were considered untreatable because they did not relate to objects but to their own egos could be understood and analyzed.

In this chapter, I will attempt to explore disruptions of early archaic levels of subject object relations, using Loewald's and Bleger's exploration of body relations. Using different language, Bion too explored both body relations and object relations. Loewald (1960) emphasizes that it is the relationship that is the source of psychic change. Both Loewald and Bion reflect on the dynamic processes of the psychic apparatus and its capacity to introject new objects. Further, I hope to elaborate Loewald's ideas about language as magical – a blending of primary and secondary process and a fusion of somatopsychic processing that furthers differentiation. Whereas unconscious to unconscious communication between self and other, between analyst and analysand, is outside of language, language-as-action which includes archaic sensory associations carries unconscious reciprocal body relations between speaker and receiver.

DOI: 10.4324/9781003544470-13

Loewald (1977) also focuses on the earliest relationship between mother and baby as a metaphor for the development of identity and the birth of the mind. The somatopsychic link between mother and baby underlies all learning and this foundational link is present throughout life. Loewald (1978) postulates that the infant does not differentiate individual words the mother speaks, but is bathed in sounds and rhythms. The infant is "immersed, embedded in a flow of speech that is part and parcel of a global experience within the mother-child field" (p. 187). I believe this global experience of body and object relationship initiates a psychic experience of time and space and dimensionality. These are represented first in the body as sensations. They are experiences, most of which may never be symbolized in images or words.

Primordial Oneness

The magical power of words comes from their link to the "primordial oneness" (Loewald, 1978, p. 188) inherent in being human. This oneness or undifferentiation or symbiosis is directly linked, I believe, to the current interest in the ontological processes inherent in the birth of a thought. It also relates to post Bionian field theory (Ferro, 1992; Ferro and Civitarese, 2015; Civitarese, 2023) and before that to the field theory of the Barangers (Baranger and Baranger, 1961) and Meltzer (1975; 1986). North Americans, after Loewald, such as Ogden (1984; 1986a; 1986b; 1989), Grotstein (1990; 2000), Eigen (1989), and recently Reiner (2012), Levine (2012; 2022), Goldberg (2020); Blum, Goldberg, and Levin (2023), amongst others, are also exploring ontological processes.

Ontological processes occur in a *somatic surround*. The somatic atmosphere that surrounds the analyst and analysand encloses them globally in time and in space. The dimensionality that evolves between and within them creates an atmospheric field. The field is the space between, the caesura, the analytic link of the dyad (Bion, 2019). The field is a phenomenological experience of undifferentiation and primordial oneness, from which something new emerges. When I speak of the field, I am describing an *Experience of Being*. The experience of the somatic surround is four-dimensional, since all components are in constant fluid motion and mark psychic time. Generated by the analytic couple, the somatic surround is an aspect of the field. Out of this, new Origins emerge.

I wonder whether Loewald's (1978) emphasis on self-understanding as an epistemological goal of analysis isn't also supplemented by a view that emerges in his writing of an ontological experience of being and in its focus on the future of becoming. In this aspect, it is the field of the analytic relationship that bears examination. The field is a reality: a somatopsychic experience. Bion (1977) says, "Investigate the break: not the analyst, not the analysand; not the unconscious, not the conscious; not sanity, not insanity, but the caesura, the link, the synapse, the (counter) transference, the transitive-intransitive mood"

(p. 99). The intransitive is object-less. Ferenczi (1949) calls this psychic place, "objectless sensation". Loewald (1977) wonders about a primordial state of nondifferentiation, where subject and object are psychically one (p. 217). Out of this place, comes the magical power of words.

To investigate the transitive-intransitive atmosphere of the analytic session is to investigate the movement between being and not being, and to notice the emotional link between two subjects or objects, no matter how faint it is. This is an inter-subjectivity beyond words. It is inter-sensory. The Zen Buddhists call it interbeing Hanh (1987). Bion (1965; 1970) calls is at-one-ment.

Time and Space

I believe we all accept that there is no time or space in the unconscious. We also recognize that traumatized persons frequently suffer from an inability to defend against their access to primal states of mind, causing them to fall out of time and experience space as collapsed. Being able to defend against the infinite sources of stimulation in actual time and space enables healthy functioning. Healthy functioning includes manageable access to all states of being in both time and space, without succumbing to the chaos of infinite time and infinite space, which are unbounded experiences. Unbounded experience often results in an experience of nothingness and meaninglessness. These states are extremely difficult to put into words, yet an approximation via a verbal description is containing.

Ontological experiences of being and becoming include being suspended in time and infinite space. Suspended time and infinite space may include experiences of undifferentiation and unintegration which when in flux can be creative or destructively terrifying. Being involves a 'moment', which Bollas (1978; 1987) calls an *aesthetic of being*. Being is outside of time. Being outside of time is not the same as falling out of time. Falling out of time is to be lost in a *"meaningless now"* (Loewald, 1971). A meaningless now "does not lose but overflows its meaning beyond meaning" (pp. 144–145).

Being involves body-mind unity and subject-object symbiosis (Loewald, 1980; Bleger, 1967; Eekhoff, 2016; 2019; 2022) that just is. The aesthetic of being is a moment outside of time. Becoming is in time. Becoming involves an evolution of the aesthetic moment and an accumulation of what went before when meaning did not overflow itself. Such accumulation occurs via the organization of experience into significant psychic groupings that include a sense of past, present, and future. Accumulation in time requires embodiment, which is accumulation in space.

Usually, the infant comes into the world somato-psychically whole, capable of multiple simultaneous somatopsychic states and capable at times of recognizing and differentiating the primordial self from (m)other. Becoming involves a process of psychic relationship between undifferentiation, differentiation, and de-differentiation from mother and father as these fluid processes occur in emotional relationship. Becoming a subject also includes the necessity of loss and the capacity to mourn that which was lost, internalize what was good, accept what was bad, and leave it behind. Leaving it behind involves mourning. Only then can one move into the future. The process of becoming is movement through somatopsychic time. Being is not. Being is the *essence of presence* (Eekhoff, Chapter 1) found in a moment.

Psychic space – the psychological distance between and within subject and object – and the awareness of it may already have mysteriously evolved in utero when the fetus perceived sounds of the mother's body and sounds of her voice. Registering the presence and absence of the heartbeat, for example, the fetus may have had a proto-mental experience of me and not me (Bion, 1970; Aulagnier, 2001; Maiello, 1995). The infant had a first experience of holding and being contained when it experienced sensations upon its skin while in the womb.

Psychic space holds these processes of being and becoming in relation to an object. From life's origins to life's end, these functions are present. Throughout life, they form the organizational structures through which we process all experience. They are not developmental processes or stages. Primary process does not go away and become secondary process; body relations do not go away and become object relations; undifferentiation does not go away and become differentiation. "Self begins as differentiated and undifferentiated" (Eigen 1986, p. 160, summarizing Grotstein). All are always present, even when unknown. Although forever present, they do evolve and transform.

Further, without denying the reality of developmental stages, I, like Klein and Bion, am identifying the vertices through which we organize life's experience as positions: the primal, the paranoid-schizoid, and the depressive positions. I believe the *total emotional situation* (Loewald, 1980, p. 179) includes all positions. Whereas regressions do occur, I more often think of what is typically called regression as foregrounding or backgrounding of positions that are always present. The organization of experience, while not named positions by Loewald, is central to his ideas about identifications, introjections, and projections as means of mediating emotional experience (Loewald, 1980, p. 238). These underlie all meaning-making and form the basis of *primordial transferences* that differ from Freud's original conception of transference, in that they are primarily somatic in nature.

Primordial transferences are foundational – originating at the birth of psychic time and psychic space – and always include both soma and psyche. They are the essence of what it is to be human. The total emotional situation (Loewald, 1980) is the total situation (Joseph, 1985) of the transference. It is also a state where the Essences of Being of two people are intermingled in an analytic atmosphere where who is who cannot be distinguished – an atmosphere of an undifferentiated somatopsychic field where unconscious and unconscious blend. The shifting vertices through which we organize experience elaborates and builds our psychic space, which is the multi-dimensional internal place in which we dwell. Indwelling (Winnicott, 1945; 1972; 1975) includes a somatopsychic relationship with all things internal and external. Indwelling enables transformations in 'O'.

The primordial transference brings life and vitality, beauty and awe to personhood. When these are defensively blocked, life "becomes sterile and an empty shell" (Loewald, 1980, p. 250) and meaning overflows into meaninglessness. Coherence and continuity of going-on-being is lost. Interconnectivity is hampered by fear and destroyed. Primordial anxieties stop time and collapse space, destroying somatopsychic unity and dimensionality.

Dimensionality

The kaleidoscopic nature of somatopsychic dimensionality is unmeasurable. As an aspect of the inner world (Grotstein, 1978), dimensionality implies constant motion. Dimensionality is the intermingling of psychic time and space (Meltzer, 1975; 1986). Whatever foregrounds or backgrounds is always present, waiting for the movement of attention to elaborate it. The resonance of primal Origins gives breadth and depth and dimensionality to current experiences including the lived experience of the primordial transference and the magical expression of language. Somatopsychic coherence, inevitable in the integration and experience of internal and external linking, creates dimensionality of the space. These links have powerful primal and perhaps primordial implications that go back to the womb.

The origin of life, the union of sperm and egg, and the dividing and multiplying of cells that ultimately lead to the umbilical cord connection between fetus and mother, may be an aspect of the somatic surround. Perhaps, the placental sac – that primal physical linking sphere – is not only sensory and somatic. Perhaps, it is already proto-mental. The *somatic surround* is holding and containing. It is ironically also a somatopsychic surround that can never be apprehended. It can be a surround of safety or a somatic/autistic encapsulation arising out of annihilatory fears. Of course, there are many other surrounds, all originating from the psychic womb.

The research and hypotheses of Maiello (1995) suggest that the first awareness of the object is the *sound object*, discovered in the womb. The sound object links the rhythm and pulsing of the umbilical cord and the sound of the mother's heartbeat as indications of the first object or, in other words, of presence and absence of otherness, creating a global experience of the field. Sound, as an *echo locator*, presents the (M)other to the fetus and the fetus to the mother. These links are repeated in any analytic session. The environmental atmosphere of the session is co-created by the analytic dyad and creates the field.

The word link has multiple implications for both sides of it. A link implies one object connected to another object. Both objects change in connection. Creativity and generativity emerge from connection. The nature of the link, be it somatic, emotional, or cognitive, or all three, determines the breadth and depth of dimensionality in subjects, objects, and between them. Embodied links are multi-dimensional and indicative of mature body relations and object relations. They are alive.

Language

We might use language as an example of a multi-dimensional linking function of the somatopsyche. The instant an image becomes a word in the mind, the link to either the word before or the word after becomes an emotional elaboration of the image. The image becomes a movie. The word becomes a phrase, a phrase becomes a clause or sentence. Sentences become paragraphs. In that emotional associative way, the moment a thought is noticed, recognized, and realized, it becomes what Bion (1962; 1963) has called the preconception for the next conception. These he links with the senses. Automatically, the *transitory link* is an experience of both time and space. The conception is realized. It is not an accident that the word conception is the same word that is used to describe the link between the spermatozoa and the ovum that creates a conceptus.

Therefore, the *aesthetic moment* is already emerging from the universe of experience, through the infinite embodiment of the universe of being. Furthermore, I believe this process of being and thinking via language functions, as Loewald (1978) hints, to create a depth and dimensionality of personality, creating a primordial power of presence. The primordial power of language is that it embodies presence. He says,

> Words in their original or recovered power do not function as signs or symbols for [as referring to] being of the same substance, the same actual efficacy as that which they name; they embody it in a specific sensory-motor medium. Sensory motor elements of speech remain bodily ingredients of language, lending to words and sentences the aspect of concrete acts and entities....
>
> (p. 203)

A little later, Loewald says, "It (language) ties together human beings and self and object world, and it binds abstract thought with the bodily concreteness and power of life. In the word primary and secondary process are reconciled" (p. 204). Language as a concrete organizer of experience integrates, bringing a psychic coherence with it by potentially moving somatic representations into oneiric and verbal symbols.

Clinical Implications

Psychoanalysis is and will always be a talking treatment. Finding language for experience contains primal agonies. We have learned much from the pre-science of our analytic ancestors and are adding depth to our analyses by including the somatopsychic realm as an aspect of the global field. Patients who previously were considered unanalyzable are being analyzed today. This is due to an interest in the primordial origins of thought. This interest enables us to search for the patient as he or she was before the pathology took hold.

Freud (1923) links body and mind, soma and psyche. His famous statement; "The ego is first and foremost a bodily ego; it is not merely a surface entity, but is itself the projection of a surface" (p. 26). This statement is developed further by Klein, Bion, and Winnicott. In the United States, Loewald and others also explore the realm of the somatic and the concrete use of language-as-sensation in the treatment of hard-to-reach patients (Joseph, 1975).

Working with patients who were traumatized in infancy and childhood demands much of us. Emotional communication and poorly represented states require suffering the pain ourselves before our patients can process their traumatic experiences. They bring us timeless psychic moments and collapsed psychic spaces with little dimensionality. They bring us their confusions regarding space, unable to experience concave or convex subject object relations as psychic representations of receptivity and productivity. They speak to us from a different level than the one we use to speak to them. From their perspective, life is not multi-faceted nor forever changing. Life is what they say it is. As a result, they are concrete and borrow language to speak to us. Borrowed language is an aspect of mimicry that is outside of the symbolic order. Timeless moments, collapsed spaces, flattened dimensionality are experiences, not thoughts.

Clinical Case: Patricia

I want to relate the beginning phases of a long and painful analysis. Patricia was a single, 31 year-old, attractive Caucasian woman who sought treatment for what she termed "social anxiety". She said she was afraid of people, did not like them very much, and expected the worst from them. She felt she had never been loved. Whereas, in my experience, other patients often feared there was something missing in them and feared they could not love, she felt fine about herself, but baffled that she had never been loved. Only after a year of treatment, did she doubt that she herself could love or "maybe even like someone".

Although she was successful in her high-tech profession, she had never had a relationship, had not finished university, and had few friends. She was an only child of a couple who purportedly rarely spoke either to her or to each other. According to Patricia, her mother was chronically depressed, having given up a career as an operatic singer at age 36 to marry a man 12 years her senior and travel with him, wherever his job in the oil fields took him. She had a child, Patricia, as part of her wifely duty. Her father was quiet and taciturn. Patricia felt she was a "perfect cloning of the two". "Nobody talks".

Their frequent moves meant that as a child Patricia had no best friend and no feeling of belonging. As an adult, she longed to fit in, but said she did not.

Each day after leaving work, she felt a profound depression. She said, "Perhaps, it is just loneliness". She valued the structure and rhythm of her work. The routine she left was important to her and the open-ended time at home made her uneasy. Although she did not say it, I wondered whether proximity to other live bodies gave her the illusion of contact.

Like her mother, she was also a singer and loved music. "I love the vibrations in my body when I hum". She said, "My whole body resonates when I sing". She frequently hummed to herself at work and this comforted her. Sound and its sensations surrounded her, "keeping me company". I came to understand from her humming on the couch how the 'sound surround' also isolated her, keeping her far from me. She lived in her own sensation-dominated world that was difficult for me to enter.

Initially, Patricia's speech lacked specificity. Her descriptions of her responses to me or to others at work were vague and general. They lacked depth. Although she had a very pleasant voice, her voice too lacked dimensionality, leaving the sound of it more important than its content. When I say her voice lacked dimensionality, I am speaking of a lack of resonance or tonality that would indicate the emotional underpinnings of her words. I tried to comprehend how she could be a singer. Often, I wondered if she had emotions. She talked about emotions but could not elicit or evoke emotion in me. I felt strangely detached and alienated from her, which was extremely disturbing. I worked very hard to find her, but felt I rarely succeeded. I observed that when I spoke, she agreed with me but could not elaborate. She told me her vocal and piano teachers often said, "More feeling! More feeling!" This confused her. From her perspective, she felt she sang with feeling. She also was confused about how to put feeling into playing the piano.

Purportedly, people valued her for her calm demeanor and clear head. I could not understand how others could describe her as such, in that with me, she seemed more dead than calm, more confused than clear. She also was extremely concrete, silently expecting me to be just like her and understand her perfectly. Her relationship with time also differed from mine. It was a pattern, which she maintained, never tardy nor early. She maintained the schedule.

In the session, I began to notice that time did not seem to move for her and experience therefore could not accumulate. She began a session where the last one left off. Initially, I thought this meant she was taking in our explorations, thinking about them, and making use of me. I was wrong. There was no time psychically between the end of one session and the beginning of the next. What was, was. Therefore, there was no need to reflect on "what was". Nothing changed.

As I began to understand my own responses to our meetings, I realized that even in the session, time did not move. By that I mean, we were locked in a perpetual moment. Each exchange was a thing in itself and could not be altered, elaborated, or reflected upon. This was extremely disorienting for me. Initially, I would experience and observe it, but then forget it. I couldn't seem to capture the process between us in words and therefore was only fleetingly aware of this experience, that may or may not have been mutual. I had to join her there, but joining her felt like death to me, a draw towards entropy, a passivity beyond passivity.

Once she remarked, "I am so passive. I think I want to stop time. If I make a decision, time is moving again. That is awful". She might have said the same thing about speaking or thinking about herself or engaging with me. She came regularly to our sessions and always on time because, "that is what I do. It's my schedule".

I found her very difficult-to-reach (Joseph, 1975). She always had things to say, but I could not find symbolic meaning in her many words. Over time, like a toy running out of batteries, she slowed down and spoke less, having little to say. She wanted me to begin every session and was tormented by always having to start. She hated silence because she said she was blank, with nothing there. She felt I wasn't there either. I imagined this had been true for her as a child with two older parents who meant well but did not talk much. I imagine she gave up trying to reach them. At the same time, she insisted on "being in the driver's seat", being in charge. This insistence did not fit with her passivity and difficulty making decisions, which was also always present.

As her analysis deepened, she began to be able to speak about herself instead of her external world. At first this consisted of descriptions of what she did, where she went, who she met, but gradually as my curiosity about her and genuine interest in finding her impacted her, her insights about herself took on emotional significance. Something was changing. She could name things, but often not remember them. I became her memory, bringing her Self back to her again and again. Over time she became able to tell me her process. Her words, which she often forgot or disregarded as mine, began to take on significance and become more than sounds and sensations.

I also felt like she was beginning to remember herself, to be less in the perpetual moment. She began telling me that she recognized she had been dissociated – her words, not mine. She said, 'I have been so disassociated. I need someone else to relate to a word and talk about it, before the word means anything to me". "Sometimes when you talk, I only hear letters, the sensation of letters, not their relationship to each other or to words". "Maybe what I hear are sounds and rhythms". "Maybe what I hear is music".

Eventually as Patricia differentiated from me, she became angry at my otherness. That is a story for another time, but the progressing from being a no-one to being a some-one was tumultuous. Differentiating was painful. She equated my not being the same as she was with my not understanding her. My differentiation from her and hence my inability to be her meant I could not comprehend her experience. From her perspective, I was always failing her. My failures made her furious. I felt her anger promoted differentiation even as it attempted to get me to conform and stop awareness of our differences.

Discussion

It is very difficult to verbalize how sensation embeds us in time. Hopefully, Patricia's story has helped with the example it provides. When, in addition, trauma has overwhelmed somatopsychic unity, sensation can be used as a defense against time. Sensation as defense is not a link when the communicating functions of sensations are absent. The meaning of words gets lost in the concrete vibrations of them. When the content and the narrative and its derivatives are our analytic focus, we pay attention to language and its symbolic meaning, not their somatic functions.

Unfortunately, sometimes when our patients have been particularly traumatized, their language is important not as symbolic derivatives, but as *somatic derivatives*. Patricia's trauma was emotional, in that she was purportedly psychically invisible to her parents. This meant that she and I were using language in very different ways. Somatic derivatives are subjective sensations that overwhelm a relationship to objects. They are an experience. Sometimes these somatic sensations replace a subjective sense of Self with vibrations, like letters separate from words. Vibrations as a primary focus stop time and collapse space into a perpetual now with no hope for a future. Patricia's humming in sessions was self-stimulation that destroyed both meaning to her and connection with me. Without a link to a live other, she was lost to herself.

I believe that somatic derivatives of trauma are representations of early psychic overwhelm. When this somatic representation occurs, other somatic sensations are used to inhibit emotional contact. The other is obliterated. Loving and being loved are difficult to experience without the psychic perception of an object to love and be loved by. It follows that the traumatized patient is left to cope alone, which often leads to a loss of a subjective sense of Self.

Psychic overwhelm originating from trauma and resulting in trauma means that signal anxiety is no longer accurately interpreted as impending danger but becomes a signal for repetitive overwhelm. If we can pay attention to the body as it represents emotional and affective storms, we often can find the point of disruption of mental processes where symbolic processing itself was destroyed and then encapsulated via sensation. Finding the point of disruption between subject and subject and between object and object provides us with a beginning point for reclaiming the representational process so necessary for healthy psychic functioning.

Primal mental states, that is states that are primarily expressed via the body, are accessed in a variety of circumstances: trauma is one of those. An expectation of care is not met. Grief over the loss of a way of life, body competency, or a lover can also promote this access. Unmediated access to primal mental states requires extraordinary defenses in order to protect oneself from overwhelming stimulation. Bodymind dissociation occurs when the higher order defenses of repression and of splitting and projection fail.

Bodymind dissociation creates perceptual distortions, particularly of time and place, that interfere with dimensionality and individuality. Fusion, not of the instincts, but of subject object relations confuses. Undifferentiated states of mind blur the psychic boundaries between inside and outside, between truth and fiction, and between self and other. Psychic fusion and undifferentiation are used then as a means of denying reality. They protect the mind from overwhelm and allow a psychic space to develop so a recognition of the Real can dawn slowly. The slow dawning of reality enables differentiation and the mourning inevitable in individuation to proceed naturally.

Conclusion

In this chapter, I have used Loewald's explorations into the magical foundations of language to explore the somatic representation of unsymbolized nonverbal emotional experience that remains in the somatopsyche all of our lives. The primal link between internal and external objects and its communication is outside of language. The unconscious link between analyst and analysand creates an emotional field. I suggest that derivatives of fusion and undifferentiation are found in the soma. In health, these become background objects of care.

I highlight Loewald's prescience in drawing our attention to somatic underpinnings in language and to archaic levels of the mind always found in relationship and assert these foreshadowed current developments in analytic thinking around object relationships. Object relationships profoundly impact the development of the mind via represented and unrepresented states. This chapter explores the undifferentiated and symbiotic (Bleger, 1967), the undifferentiated and archaic (Loewald, 1979) analytic relationship and its therapeutic function in the ongoing development of the mind.

It expands on Loewald's "archaic level" of the analytic relationship, focusing on what has frequently been termed "the psychotic core" (Eigen, 1986) of the dyad. I concur with Loewald that these levels manifest as normal aspects of relationship all of our lives. These deeply unconscious links influence the therapeutic action at a nonverbal level. The communication of the primal link is unconscious to unconscious and outside of language. The derivatives, I believe, are in the soma. When outside of language, words are used as words for their sensual qualities and their associative link to the lost mother of infancy. They are not primarily used for their symbolic meaning. Words are also used as links to primordial unity and the *somatic surround*. The chapter explores the defenses of stopping time and space as a means of de-differentiating.

I have explored how in instances of traumatic overwhelm, the background object of care is absent. Extraordinary defenses against psychic overwhelm are needed. These defenses interfere with healthy development of the Self and subject object relations. I describe how the somatopsychic environment is disrupted following trauma via the defenses of stopping time and collapsing space in order to avoid awareness of reality and mourning of loss. Further, the chapter links the undifferentiated aspect of relationship to post-Bionian field theory.

A clinical example from the early analysis of a difficult-to-reach patient illustrates the lack of differentiation, the loss of time and space, and the dissociation of soma and psyche that characterizes a loss of depth and dimensionality found in patients who have been traumatized in infancy and childhood.

References

Aulagnier, P. (2001). *The Violence of Interpretation: From Pictogram to Statement*. Sheridan, A. (Trans.). Hove, UK; Philadelphia: Brunner/Routledge. [Originally published in French: Paris: Presses Universitaires de France, 1975.]

Baranger, M. and Baranger, W. (1961). *The Work of Confluence: Listening and Interpreting in the Psychoanalytic Field*. London: International Psychoanalytical Association, Karnac, 2009.

Bion, W. R. (1962b). *Learning from Experience*. London: Heinemann. [Reprinted London: Karnac, 1984.]

Bion, W. R. (1963). *Elements of Psycho-Analysis*. London: Heinemann. [Reprinted London: Karnac, 1984.]

Bion, W. R. (1965). *Transformations*. London: Heinemann. [Reprinted London: Karnac, 1984.]

Bion, W. R. (1970). *Attention and Interpretation*. London: Tavistock. [Reprinted London: Karnac, 1984.]

Bion, W. R. (2019). *Two Papers: "The Grid" and "Caesura"*. London and New York: Routledge.

Bleger, J. (1967). *Symbiosis and Ambiguity: A Psychoanalytic Study*. Churcher, J. and Bleger, L. (Eds.); Rogers, S., Bleger, L., and Churcher, J. (Trans.). London and New York: Routledge.

Blum, A., Goldberg P., and Levin, M. (2023). *Here I'm Alive: The Spirit of Music in Psychoanalysis*. New York: Columbia University Press.

Bollas, C. (1978). The Aesthetic Moment and the Search for Transformation. *Annual of Psychoanalysis*, 6: 385–394.

Bollas, C. (1987). *The Shadow of the Object: Psychoanalysis of the Unthought Known*. New York: Columbia University Press.

Civitarese, G. (2023). *Psychoanalytic Field Theory: A Contemporary Introduction*. London and New York: Routledge.

Eekhoff, J. K. (2016). Introjective Identification: The Analytic Work of Evocation. *American Journal of Psychoanalysis*, 76: 354–361.

Eekhoff, J. K. (2019). *Trauma and Primitive Mental States: An Object Relations Perspective*. London and New York: Routledge.

Eekhoff, J. K. (2022). Psychic Equivalency as an Aspect of Symbiosis. In Levine, H. and Moguillansky, C. (Eds.), *Psychoanalysis of the psychoanalytic frame Revisited" A New Look at Bleger's Classical Work*. London and New York: Routledge/IPA.

Eigen, M. (1986). *The Psychotic Core*. Lanham: Jason Aronson, Inc.

Ferenczi, S. (1949). Notes and Fragments [1930–32]. *International Journal of Psycho-Analysis*, 30: 231–242.

Ferro, A. (1992). *The Bi-Personal Field: Experiences in Psychoanalysis.* London: Routledge (1999).

Ferro, A. and Civitarese, G. (2015). *The Analytic Field and Its Transformations.* London: Karnac.

Freud, S. (1923). The ego and the id. *SE 19*: 3–68.

Grotstein, J. S. (1978). Inner space: Its dimensions and its coordinates. *International Journal of Psychoanalysis*, 59: 55–61.

Grotstein, J. S. (1990). The "black hole" as the basic psychotic experience: Some newer psychoanalytic and neuroscience perspectives on psychosis. *Journal of the American Academy of Psychoanalysis*, 18: 29–46.

Grotstein, J. S. (2000). *Who is the Dreamer Who Dreams the Dream? A Study of Psychic Presences.* Hillsdale, New Jersey and London: The Analytic Press.

Hanh, T. N. (1987). *Interbeing: Commentaries on the Tiep Hien Precepts.* Berkley: Parralax Press.

Joseph, B. (1975). The patient who is difficult to reach. In Feldman, M. and Spillius, E. B. (Eds.), *Psychic Equilibrium and Psychic Change: Selected Papers of Betty Joseph* (pp. 75–87). London: Tavistock/Routledge, 1989.

Joseph, B. (1985). Transference: The Total Situation. *International Journal of Psychoanalysis*, 66: 447–454.

Levine, H. B. (2012). The colourless canvas: Representation, therapeutic action and the creation of mind. *International Journal of Psycho-Analysis*, 93: 607–629.

Levine, H. (2022). *Affect, Representation and Language: Between the Silence and the Cry.* London: Routledge.

Loewald, H. W. (1960). On the therapeutic action of psychoanalysis. *Int. Journal of Psychoanalysis*, 41: 16–33.

Loewald, H. W. (1971). The Experience of Time. In *Papers of Psychoanalysis* (1980, pp. 138–147). New Haven and London: Yale University Press.

Loewald, H. W. (1977). *Instinct theory, object relations, and psychic structure formation.* In *Papers of Psychoanalysis* (1980, pp. 207–218). New Haven and London: Yale University Press.

Loewald, H. W. (1978). Primary process, secondary process, and language. In *Papers of Psychoanalysis* (1980, pp 178–206). New Haven and London: Yale University Press.

Loewald, H. W. (1979). Reflections on the psychoanalytic process and its therapeutic potential. *Psychoanalytic Study of the Child*, 34(55): 155–167.

Loewald, H. W. (1980). *Papers of Psychoanalysis.* New Haven and London: Yale University Press.

Maiello, S. (1995). The Sound-Object: A Hypothesis about Prenatal Auditory Experience and Memory. *Journal of Child Psychotherapy*, 21: 23–41.

Meltzer, D. (1975). Dimensionality as a parameter in mental functioning: Its relation to narcissistic functioning. In Meltzer, D., with Bremner, J., Hoxter, S., Weddell, D., and Wittenberg, L. *Explorations in Autism* (pp. 6–29). Strath Tay, Perthshire, UK: Clunie Press. [Reprinted for the Harris Meltzer Trust, London: Karnac, 2008.]

Meltzer, D. (1986). *Studies in Extended Metapsychology: Clinical Applications of Bion's Ideas.* Perthshire: Clunie Press for The Roland Harris Educational Trust, London.

Ogden, T. H. (1984). Instinct, phantasy, and psychological deep structure: A reinterpretation of aspects of the work of Melanie Klein. *Contemporary Psychoanalysis*, 20: 500–525.

Ogden, T. H. (1986a). *The Matrix of the Mind: Object Relations and the Psychoanalytic Dialogue.* Lanham: Jason Aronson, Inc.

Ogden, T. H. (1986b). *The Primitive Edge of Experience.* Lanham: Jason Aronson, Inc.

Ogden, T. H. (1989). On the concept of an autistic-contiguous position. *International Journal of Psycho-Analysis,* 70: 127–140.

Reiner, A. (2012). *Bion and Being: Passion and the Creative Mind.* London and New York: Routledge.

Winnicott, D. W. (1945). Primitive emotional development. In *Through Paediatrics to Psychoanalysis* (pp. 145–156). New York: Basic Books, 1958.

Winnicott, D. W. (1972). Basis of self in body. *International Journal of Child Psychotherapy,* 1: 7–16.

Winnicott, D. W. (1975). *Through Paediatrics to Psycho-analysis.* London: Hogarth Press/Institute of Psycho-Analysis.

Chapter 14

Catastrophe and Creativity
From Fragmentation to Emergence

Today, I am using Ferenczi's search for truth and the courage he exhibited in seeking it to explore catastrophe and creativity. Further, I am following Ferenczi's (1909; 1914) lead into the primordial, exploring a search for truth that if successful will result in both a catastrophic loss and creative gain. In entering the primordial, Ferenczi (1909) takes us into the body, and into what he calls "the symphony of life" and "the primordial music of the instincts" (p. 62). He also takes us into our own experiences of undifferentiation and differentiation, bringing us to an exploration of the very origins of self. It is an ontological journey outside of time and space. It is an exploration into our essence or spirit or what some might name soul. Such an exploration is both terrifying and awe-inspiring.

Ferenczi suggests that familiarity with the primordial never leaves us, but rests silently in our bodies as background for truth. We access the primordial in moments of beauty, discovered in art, poetry, music, or sexuality. We access it in psychoanalysis in the profound intimate relationship between patient and analyst. Love, hate, and curiosity are expressions of the primordial. We access it in moments of grief, as our primordial states rise to comfort us. Loss, and the comfort our bodies can bring us, recall our earliest loss of our mother's womb, but the womb comforts. Loss just is – a truth with which we must reckon. Just as truth and loss go together, so too do truth and beauty. Truth and beauty cannot be separated.

Unfortunately, both truth and loss and truth and beauty can be attacked with disastrous consequences. Attacks on truth are as catastrophic as is truth itself. During attacks, we also access the primordial. Each of us knows this from our personal experiences with our patients and each other, as well as from our observations of the political and natural catastrophes around us. We also know these disastrous consequences from the years when Ferenczi's ideas were banned from psychoanalytic discussion.

A catastrophe is different than a trauma. A trauma overwhelms our defenses and leaves us without our minds to help us. The loss of self includes the fragmentation that separates body from mind. A catastrophe is life changing. It may be either internal or external. While disorienting and disturbing,

DOI: 10.4324/9781003544470-14

a catastrophe does not necessarily destroy the mind or the body mind union. Instead, a catastrophe changes internal or external structures. Both trauma and catastrophe evoke the primordial – that is our earliest experiences of sentience. Another difference is that trauma co-opts the primordial senses, turning them into defenses against reality. A catastrophe might use the senses to survive.

The primordial defenses also are accessed when the higher-order defenses of repression, of splitting, projecting, and introjecting fail. When these defenses are absent, psychotic processes protect us from reality. Unfortunately, without the higher order defenses, primitive intense affects are unmediated by the mind. Being in touch with life and with death creates a catastrophic upheaval of our assumptions and beliefs. In doing so, the unconscious structures of our somatopsyche are potentially altered, something that ultimately with relationship can be turned to creative renewal.

Somatic defenses arising from the primordial can replace emotion. The primordial, linked intimately with the body, puts us in touch with our animal natures – "the music of our instincts". The primordial is a constant foreverchanging natural wonder that supports life in all its mystery and fluidity. Primordial rhythms are the source of our creativity. Emotional vibrations link body and mind. Unfortunately, when co-opted by trauma, the senses are no longer reliable sources of information about reality.

Ferenczi understands this. Ferenczi (1918) recognizes that even if "humanity remained a victim of its own unconscious to the end", truth is compensation. Through discourse with one another, truth can be found. However, discourse is not always possible. For example, in war, there is no discourse. The emotional psychic drivers are primordial survival instincts. War is a fight to the death. In war, actual physical survival is threatened. The fear of dying heightens a fear of being wiped out of existence psychically. To call this annihilation anxiety is to minimize its primordial links. Psychotic processes dominate.

We also find a lack of discourse in terrorism where random attacks on chance innocents shock and horrify us. A lack of discourse is not only about speaking a different language, it is also about not being able to represent experience in language. It is about not being able to think, using Bion's (1958; 1962a) definition of thinking – that is with the aid of love, hate, and knowledge, of being able to dream. A lack of discourse includes a concretization of emotion that makes action the language. Such concretization leaves no room for dialogue or for learning from experience (Bion, 1962b). Words themselves lack meaning and are merely words about other words.

Language without thinking also destroys discourse, while seemingly seeking communication. Language without thinking, words about words, may hide a cruel reality of a lost or absent subject. Herein begins the lie. Discourse from a dissociative state, without a thinking mind or without a subjective embodied sense of self, furthers polarization. It makes truth a subjective certainty that each side claims. Discourse as a lie that imitates openness results in an impasse. Impasses feed violence, since violence arises as a defense against truth and a concretization of overwhelming affect. Impasses feel solid, unmovable and unchangeable. They are a source for despair, even as they paradoxically provide comfort in their immobile constancy.

Creative or Destructive Catastrophe?

A psychic catastrophe, that is an emotional breakdown, not only comes from lies, but happens to and from truth. Bion's (1968; 1970) idea of catastrophic change that occurs when two people truly meet is relevant here. Again, I believe Ferenczi (1932a; 1932b; 1952; 1988, foreshadowed this awareness, speaking as he did of catastrophic truths he learned about himself from his patients. Truth exists in relationship. Awareness of truth arrives via the emotional exchange between two people. However, discovering truth requires both people to be psychically present, open to themselves and each other.

For catastrophic psychic change to happen, something internal occurs: there is an unconscious and conscious breakdown of preconceived notions, a break-up of old patterns of organizing experience. There is a devasting psychic war. These breakdowns are catastrophic for our organizing structures. However, they are also breakthroughs opening us to creative new insights and potential new ways of organizing our experiences. Language and discourse are the conscious expression of the emotional links that catastrophically and creatively change us. Discourse in the symbolic realm is a transformation of emotional psychic reality that may or may not be put into language. It is expressive of primordial affects calmed and used for growth and development, not destructiveness.

Ferenczi (1910) wrote to Freud,

> The final consequence of such insight—when it is present in two people— is that they *are not ashamed in front of each other, keep nothing secret, tell each other the truth without risk of insult or in the certain hope that within the truth there can be no lasting insult.*
>
> (p. 220)

Ferenczi is saying the truth of the joint experience does not need to be one of agreement. It needs to be one of honesty. I would add that it requires courage to face oneself through the eyes of another person. The context for this quote is one where he is exploring the application of Freud's ideas of the unconscious as found within psychoanalysis. A catastrophic psychic break-up occurs on either side of emotional contact – being either too close or too far from each other. A catastrophe happens when one or both members of a dyad are too frightened to acknowledge the joint experience in the moment. It also happens when they do.

The catastrophe implied from this quote occurs when two people unconsciously are dishonest and so do not emotionally meet. I believe both Ferenczi (1952) and Bion (1965) are in touch with the emotional reality of our ongoing need for intimacy and the inevitable change intimacy evokes. Both men explore the context and the process of relationship and discourse. Both are examining the conscious and the unconscious processes leading to symbolization and the ability to think. A creative catastrophe happens when truth is revealed. A destructive catastrophe happens when a lie keeps us isolated from each other. The lie keeps internal structures unchanged. Some of this catastrophe occurs on a primordial level. Some of it occurs at a symbolic level and leads to a creative breakdown.

Fragmentation

In his search to help his patients, Ferenczi (1933) describes breakdown as fragmentation. He explores fragmentation and atomization so extreme that a sense of existence itself is lost. If existence is lost, emotional relationship with another person is absent and only the concrete functional transaction continues. Evidence of a catastrophe occurs when two people are not meeting as equals. If one is fragmented and the other is not, no meeting of equals is possible. Perhaps emotional meeting itself is fleeting. In a moment, we will see an example of this with my patient Ava.

Truth emerges as a function of loving, hating, and knowing another person. Love, hate, and knowledge lie outside the symbolic order, as well as within it. These emotions are bridges between body and mind, present in the birth of representation. I say this, recognizing with Bion (1962a; 1962b), that sensual perceptions require only one person. Lies require only one as well. Emotional links as symbols where truth and beauty emerge require two.

A truthful discourse then would be without a manic or aggressive stance. It would include passion without sexuality, tenderness without expectation, respect without condescension. It would not be discourse if one person asserts an imperative. Ferenczi (1910), again in a letter to Freud, agrees with him that imperatives are paranoic. I would add, and therefore imperatives are intrusive. Winnicott (1965; 1986) asserts that intrusion creates trauma. As I have said earlier, trauma and catastrophe are not the same. When we assert our opinions about what our patients should do, we are implying our superiority and their inferiority. Such behavior impedes true change and does not represent truth. It traumatizes via intrusion.

A truthful discourse when working with trauma is difficult, because primal defenses have confused truth with lies (Eekhoff, 2021; 2025, Chapter 10). These very unique and personal defenses often serve to collapse psychic boundaries, erase differences, and confuse who is whom. When boundaries are confused and differences erased, two subjects are not in relationship with each other. Subjectivity itself is lost when the response to a trauma includes atomization, an extreme form of fragmentation (Ferenczi, 1918; 1932b; 1933). Subjectivity is lost during somatopsychic dissociation. A true intersubjective relationship with an object requires separateness and difference. A relationship requires a subjective sense of self.

We are moving now into a different arena: from a neurotic processing of experience, where truth is possible to discern to a psychotic one where it is not. We are moving from intersubjective contact to intrasubjective alienation. We are moving from a differentiated state to a paranoid or schizoid state or an even more primordial state of sporadic undifferentiation as is seen in autistic states of mind. These states make discourse difficult and sometimes impossible because they deny that the other or ultimately the self exists.

Emergence

Emerging from these defensive somatic undifferentiated states and being free to move back and forth between them enables creative interaction with self and other. Access and emergence results in art, music, dance, and poetry. Access and emergence are the center of psychoanalytic relationship. Art, music, dance, poetry, and psychoanalysis integrate the primordial soma with psyche via contact with primordial affects and primitive emotions. The arts both originate in the primordial and give access to primordial selves. Universal primordial places evoke contact within each participant, enabling us to penetrate a little further into the outer reaches of our inner spaces, furthering integration and creation.

A state of analytic openness to the other in analysis, akin to a mother's primary preoccupation with her infant in the pre and post months of birth, while necessary, is terrifying. Both analyst and analysand become preoccupied unconsciously with each other. Their primordial natures emerge, becoming the reality of the moment, existing together in time and space. Proximity and sensuality unite. The dyad moves between psychotic and nonpsychotic states of mind. Undifferentiated states blend with differentiated states generating a creative flow between them. Truth is happening then. This is not traumatic, but may be catastrophic, because it disrupts set internal structures, which is why it is terrifying.

Creative thinking is thinking that includes the emotions and a capacity to tolerate not knowing. It involves an ability to move into the gap between people, emotions, and/or ideas. When Ferenczi was attempting to understand E. Severn, he was attempting to put himself in her shoes, to bridge the gap of their differences so he could emerge again and think about how to help her. His attempt was what Bion (1970) has called at-one-ment. Intuitively, Ferenczi was attempting to return to the origin of Severn's creativity via what Bleger has called symbiosis (Bleger, 1967). He was willing to open himself radically to her experience – including her experience of him. He became acutely aware that in spite of his best intentions, he could genuinely hurt her. His contact with Severn resulted in catastrophic change for him.

He was willing to face the catastrophe of letting go of his own set ideas and beliefs about himself, about her, and about psychoanalysis. Doing so was both catastrophic and creative. It was catastrophic both personally and professionally. He paid dearly for his courage, suffering his patients' pain and looking at his own participation. He listened to himself and to them simultaneously, learned from them, and in Severn's case, they both changed creatively.

Ferenczi also suffered for them by losing credibility with his colleagues, becoming estranged from Freud, proceeding in the face of his doubts. He suffered from speaking his truth as he knew it. Today we know that Ferenczi's willingness to look at himself, to pay attention to himself paying attention to his patients and to listen to what they taught him about how to help them was both courageous and creative. Yes, he made mistakes. We all do. Hopefully we learn from them.

In health, concrete thinking and creative thinking are linked to each other. Each is necessary. When working together, the concrete and the creative result in learning from emotional experience. Surrendering to emotional relationship and the chaos it brings, while life-affirming and vitalizing, is especially terrifying and catastrophic for those who have suffered early trauma. The uncertainty emotions bring can be threatening and feel dangerous. Emotions are communication to ourselves and to others. Often, they carry messages we do not want to hear.

Analysts working with patients who have been traumatized must think creatively and give up their set notions of what needs to happen (Ferenczi, 1928). They must be willing to disturb and be disturbed. Without this, positive catastrophic change cannot occur and old patterns will re-emerge in new forms, leaving the patient and the analyst as they were – perhaps within a cycle of collusion, confusion, and disillusion. Instead of true emotional contact with creative discourse, they may be caught in a mutual misconception of symbiosis as an attempt to hold themselves together and prevent fragmentation.

Ava and the Catastrophic Breakup of the Black Hole

Ava, a patient I (Eekhoff, 2021 wrote about in a paper entitled "The Black Hole: Alarm Signal of Catastrophe" purportedly suffered from early sexual abuse plus maternal and paternal misattunement. The black hole, her words for a sensation of imploding and being alone inside a dense sucking place of no exit, had been a frequent place of despair in her analysis. Alone even in the presence of others, myself included, left Ava safe but desperate.

As a child, Ava was extremely anxious and clinging, always terrified of separating from her mother. As a young adult, she was avoidant of others. She over-rode her anxiety to be social. She was bright, attractive, and could mimic appropriate social behavior. This enabled her to marry, have a successful career, and then have two children. She loved being a mother, but felt 'triggered' by her children's helplessness and total dependence upon her.

Later, I came to understand that the love she felt and received from them was disorganizing for her. Although her analysis was completed before COVID, the pandemic further evoked access to her 'black hole', leaving her paranoid about her husband's faithfulness and obsessive about the well-being of her children. She returned for further analytic work discouraged, angry, and occasionally suicidal.

She did not want to come four times a week nor use the couch. She said she needed to see me since she didn't believe I was real. I was struck by how different she seemed than when first I'd met her. I could see that her analysis had made a difference. No longer did she hide behind her hair, or pull the blanket over her head, and murmur words softly. No longer was her speech vague and tangential. She looked at me, and spoke clearly and directly. She recognized her reactions to her husband, her children, and me as being excessive and was seemingly able to reflect upon her behavior.

What was so disturbing to her were spells of deep lethargy and passivity, what she called her "return to the black hole", which actually comforted her. Initially I was quite taken with her reflectiveness. However, later I recognized some of her words as mine. I could not find her emotionally in the verbal processing nor in the action of the hour. We seemed caught in an impasse where thought and interpretation brought agreement and apparent elaboration without bringing creative catastrophic change. Ultimately, I felt I could not reach her in the black hole of her depression and extreme withdrawal.

Still, I remained hopeful. In her profession and her mothering, Ava remained creative. She was able to envision new programs at work, intuit her infants' needs, and speak almost poetically about herself. In spite of how busy she was, she wrote poetry and journaled. Her husband was a musician and they sang together.

Was this creativity real? By real I mean, did it come from truth within her? Or was her creativity a mimicry itself, serving a function of meeting an internal ideal? Was it too a compensatory defense? If her creativity was real, then what if anything had her analysis done to help her register and express it? And what was her black hole, returned again from years before? I felt we had had genuine contact by the end of her analysis, yet now, reaching her was so difficult. What was this deep, depressive, and seemingly destructive place she had once again accessed? As before, I experienced these black hole states with her as a collapse of time and space and being sucked into infinity. To bear these, both of us had to stretch in our abilities to tolerate reality.

Was this depression a final bastion of Ava's black hole? Or would her black hole always be with her? Being outside of time and space and outside of relationship meant she was terribly, but unfortunately comfortably, alone, where not even I could find her. Would I too always now register a dark, solid, unchangeable aspect of myself? Was the black hole in everyone, just unregistered? Was it some aspect of an inner inaccessible (Bion, 1970) place most of us never contact? She appeared unreachable there, fooling me with her mimicry of me.

It was me really who fooled myself and perhaps wanted to be fooled by her. My love for her and my hatred of the black hole made me want to be hopeful. I feared imploding. I did not want to be a companion in her black hole. I did not want to go with her into that dark, solid sucking place. I feared never emerging, as did she. We both despaired. I needed to register my terror and horror, rather than defend with a manic denial of my dread and hopelessness.

Yet, at the same time, I recognized that we were making progress creatively together. We had registered the event horizon, which was the chaotic somatic nameless sensations being evoked in the hour in both of us. These occurred just before her implosion. Now, some might say this is my imagination, my creativity, re-framing a catastrophe into progress. Perhaps. At the time, my subjective experience told me we were both reacting to these registrations by attempting to defend in very primitive ways. However, we were meeting each other honestly in our reactions.

Both Ava and I responded to our somatic sensations. We could not repress them because they were too fleeting and unprocessed to be relegated to the unconscious. We could not split and project them out because their chaotic nature meant they had not come together enough to be split apart and projected. They emerged as somatic registrations of the primordial. At best, the somatic sensations were traces that had been atomized (Ferenczi, 1933; 1988). Ava's subjective sense of self had vaporized. I watched myself through the mist of her. I believed there was an ontological birth occurring. Neither of us had words. Meaning might follow.

Since Ava had had what seemed to me "a good-enough" analysis, she was able to describe and name that which I also was eventually able to name. In a session that marked a turning point, she was almost whispering. I had to strain to hear her. She spoke in phrases without links attempting to describe her experience of being sucked into the black hole. The event horizon, in the session, that had triggered this was a moment of deep connection and beauty between us. We had looked deep into each other's eyes and met there. We both had felt love.

Then Ava disappeared, her face and eyes going blank. She eventually struggled to find words.

> Ava: [Breathing shallowly, following a long silence]. Atoms…molecules… I'm disappearing…atoms.
>
> (She is silent for several minutes during which I feel very shocked at the sudden shift and anxious.)
>
> Elements inchoate…to become aware of chaos, with an observing mind. It's…I don't know. Gone…back…gone again. So alone, so solid and dark and dense…how can I be atoms?
>
> There's a potential. Like oh. [She is silent.]
>
> (Then with pressure and volume, she says:)
>
> You're here… oh. Oh. Ooohhh. You're here, then later it's like you're gone. I don't know.

Analyst: Hmm.

Ava: O, oh, oohhhhh. [She is silent.]

It's like a different kind of nothingness. It just is. A fact I condone when I'm aware I need you. You have to go. I understand. It's life. You'll come back, but there's this moment of nothingness. I can kind of imagine nothingness from a place of observation.

Analyst: You and me.

Ava: A momentary observation, then an immediate light and I'm in a black hole, atomized, gone. That's a defensive nothing. The other nothing is where I was before all of this.

Was? Was I? Am I? No me there. I don't think. Could be defensive too. (For several moments, there is silence.)

No sound, no sensation, no image. No words. Just pain. Oohhhh. [silence.]

Analyst: I am here.

Ava: Implosion. No color. Psychic. I'm crying, but I don't recognize what it is. No recognition. I cry, but it's just sound coming out of my mouth. Tears.

Some flicker occurred: Why are you crying? I don't know.

Oh, you are here. I cry some more. Stop. This isn't a big deal, but I do feel so sad.

Surprise, confusion, a glimmer of hope, but mostly something missing. To think you've been here all along and I haven't. [Silence.]

I haven't. Confusion, such confusion. Where am I?

Now that you are here, you'll leave.

I'm just eyes, big eyes, seeking comfort. That's terrifying.

(She's silent. She looks at me and away – the contact is seemingly too much.)

The rug. Creating patterns. Going away into a constellation, stars, clouds, going into outer space to be ok. [She leaves without looking at me.]

The following Monday, she is very quiet. Surprisingly, she lies on the couch. I can barely hear her and when I wonder why, she says she is not here. The session slowly evolves. She remains distant. We explore how she has lost me over the weekend. She has snippets of memory from Friday, but not enough for a narrative.

At the end of the session, she says it is as if she is at the very cusp of being, then realizes I am here.

AVA: The 'You are here' is too overwhelming. Like it is so true and so beautiful and I...poof! I'm gone.

ANALYST: Somehow being with me is too much for you.

AVA: So sad, alone. Yeah.

ANALYST: Alone even knowing I am here.

AVA: (She agrees)

The Friday session marked a turning point because she managed to find words and fragmented sentences to share with me. Our true emotional contact triggered withdrawal and collapse into a black hole. This was a repetition of what was happening when she truly connected with love to her husband and her children. The truth of their love was overwhelming to her given her early experience of traumatic mis-attunement and catastrophic loss. My concrete presence became an emotional truth for her that initially was too much. The pain of what she had not known – both with me and before me – could be registered, then remembered and processed between us. The catastrophe was that now the truth of potential loss could be realized.

Her collapse into the black hole was not attacking the link (Bion, 1959) within her or between us. She simply vaporized and disappeared. In the process, she could not experience me as present. The primordial projection – the first one – comes before the fear and the paranoid projections that are recognitions of the existence of the other, the beauty of the other. The enormity of the beauty and truth of our connection was horrible in its transience. She could not yet bear its coming and going. The loss was too great. She disappeared. Meltzer and Williams (1988) describe the apprehension of beauty, where the presence of the object is potentially as overwhelming as is the absence.

Discussion

Ferenczi (1909) asserts that object love and object hate are primordial instincts that are the source of introjection, again implying they are necessary for our connections with each other, for thinking and dreaming. They are necessary for symbolization (Ferenczi, 1952). Lack of discourse arises when the participating parties are on different psychic levels and one or both collapse into concrete processing, losing a capacity to symbolize. The collapse into concrete organization of experience places physical proximity as the primary relationship. Concrete organization via proximity replaces mind and emotion with body and sensation. The concrete also replaces emotion and thinking with action. Relationship is practical and functional, not emotional.

For discourse to be possible, two subjects must engage each other emotionally. Fear of the presence of the other as well as longing for the beauty of the other can inhibit a subjective sense of self. With this inhibition, the threat of loss is denied. This is especially true in those who have been traumatized as children. Then action – sometimes explosion, sometimes implosion – replaces emotion, connection, and creativity with fragmentation and collapse. Emergence can only come with contact with another. This we learned from Ferenczi, who faced catastrophic loss in order to bring us this truth about relationship.

We normally think of catastrophe as being related to trauma. When a childhood consisted of accumulated trauma, as was true of Ava's, in order to psychically survive these traumas, extraordinary protections arose to defend against overwhelming sensation and emotion. The protections were catastrophic for her development. Perception itself had to be altered in order to psychically survive. Reversals occurred. Love and concern became misinterpreted as dangerous. Perhaps they were dangerous in that they challenged the internal extraordinary protections that had built a psychic structure that co-opted the primordial.

Conclusion

This chapter has explored Ferenczi's path towards truth: the link between patient and analyst that occurs first and foremost on a body level. The body does not lie. The chapter explores truth as it relates to the beauty of love and the catastrophe of loss. It follows emotion in relationship, thought as a reflection of intersubjectivity, and the role these play in structuralizing of mind. All these processes are both catastrophic and creative. They are essential for truth to be found.

References

Bion, W. R. (1958). On hallucination. *International Journal of Psycho-Analysis*, 39: 341–349.

Bion, W. R. (1959). Attacks on linking. *International Journal of Psycho-Analysis*, 40: 308–315.

Bion, W. R. (1962a). A psycho-analytic theory of thinking. *International Journal of Psycho-Analysis*, 43: 306–310. [Reprinted as "A theory of thinking", in Bion, W. R., *Second Thoughts*. London: Karnac, 1984 (pp. 110–119).]

Bion, W. R. (1962b). *Learning from Experience*. London: Heinemann. [Reprinted London: Karnac, 1984.]

Bion, W. R. (1965). *Transformations*. London: Heinemann. [Reprinted London: Karnac, 1984.]

Bion, W. R. (1967). *Second Thoughts: Selected Papers on Psychoanalysis*. London: Heinemann. [Reprinted London: Karnac, 1984.]

Bion, W. R. (1970). *Attention and Interpretation*. London: Tavistock. [Reprinted London: Karnac, 1984.]

Bleger, J. (1967). *Symbiosis and Ambiguity: A Psychoanalytic Study*. Churcher, J. and Bleger, J. (Eds.); Rogers, S., Bleger, L., and Churcher, J. (Trans.). London and New York: Routledge, 2013.

Eekhoff, J. K. (2021). *Bion and Primitive Mental States: Trauma and the Symbiotic Link*. London and New York: Routledge.

Eekhoff, J. K. (2022). Psychic Equivalency as an Aspect of Symbiosis. In Levine, H. and Moguillansky, C. (Eds.), *Psychoanalysis of the psychoanalytic frame Revisited" A New Look at Bleger's Classical Work*. London and New York: Routledge/IPA.

Eekhoff, J. K. (2025). Truth and Lies: The Perversion of Truth and the Disruption of Passion. In Fortuna, T. (Ed.), *Truth and Lies in Psychoanalysis*. London: Phoenix Publishing House.

Ferenczi, S. (1909). *Introjection and transference. In: First Contributions to Psychoanalysis* (pp. 35–93). New York: Brunner/Mazel, 1980.

Ferenczi, S. (1910). Letter from Sándor Ferenczi to Sigmund Freud, October 12, 1910. *The Correspondence of Sigmund Freud and Sándor Ferenczi, Volume 1, 1908–1914,* 25: 224–226.

Ferenczi, S. (1914). Letter from Sándor Ferenczi to Sigmund Freud, February 18, 1914. *The Correspondence of Sigmund Freud and Sándor Ferenczi, Volume 1, 1908–1914,* 25: 541–542.

Ferenczi, S. (1918). Letter from Sándor Ferenczi to Sigmund Freud, December 26, 1918. *The Correspondence of Sigmund Freud and Sándor Ferenczi, Volume 2, 1914–1919,* 26: 319–320.

Ferenczi S. (1928). The elasticity of psycho-analytical technique. In *Final Contributions to the Problems and Methods of Psycho-Analysis* (pp. 87–101). London: Karnac, 1955.

Ferenczi, S. (1932a). 14 June 1932. Permanent disturbance of object-libido. In Dupont, J. (Ed.); Balint, M. and Jackson, N. Z. (Trans.), *The Clinical Diary of Sándor Ferenczi* (pp. 122–124). Cambridge, MA: Harvard University Press, 1985.

Ferenczi, S. (1932b). 18 June 1932. A new stage in mutuality. In Dupont, J. (Ed.); Balint, M. and Jackson, N. Z. (Trans.), *The Clinical Diary of Sándor Ferenczi* (pp. 129–131). Cambridge, MA: Harvard University Press, 1985.

Ferenczi, S. (1933). Confusion of the tongues between the adults and the child (The language of tenderness and of passion). In *Final Contributions to the Problems and Methods of Psycho-Analysis* (pp. 156–167). London: Karnac, 1994.

Ferenczi, S. (1952). Introjection and Transference. *First Contributions to Psycho-Analysis,* 45: 35–93.

Ferenczi, S. (1952). Symbolism. *First Contributions to Psycho-Analysis,* 45: 253–281.

Ferenczi, S. (1988). *The Clinical Diary of Sándor Ferenczi.* Dupont, J. (Ed.); Balint, M. and Jackson, N. Z. (Trans.). Cambridge, MA: Harvard University Press.

Meltzer, D. and Williams, M. H. (1988). *The Apprehension of Beauty: The Role of Aesthetic Conflict in Development, Art, and Violence* (pp. 1–258). London: Karnac Books.

Winnicott, D. W. (1965). Psycho-Analysis and the Sense of Guilt (1958). *The Maturational Processes and the Facilitating Environment: Studies in the Theory of Emotional Development,* 64: 15–28.

Winnicott, D. W. (1986). Holding and Interpretation: Fragment of an Analysis. *Holding and Interpretation: Fragment of an Analysis,* 115: 1–194.

Index

For Product Safety Concerns and Information please contact our EU
representative GPSR@taylorandfrancis.com
Taylor & Francis Verlag GmbH, Kaufingerstraße 24, 80331 München, Germany

www.ingramcontent.com/pod-product-compliance
Lightning Source LLC
Chambersburg PA
CBHW050343270326
41926CB00016B/3584